M000036175

# THE GIST OF READING

# THE GIST
# OF READING

**Andrew Elfenbein**

STANFORD UNIVERSITY PRESS
STANFORD, CALIFORNIA

Stanford University Press
Stanford, California

©2018 by the Board of Trustees of the Leland Stanford Junior University. All rights reserved.

No part of this book may be reproduced or transmitted in any form or by any means, electronic or mechanical, including photocopying and recording, or in any information storage or retrieval system without the prior written permission of Stanford University Press.

Printed in the United States of America on acid-free, archival-quality paper

Library of Congress Cataloging-in-Publication Data

Names: Elfenbein, Andrew, author.
Title: The gist of reading / Andrew Elfenbein.
Description: Stanford, California : Stanford University Press, 2017. | Includes bibliographical references and index.
Identifiers: LCCN 2017007207 | ISBN 9781503602564 (cloth : alk. paper) |
ISBN 9781503603851 (pbk. : alk. paper) | ISBN 9781503604100 (epub)
Subjects: LCSH: Books and reading—Psychological aspects. | Books and reading—History—19th century.
Classification: LCC Z1003 .E46 2017 | DDC 028/.9—dc23
LC record available at https://lccn.loc.gov/2017007207

Typeset by Bruce Lundquist in 10/14 Minion Pro

*For Textgroup, past, present, and future*

# CONTENTS

# ACKNOWLEDGMENTS

What interdisciplinarity feels like: traversing the length of campus in subzero weather to meet with your collaborators; writing embarrassed notes to your statistics teacher explaining that you did not notice the last problem on the homework; resigning yourself to the fact that everyone else in the room will interpret a complex interaction graph more easily than you will; spending a shocking amount on updating SPSS; patiently explaining (again) why psychology can be useful. Luckily for me, I have worked with a remarkable group of psychologists, who made the benefits of interdisciplinarity outweigh its challenges.

My first thanks go to Paul van den Broek, who invited me to audit his class when I inquired about reading comprehension in psychology; that was the beginning of a long journey and an important friendship. Through Paul I came to know past and present members of Textgroup at the University of Minnesota, and I dedicate this book to them. Particular thanks go to Sashank Varma, David Rapp, Elaine Auyoung, Brooke Lea, Randy Fletcher, Sid Horton, Mike Mensink, Panayiota Kendeou, Catherine Bohn-Gettler, Reese Butterfuss, Mark Rose, Ben Seipel, Virginia Clinton, Andreas Schramm, Mary Jane White, Mija Van Der Wege, Sarah Carlson, and Katrina Schliesman. Sashank, David, and Brooke offered superb advice about this book and corrected many of my errors. Elaine is a treasured colleague, and being able to discuss this book and her own work has been a joy.

As I have presented my work, especially at the Society for Text and Discourse, I have received interest and support from many, especially Walter Kintsch, Arthur Graesser, Susan Goldman, Danielle McNamara, Joseph Magliano, Keith Millis, and John Sabatini. Richard Gerrig deserves a special mention for his detailed, critical commentary on several chapters. Patient instructors at the University of Minnesota introduced me to inferential statistics: Mark van Ryzin, Michelle Everson, Robert delMas, Andrew Zieffler, Michael Harwell, and Michael Rodriguez. Chairs of English at the University of Minnesota have supported this project: Michael Hancher, Paula Rabinowitz, and Ellen Messer-Davidow. Leslie Nightingale, Trent Olsen, and Katelin Krieg were excellent research assistants for tracking Victorian readers; Douglas Addleman has been exceptional in preparing the final manuscript. Emily-Jane Cohen at Stanford University Press has, once again, been a model editor, and I am lucky to have benefited from the careful copyediting of Joe Abbott.

Several scholars have invited me to present my work: Alan Liu at the University of California, Santa Barbara, Catherine Robson and James Eli Adams for the Dickens Universe, Elaine Scarry at Harvard, Asha Varadharjan at Queens University, Gerald Cohen-Vrignaud at the University of Tennessee, Charles Rzepka at Boston University, Leigh Dale and Jennifer McDonell at the University of Wollongong, Amy Muse for the International Conference on Romanticism, and Alan Bewell at the University of Toronto; I am also grateful to audiences at conferences organized by the North American Victorian Studies Association and the Dickens Universe. I have been fortunate to have the support and friendship of Susan Wolfson, Herbert Tucker, and Deidre Lynch; Alan Richardson deserves special mention for his pioneering work on cognitive science and literature and his early encouragement of my work.

Sabbatical fellowships from the American Philosophical Society and the American Council of Learned Societies have made this book possible, as well as travel grants and grants-in-aid from the College of Liberal Arts at the University of Minnesota. Earlier versions of portions of this book appeared in *PMLA*, *MLQ*, and *A Companion to the English Novel*, edited by Stephen Arata, Madigan Haley, J. Paul Hunter, and Jennifer Wicke (New York: Wiley-Blackwell, 2015). I am grateful to all for permission to republish; Leane Zugsmith's "The Three Veterans" appears in an appendix to Chapter 3 by the kind permission of the *New Yorker*/Condé Nast. Considerations of cost prevented including a bibliography in this book; those who are interested may find one at my faculty webpage: http://cla.umn.edu/about/directory/profile/elfen001.

Several cats past and present have woven themselves into my life as I wrote: loving but troubled Muffin, regal Brandy, and now Charlotte, who inspires me with a clear sense of priorities. My son, Dima, has grown into a man in the time it has taken me to write this, and I could not be more proud. After thirty years of living with me, my husband John Watkins remains my sharpest critic, and I thank him for supporting me as my career has taken directions that neither of us could have anticipated.

# THE GIST OF READING

# INTERDISCIPLINARITY

## I, Too, Dislike It

**DISSATISFIED** with discussions of reading in literary criticism, I became interested in how cognitive psychologists understood it. As I became acquainted with a new field, I found myself tripping over a stumbling block that took me a while to identify. Objections that seemed smart to me seemed beside the point to the psychologists with whom I studied. The difference in viewpoints arose from a core disciplinary distinction between us about the value of the particular versus the general. As a literary scholar, I sided with the particular. Although I could generalize about periods like romanticism, genres like the ode, or the oeuvre of an author like Byron, the core of my expertise was discussing what made a text, line, word, or even phoneme special. Literature consisted of irreducible particularities, and my job was to recognize them. Without sensitivity to them, there seemed no reason for scholarship at all.

When I came to study psychology, I confronted a different outlook; in Ellen Messer-Davidow's words, the "schemes of perception, cognition, and action that practitioners must use" were not the ones I knew.[1] What psychologists explored was not a particular work but the mind. For psychologists, people are different from each other—but not too much. If psychologists believed that people in general were like canonical authors, each uniquely special, no experiments would be possible because differences would overwhelm commonalities. Psychological claims depend, instead, on demonstrating that, while there are major individual differences between people, core cognitive architectures, such as memory systems or functions of executive control, have much in common.

As Keith Stanovich notes, it may be easier for nonpsychologists to accept such commonalities when they concern the body rather than the mind.[2] Few academics would bother to debate that smokers are at higher risk for certain forms of disease than nonsmokers. Yet I had learned to suspect comparable psychological claims, especially about reading. When, for example, Danielle McNamara and Joseph Magliano write, "Reading is an inherently goal-directed activity and like many such activities, readers have control over their attentional resources," my instincts as a literary critic taught me to pounce with "gotcha" questions like "Who decides what counts as 'goal directed'?" and "Just which readers have 'control over their attentional resources'?"[3]

My irritation came from psychology's probabilistic claims, which describe general tendencies across a wide variety of individuals that are often, though not always, true. Especially since I, as an academic critic, did not represent a general reading population, I felt that psychological findings about reading did not describe me. What I learned was that it was a mistake to dismiss psychological findings for this reason. Instead, they had great value in capturing widely shared aspects of reading across a huge variety of readers and were useful for someone like me, who cared about reading and its history. More importantly, the difference between my reading and that described in psychological articles was not as vast as I had first believed. I had developed, through long practice, a set of strategies for understanding imaginative literature, but the cognitive architecture underlying these strategies was shared with many readers. I just had sharpened a certain subset of them, so that my reading shifted between strategies common to many readers and those belonging to literary scholars. Psychological vocabulary was especially helpful in understanding my challenges when faced with difficult or unfamiliar texts, moments at which my accustomed modes of reading were less helpful than I hoped.

Psychological claims about reading are rarely just about reading: studying reading helps psychologists build larger theories about memory, cognition, inference making, social intelligence, decision making, and judgment. The study of reading in psychology links to larger cognitive issues, such as readers' susceptibility to learning false facts from fiction or to what Richard Gerrig calls anomalous suspense, the ability of stories to suppress, even if just slightly, what ought to be familiar knowledge; for example, readers are slower to confirm that George Washington was the first president of the United States after reading a story that makes it seem doubtful that he will succeed to the presidency.[4] The fact that psychologists do not set out to describe how literary critics read and are often not interested in literature should not make their work irrelevant. Instead, it should highlight aspects of reading masked in literary scholarship by an exclusive focus on literariness. It may seem unfair of me to blame literary scholars for caring about literature. Yet literary reading is a subset of reading more generally, and an understanding of the first requires an understanding of the second.[5]

Since psychologists aim to explain common behaviors, the default settings inflected by differences in personality, setting, mood, physical state, and developmental stage, their experiments constrain individual difference through uniform lab settings and random assignment of participants to control and experimental groups.[6] If differences between the two groups as a whole are greater than the differences between the participants in each group, and those differences generalize statistically to a larger population, then psychologists have a valid finding. Often, to those like me, coming from a different discipline that prizes striking or unusual interpretations, these findings can seem thuddingly obvious. For example, Edward O'Brien and his collaborators have developed a long and highly regarded stream of research on the "inconsistency effect," the tendency for readers to slow down when they read about characters whose behavior is not consistent with facts about them encountered earlier in the text. Simple as the finding is, O'Brien has used it as a springboard for surprisingly rich work on memory.[7]

While literary critics, as inheritors of New Criticism, prize arguments that feature paradoxes, tensions, and ambiguities, psychologists usually suspect findings, especially new ones, that seem too interesting. Confronted with data, good psychologists are skilled at giving the simplest explanations.[8] While psychology does contain many counterintuitive findings, the average article in psychology often demonstrates what could have been predicted in advance. Setting out to prove the obvious is not intrinsically bad—especially since experiments do not always confirm it. It is just a different disciplinary emphasis from literary criticism. Accustomed to sensitively revealing interpretations of individual works, I had to learn to appreciate baseline commonalities that crop up across differences.

Doing so helped me get past one of the easiest charges to make against psychology: it is reductive. *Reductive* has a peculiar taint in literary criticism as an adjective for work that is obviously flawed. Such quick condemnation masks how central and how useful reductiveness is to all disciplines. Since literary scholars accuse even each other of reductiveness, it is not surprising to find psychological work, which painstakingly aims to be reductive, accused of the same perceived sin; as one critic writes, "So, whilst cognitive science may enable us to start to understand how a reader actually processes a text, it can too often be neglectful of the processes at work both in a text and a reader; the social, political, economic and cultural forces that mean we cannot see the text, nor the reader, in isolation."[9] For this author, since cognitive science does not acknowledge "social, political, economic and cultural forces," it must be too reductive to say much about reading. Part of this author's mistake is assuming that cognitive science lets us "understand how a reader actually processes a text." Psychologists, as I have argued, are not interested in "a reader." Instead, they care about processes common to readers across reading situations, including the differences that matter to this critic: that is why they use randomized samples.[10]

Psychological analysis focuses not on forces but on data, because they are the evidence needing interpretation. Data give rise to questions about the size of the difference between results from experimental and control groups (in reading research, such differences often amount to milliseconds), how much variability the data have, what results are unexpected, what interactions between variables are significant, and which existing theories the findings support or challenge. Generalizations have to come from data, which are often messier than the stories that psychologists tell about them. When humanists object to psychologists' inattention to "social, political, economic and cultural forces," psychologists can feel as if such objections miss the point. If participants are randomly assigned to control and experimental groups, then variations arising from social, political, economic, and cultural forces should affect them equally: if the two groups are nevertheless different, then the difference must result from experimental manipulation. Good questions to ask about a piece of psychological research are not necessarily about those forces but about the experiment's materials and procedures, the possibility of generalizing from it, and the number of replications it has received.

Literary scholars may assume that, to psychologists, reading processes depend on biological essentialism, a belief that reading is hard-wired into the brain and can therefore trump culture. But psychologists generally avoid such claims, especially after the rise of cultural psychology, a flourishing subfield that distinguishes between mental processes that are affected by culture and those that are not.[11] Psychology proves its claims not through essentializing assumptions about biology but through convergent evidence: if the same behaviors turn up in experiment after experiment, which have used different methodologies and randomly assigned samples from many different populations, then such behaviors are widespread and are less affected by "social, political, economic, and cultural forces" than literary scholars might want to believe.

Having found such widespread behaviors, psychologists will next search for individual differences. Once they have found an effect that obtains in many readers, they may examine why it does not happen in all of them: what characterizes readers who, for example, do not slow down when they read inconsistent information? Psychologists may also change the text or the laboratory setting to see if they can make an effect disappear. To construct the necessary manipulations, they may learn more about participants (in the case of reading research, their comprehension skills, vocabulary, enjoyment of reading, personalities, need for cognition, world knowledge); they may also change wording to foreground some information and background the rest or include more or less filler. Through manipulations, they hope to understand, for example, why some readers notice plain contradictions and others do not, or why some readers remember details in a passage and others do not. But such questions are interesting only in light of a finding that, initially, applies across many participants.

After exploring such commonalities and their limits, psychologists connect their findings to others in psychology that advance or criticize a developing theory. Literary scholars may be surprised to learn how central theory is to psychology; psychologists use *descriptive* in the way that humanists use *empirical*, to dismiss work that does not engage theory enough. Yet theory in psychology differs from theory in literary criticism because a good psychological theory is falsifiable. A theory has to be specific enough to yield a testable hypothesis yet general enough to account for phenomena across the enormous variability of people. A theory, often as represented in a model, makes predictions.[12] These should differ from those made by a competing theory, so that an experiment can test both by hypothesizing two possible outcomes for two different theories. If the experiment works, one model or the other may be upheld in whole or part, or one or both may be dismissed. When psychologists write up their experiments, they make these competing hypotheses explicit so that the stakes of falsifiability are clear.

A challenge for those from a different discipline is that, out of their original context, findings lose their edge because the original hypothesis competition disappears. A claim beginning "psychologists have found that . . ." can make psychology look like a source of eternal truths rather than, as is obvious from reading any empirical article, a source of findings subject to change and renegotiation. This is why I recommend that humanists interested in psychology read actual articles rather than overviews popularizing scientific findings: the closer you come to procedures, materials, and data, the better sense you have of just how pertinent findings may be.

Falsifiability has a corollary: lack of originality is useful. If a finding is falsifiable, then someone else should be able to copy what the original researchers did and either confirm their findings or not. Psychologists test falsifiability through replication. Often papers present a series of experiments, and, typically, at least one will repeat findings from another psychologist. Only after a finding has received many replications, in different labs, is it considered robust. (In a development that has been fascinating for me as an outsider, psychology during the years I have been writing this book has been shaken by high-profile articles underscoring the questionable replicability of widely disseminated findings. The field as a whole has responded with impressive speed to promote greater rigor and transparency.)[13] The need to replicate encourages psychologists to state findings not in the densely individualizing style of literary scholarship but in broad terms that enable a theory to be tested.

In experiments, tightly controlled differences between control and experimental groups support causal inferences. If an experimental manipulation is the only difference between two groups of participants, and they behave differently, then psychologists argue that the manipulation caused the difference. As a literary critic, I initially found such explanations impoverished because I had learned to love rhetorics of infinite detail: the more complex an argument, the truer it felt. As Alan Liu has argued, the rhetoric of detail creates a "logical order that is pseudo-syllogistic" in the absence of "any foundational major premise or conclusion."[14] Liu's point is that cultural criticism allows any detail to become a cause for any other detail, and the more, the better, in a way that he compares to the romantic sublime.

As a literary scholar, I was used to concepts like Foucault's understanding of power, a network of discourses and practices so interwoven as to be almost unanalyzable.[15] With regard to reading, Roland Barthes eloquently summed up reading as such a network: "It is commonly admitted that to read is to decode: letters, words, meanings, structures, and this is incontestable; but by accumulating decodings (since reading is by rights infinite), by removing the safety catch of meaning, by putting reading into freewheeling (which is its structural vocation), the reader is caught up in a dialectical reversal: finally, he does not decode, he *overcodes*; he does not decipher, he produces, he accumulates languages, he lets himself be infinitely and tirelessly traversed by them: he is that traversal."[16] Barthes envisions a reader ecstatically surrendering to "freewheeling" forces and secularizing the penitent's surrender to God's vastness. His vision battles against those who insist on a single correct reading—but nobody can actually do what he describes. Psychology led me to see the move to infinity in descriptions like Barthes's not as acknowledging complexity but as reducing it because the rhetoric of infinity is too easy. It will not risk naming what factors matter most for reading in a given context.

In learning about the psychology of reading, my own reading could be as much a hindrance as a help. I was a good enough reader to be able to get some meaning out of articles in psychology, but I did not always know enough to understand the bigger stakes or the disciplinary history. As an example of how literary critical expertise can hamper cross-disciplinary work, I take Eve Kosofsky Sedgwick and Adam Frank's attack on the cognitive psychology of emotion. In *The Oxford Companion to the Mind* George Mandler describes a link between cognition and emotion: "Current wisdom would suggest that any discrepancy, any interruption of expectations or of intended actions, produces undifferentiated visceral (autonomic) arousal. The *quale* of the subsequent emotion will then depend on the ongoing cognitive evaluation (meaning analysis, appraisal) of the current state of affairs."[17] Like many psychologists, Mandler imagines a time course to emotion: an emotion begins as pure arousal based on surprise ("any interruption of expectations") that is then channeled into a specific emotion through cognitive evaluation.

Sedgwick and Frank demolish Mandler's passage as an example of psychology's silliness:

> So ask yourself this: How long does it take you after being awakened in the night by (a) a sudden loud noise or (b) gradual sexual arousal to cognitively "analyze" and "appraise" "the current state of affairs" well enough to assign the appropriate *quale* to your emotion? That is, what is the temporal lag from the moment of sleep interruption to the ("subsequent") moment when you can judge whether what you're experiencing is luxuriation or terror?
>
> No, it doesn't take either of us very long, either.[18]

Sedgwick and Frank imagine some poor soul, awakened in the night, obliged to sit in bed busy analyzing or appraising what emotion to feel. Their point, not stated directly, is that no such analysis is necessary: the right emotion should be obvious. Their common sense is meant to unseat the overly involved models of psychologists.

But Mandler is not as silly as Sedgwick and Frank imply. If you are awakened by a loud noise and figure out that that noise came from (1) your cat knocking over a vase or (2) a tree falling on your house, you may well respond differently. If you are awakened by gradual sexual arousal that comes from (1) a spouse or (2) a one-night stand, you may also have different responses. The quarrel arises from different parsings of "cognitive appraisal." For Mandler, such appraisal has a specialized meaning within psychology: appraisal happens quickly because human beings learn early in their development how to assess a scene for the appropriate responses and how to revise first perceptions in light of later information. Since they do it often, they become so practiced that appraisal usually takes almost no time. Sedgwick and Frank, in contrast, assume the connotations that "appraisal" has in ordinary language, in which it suggests a time-consuming, laborious process. But, in the psychological sense that Mandler assumes, we appraise most of what we encounter in a day without massive introspection; if we did not, we could hardly cope.

Sedgwick and Frank's attack on Mandler typifies the challenge that humanists meet when faced with a new discipline: they interpret new material in terms of what they already know, as do all learners.[19] They read a phrase that looks familiar in the most easily accessible context, even though the valence of "cognitive appraisal" in psychology may be quite different than it seems. Grasping the unfamiliar in terms of the familiar leads not only to dismissals like Sedgwick and Frank's but also to the objection that nothing about cognitive approaches to literature is new: such reactions filter out the unfamiliar to focus on what looks familiar.

Despite the stumbling blocks I encountered in redisciplining myself as a psychologist, the interdisciplinary work had a payoff: the ability to write this book about reading from a new perspective. The two chief modes of discussing reading in literary scholarship, reader-response criticism and archival work on real readers, felt inadequate to me. Reader-response criticism did not progress beyond the recognition that meaning arises from an interaction between reader and text, whereas work on real readers amassed archival evidence with few principles about how to make sense of it. Psychology let me see what reading looks like when approached with a different set of assumptions. I realized that my starting point had to be reading per se rather than literary reading, as assumed by previous reader-response critics. This starting point separates my approach from that of most other scholars working in cognitive literary studies. They start with books and literature, or at least narrative, and look for findings in psychology to help understand them. In contrast, rather than assuming that literary reading needs to be cordoned off from other reading, I argue that literary reading involves a specialized subset of skills used both in reading more generally and in cognition as a whole.

Recognizing this point matters because literary reading cannot be adequately understood without understanding how it draws on and is constrained by general mental activities. Not seeing the larger picture would be like studying the reception of music but ignoring how the brain responds to sound, or like studying the reception of visual art without noticing vision. Moreover, having learned to place reading in a broader cognitive perspective, I gained a better sense of psychology's assumptions and conventions. If my early questions about psychological experiments seemed irrelevant, they eventually became better focused on the goals of experimenters. My background in literary criticism in time even provided a useful perspective for understanding and critiquing scientific research—but it took a lot of work to get there.

Nothing that I have said about my own learning exempts psychology from criticism, even though most criticisms that humanists raise, especially about the psychology of reading, have appeared within psychology itself. As psychologists are well aware, their findings face problems of ecological validity (how well results in the lab translate to findings about real-world experience), of using oversimplified textoids, of emphasizing some areas over others because they are easier to study, and of potentially confusing definitions.[20] These problems lead me, again, to stress that anyone interested in the field should read actual research articles.

The benefits of interdisciplinary work were a sense of reading apart from literary reading, a vocabulary for asking questions about reading masked by disciplinary convention, and the ability to separate reading from interpretation. But, as my chapter's subtitle suggests, I, like Marianne Moore writing about poetry, also have faced challenges in working across disciplines. Literary scholars who use psychological findings commonly encounter loud objections from other literary critics, such as, "One has the feeling this book is meant for beginners"; "tailoring the object of inquiry to the mode of inquiry entails refashioning the former in ways that fail to do it justice"; and "excellent descriptions of developments in literary criticism alternate with what I persist in regarding as unnecessary scientific explanations."[21] Objections fall into three categories: problems with interdisciplinarity, problems with psychology, and problems with procedure. The first arises from discomfort with borrowing ideas and findings that originally had nothing to do with literature; the second, from a long-standing antiscience rhetoric in the humanities; the third, from discomfort with the tone, jargon, and stylistic awkwardness that working across disciplines creates.

Dismissals of interdisciplinarity arise because cognitive work in literature asks critics to question the often-unstated border work of all disciplines.[22] Disciplines mark off what will and will not be studied. Over time, as practitioners learn their discipline, such borders become taken for granted as tacit knowledge. Interdisciplinarity renders those borders more permeable in ways that are not always welcome: "Scholars may resent what they take to be poaching on their scholarly terrain and may dismiss challenges to their authority from those in other fields who ask different questions and seek answers through different methods."[23] Writing within a discipline occurs on common ground between author and assumed audience. As I noted earlier, my training led me to know well a body of works familiar to those reading my scholarship. When crossing disciplines, such common ground disappears. Should a book about psychology and literature, for example, make its case to those interested in practical criticism or in theory? Should it assume readers who like findings from other disciplines, or ones who need to be convinced that such findings are relevant? How does one acknowledge the strengths and the shortcomings of disciplines without making readers defensive? Knowing the mind of an audience is never easy, but interdisciplinarity makes it even harder.

I have imagined a reader for this book who also feels that long-held assumptions about reading can benefit from being challenged. I do not assume a reader familiar with previous cognitive approaches to literature or with psychology. As a scholar of nineteenth-century British literature, I assume knowledge of it as home base, although I hope my findings will interest those specializing in other national literatures and periods. I have also presented my findings to different audiences, from different disciplines, to anticipate potential stumbling blocks, even as I know that a complete accounting is impossible.

To a degree, much in this book should be familiar. Although psychological details of reading are not part of standard literary critical study, they have hardly been ignored: Peter Rabinowitz's work on the rules assumed by interpretation; Norman Holland on reading and brain processes; Wolfgang Iser on the filling of textual gaps; Stanley Fish on the temporal process of reading; and Nicholas

Dames on novel reading in Victorian psychology are all important inspirations for my work.[24] Yet my treatment of reading also includes less familiar frameworks, such as "good-enough processing," the relation between top-down and bottom-up processing, automaticity, and the limitations on cognitive resources. Bringing such material into a single book may seem like an onslaught of unfamiliarity, though I hope that much may be less unfamiliar than it seems initially.

In the background of objections to cognitive psychology and literary study sometimes lurks the concern that, when the humanities have less money and fewer students than ever before, engaging empirical work looks like going over to the enemy. Literary critics who work closely with contemporary science supposedly accept that scientific investigation alone produces truth. Theodor Adorno long ago attacked the social sciences for not recognizing the social ground of facts: "Knowledge derived from an uncritical acceptance of empirical facts becomes a pure reproduction of existing relations of society."[25] Yet no scientific article has treated facts as speaking for themselves. Equations determine the statistical validity of a generalization from sample to population, but people (trained and disciplined) determine what that validity means. Any distinction between "fact-based disciplines" and "interpretation-based disciplines" is nonsense: all disciplines are interpretation-based. Data require interpretation because they cannot speak for themselves.

Another objection is anachronism: findings arising from twenty-first-century experiments may be valid for the twentieth-first century, but they should not apply to earlier readers, who read under different conditions. This objection assumes a law of the excluded middle: either psychological findings apply to earlier periods, or they do not. But those are not the only options. Different aspects of reading are more or less susceptible to change. Evolution proceeds slowly enough that we can assume that low-level visual cognition operated for the Victorians much as it does for us and will continue to do so for the foreseeable future. In contrast, higher-order, more constructed, aspects of reading, such as readers' background knowledge, vary historically. For example, the average Victorian educated, middle-class reader would have had quicker access to the language of the King James Bible and (possibly) the Book of Common Prayer than does the average twenty-first-century American college student. Such access may indeed have affected the inferences that readers made. Nevertheless, despite this difference, readers then and now use background knowledge to comprehend what they read. The cognitive architecture remains transhistorical, but the contents on which it draws do not.

As for the objection that cognitive psychology feels like a coldly analytical tool for the cauldron of emotions in literary reading, it is true that psychological studies of reading, with a few important exceptions, have not engaged with emotion as thoroughly as they should. Cognitive psychology came of age in the 1970s, when links between psychology and artificial intelligence were close and the metaphor of the mind as computer fueled exploration. With time the fields have grown apart, but the chilly view of reading installed in that founding moment has not dissipated. Within cognitive psychology itself emotion has received attention, but that research has not yet fully intersected research on reading, in part because testing a reader's emotions in a lab is difficult. One goal of my book is to use historical evidence to point out directions that psychologists studying reading might follow to understand emotion better.

The least-discussed but, I believe, most deep-seated objections arise not from substance but from style. Cognitive approaches often do not feel smart. Literary critics recognize a rhetoric of smartness even if they cannot list its traits; prizing infinite detail, as I discussed earlier, is one manifestation. When literary critics borrow findings from psychology, the move from one discipline to another has a cost. In its original setting an experiment is a small moment within a large research stream. When such findings move out of psychology, literary critics may feel that they are being asked to accept obvious or even trivial points as if they were major revelations. The result can make interdisciplinary work drawing on psychology feel unsmart next to scholarship that stays more securely within its discipline. Even worse, adopting jargon from psychology introduces an array of clunky terms, a bad heteroglossia that feels awkward and alien in literary analysis.

Yet "cognitive approaches to literature" is a big enough tent that generalizations about the field are likely to be inadequate: some work engages with cognitive approaches to metaphor, with theory of mind and its relevance to character, with evolutionary psychology and the mental uses of narrative form, with findings from neuroscience about the brain and emotion, and with narratology and cognition.[26] These interests skew cognitive psychology as a whole, since critics have hardly touched on some of the field's key preoccupations, while relatively minor issues take an outsized place in their literary critical reception.

In this book I draw on empirical work with reading, a tiny subfield within a much larger discipline. I focus on research that has received little attention within cognitive literary studies, and I hardly touch on concerns central to other literary critics interested in cognition. For example, I have nothing to say about evolution, largely because reading postdates the brain's evolution. From an evolutionary standpoint, reading brings together different cognitive networks (such as visual perception, phonological processing, pattern recognition, and inferencing), each of which developed for purposes other than reading and still have those other purposes as their primary uses. Even within the study of reading, most of my discussion will focus on only a part of the existing research, since psychologists study reading at different levels: phonological, lexical, and semantic recognition; sentence comprehension; intersentential connections; and the situation-model representation of texts (usually very short ones). I am primarily interested in the last of these because its concerns are closest to those of literary scholars.

At the same time, while text comprehension is a small subfield, it connects with much larger areas of investigation, such as memory, decision making, conversation comprehension, inferencing, event representation, and mental imaging. Some psychologists have reading as their chief interest, while others use reading to learn more about processes other than reading. The empirical study of text comprehension, although a small subfield, is also a testing ground for major concerns. The findings on which I draw in this book come both from scientists interested specifically in reading and from those who use reading as a pathway to bigger issues.

I titled this book *The Gist of Reading*, and the title has two meanings. The first involves *gist* in the ordinary sense of essence or core: I will argue in the first three chapters that this core arises from a combination of automatic and controlled mental processes. Yet in Chapter 3 I also introduce *gist* in a more technical sense, as the simplified mental representation that the mind retains in long-term memory. When faced with a complex visual scene, or even a moderately long sentence, the mind does not remember everything it has perceived. Instead, it holds on to a drastically reduced, simplified version, something like a sketch rather than a full representation. I explore this second sense of *gist* in the final four chapters, which argue that understanding gist is central to the social, psychological, and political impact of literary works.

My first chapter takes a bottom-up approach to reading. It looks at the nuts and bolts of the processes that the mind coordinates in order to comprehend. Although these processes have not traditionally been part of the scholarly understanding of literary reading, I argue that understanding them helps us to analyze hitherto-neglected aspects of reader response even in long, complex literary texts. The vocabulary developed to describe bottom-up processing helps scholars pay closer attention to readers' actions during and after reading.

Top-down processes complement bottom-up ones. These are processes over which readers usually have more conscious control and may be more familiar to literary critics. To understand them, I look in my second chapter at three exemplary readers, one fictional and two real. In each case I analyze reading moment-by-moment, accompanying readers as they progress through a work to argue that the same conceptual framework allows us to understand very different readers. The first is Mr. Knightley in Jane Austen's *Emma* as he reads and responds to Frank Churchill's letter. Austen makes visible in this passage core aspects of top-down reading that have nevertheless been often overlooked by critics. Next, I turn to the most famous reader-response critic, Stanley Fish, and to his interpretation of a sentence by Walter Pater. Fish's reading manifests some of the difficulties that reader-response criticism has faced; I use vocabulary from psychology to disentangle reading and interpretation in Fish's passage. Finally, I examine a reading protocol from a student reader struggling with a challenging short story, Leane Zugsmith's "The Three Veterans." I look at when and why this reader has trouble with the story to fill out the picture of what top-down processes in reading can involve.

My third chapter describes how bottom-up and top-down processes combine for four nineteenth-century readers confronted with a particularly tough book, Robert Browning's *Men and Women*. This chapter also introduces standards of coherence as a concept enabling a crossing-point between psychology and history. Its second part moves from online to offline reading to examine reader memory. A genre of poems designed to represent the state of a reader's mind after reading demonstrates the rise of the imagined author as a retrieval cue for long-term memory. I use the imagined author to analyze late Victorian criticism usually dismissed by academic critics as belles-lettristic. Such criticism uses the imagined author to capture the overall gist impression that a complex work creates in long-term memory.

The fourth and fifth chapters historicize the idea of standards of coherence by outlining a long-standing debate in Britain about whether reading should be hard or easy. Chapter 4 starts with the hard side. This tradition stemmed from guides to reading the Bible, was secularized by Ruskin, and then enshrined by the school curriculum: the American high school reception of George Eliot's *Silas Marner* demonstrates how "hard reading" was crystallized in reading practices meant to demonstrate college readiness. Chapter 5, in contrast, explores the standards of those who wanted reading to be easy. Easy reading was a long-standing value in eighteenth-century rhetoric and became a prime value of novel writing as developed by Walter Scott. I use extensive archival records of Victorian novel readers to understand the quantitative and qualitative aspects of easy reading during the nineteenth century.

The final two chapters are more speculative. I analyze two aspects of reading understudied in the empirical literature: reading for entertainment and reading for literary influence. To explore entertainment, I examine how Victorian readers reacted to novels that reviewers agreed were the worst that they had ever read (Gustave Strauss's *The Old Ledger* and Eliza Humphreys's *Like Dian's Kiss*). These novels were so bad that readers' reactions are especially revealing about what they thought had gone wrong: in the process they model what nineteenth-century readers believed made reading entertaining. I use their reactions to examine a better-known novel, Charles Dickens's *The Old Curiosity Shop*, and its metamorphosis from one of Dickens's least successful works to one of his hits. The final chapter uses literary influence to explore some of the shortcomings of the empirical study of reading and speculate about questions that are as yet not easily answered within its terms. My case study is Oscar Wilde's *The Picture of Dorian Gray* and its extensive engagement with prior literature at the level of both passing allusion and large-scale plot structure.

No book on a topic as complex as reading can be definitive. I hope that *The Gist of Reading* will allow those interested in reading to rethink some familiar assumptions about what reading is and how it happens. Within literary scholarship as a whole, the study of reading is frozen in paradigms that are now several decades old. My engagement with psychology, awkward and laborious as it has been, has led me to believe that wrestling with, adapting, and playing with psychology can teach us to read reading with the same care that we have learned to read texts.

# CHAPTER 1

# DOING WHAT COMES AUTOMATICALLY

**EVOLUTION** hard-wired us to do remarkable things, and reading is not one of them. Reading arrived long after we evolved into our current form. We might have wish lists of what our brains and bodies might be if only we had evolved to read: extra hands for holding books, perfect memories, concentration less subject to distraction, eyes that could take in a larger visual field, maybe a built-in night light. But it was not to be, and we are stuck with what we have. Hands and eyes tire quickly, linguistic abilities are easily confused, memories are imperfect, attention drifts from the text at hand, and brains are happy with minimal effort.

For reading to occur, we rewire the brain from what it was built to do to what we want it to do, and we face an uphill battle. As Stanislas Dehaene puts it, "During education, reading processes must invade and 'recycle' cortical space devoted to evolutionarily older functions."[1] Such recycling is not in itself unusual. We often ask the brain to do what it did not evolve to do: play chess, drive a car, bake cookies. Reading stands out, though, for the density of what has to happen almost simultaneously: moving eyes to perceive symbols, assembling symbols in words, parsing words as sentences, translating sentences into a mental language, creating a mental model of what has been read, supplementing it with inferences drawn from semantic memory (typically, general factual knowledge) and episodic memory (memory for events that we have seen or experienced), finding appropriate emotional reactions to that model, reasoning or making decisions about what has been read, and much more.[2] As I learn about the juggling act of reading, difficulties surprise me less than successes, especially at an early age.

The sheer improbability of ever getting reading right may explain part of its outsized role in some religious practices meant to provide meaning for human life: the ability to read taps into human potential in ways not obvious on the surface. Its importance comes from the centrality of scriptures in some religions for transmitting belief, so that reading becomes inseparable from religious experience. Secularization has had only a partial effect on disassociating reading from religion because the step from valuing reading holy books to valuing reading per se is small. Even for secular readers, reading books, at least in some circumstances, sounds like a religious experience: "Ideally, we lose ourselves in what we read, only to return to ourselves, transformed and part of a more expansive world—in short, we become more critical and more capacious in our thinking and our acting."[3] The writer (Judith Butler) secularizes the familiar Christian notion of losing oneself to gain oneself, or dying to live, and applies it not to transcendent salvation but to reading.

While reading may, at times, be such a transformative process, it is many other things first. Above all, it is something we do often. If we read well, we do so less because we are smart or motivated than because we have read over and over again. Although a print-filled environment is recent in human history, for those who live surrounded by words, to see the world is to read. Places with nothing to read may require effort to reach, and once we get to them, we (or at least I) need all our determination not to look at text. More typically, ambient text surrounds us: the eye cannot choose but read.[4]

So practiced is reading that most of us read automatically. I do not mean that we involuntarily drift through *The Magic Mountain* but that, if you are an experienced reader of English, you would find it impossible to look at a common word projected on a screen, such as *blue*, and not read it, within milliseconds. Certain conditions could interfere with the process: lack of light, small type, unfamiliar font, tired eyes. But with average operating conditions you will read a familiar word quickly because you have read it many times before. Not only has word recognition become automatic, but so has sentence parsing. If I flashed on a screen, one word at a time, the word list *the, dog, ran, to, the, ball*, you would process it differently from the word list *five, over, blue, quickly, truth*. With the first list, if you are an experienced reader, you will assign the words different syntactic roles as part of a sentence; the second you would treat as just a list. Syntactic parsing is so automatic that grammatically correct but deliberately tricky sentences, such as "The old man the boats," feel irritating, as if they hardly merit the extra effort needed for them to make sense.

In using the term *automatic*, I am borrowing a technical, and controversial, term from psychology.[5] The psychological model of automaticity that works best for findings about reading is one that Agnes Moors refers to as the "triple-mode view." This model describes three modes of processing:

1.  Nonautomatic processing: attentive and effortful processing over which the subject has conscious control;

2.  Bottom-up automatic processing: unconscious, fast, passive processing that is inaccessible to consciousness and happens immediately after the presentation of a stimulus (in this case, text).

3.  Top-down automatic processing: processes that have become automatic as a result of training and repetitive practice. As Moors notes, such processes "are usually unconscious, but they are not inaccessible to consciousness. They can become conscious when attention is directed to them."[6]

Bottom-up automatic processes in reading, such as visual perception and associative memory searches, do not belong exclusively to reading: they are so fundamental as to be building blocks of cognition. They happen at such a low level that literary scholars are hardly aware they exist—although, as I will argue, they can have interesting effects. To be considered automatic, a mental process must involve a lack of conscious effort, rapid speed, autonomy (once started, it cannot be stopped), minimal demand on processing resources, and inaccessibility to consciousness (you are not aware of the work). Top-down automatic processes, in contrast, may or may not be specific to reading, and, as Moors points out, may become accessible to consciousness. Some of these may include decoding (translating graphemes into words), parsing (making syntactic sense), comprehending (understanding the meaning of what is read), and situation model building (integrating what has been read with general world knowledge, cognitive and emotional inferences, predictions, and evaluations). A good analogy is language production: for the most part we produce responses in conversation without much conscious awareness. Yet we recognize situations when, for various reasons, we have to choose our words carefully. Reading is similar: having done it so often, we have a good set of tools for reading with minimal conscious effort. Yet every so often, those tools do not work quite as well as we want them to, so we give reading extra attention.

I focus here on automatic processes because they are least familiar to literary scholars, even though reading would be impossible without them. My goal is to show just how consequential they can be. To do so, I will present some psychological experiments in detail—maybe, for some, too much detail. Yet I want to acknowledge the practices that give rise to psychological claims rather than presenting experimental conclusions as truth. For example, in a form of what is known as masked semantic priming, participants are presented, in order, with (1) a blank screen; (2) a screen with a neutral display, such as "######"; (3) a prime, such as the word *doctor*; (4) the neutral display again; and (5) a target word, such as *nurse*. (While there are many variants of such priming, they share the research design of a prime word that has either a stronger or a weaker relation to a target.) Participants are asked to react to the target, sometimes by reading it aloud and sometimes by making a judgment about it, such as whether or not it is a real word. When the prime is related to the target word (semantically, morphologically, or orthographically), participants are faster to respond to it than if the prime does not match the target.[7]

This finding is not especially surprising. It seems intuitively obvious that it would be easier to read a word in capitals, for example, if you have previously seen it in lower-case letters. The surprise is that the prime is onscreen for a breathtakingly short time, as little as 43 ms (less than a twentieth of a second).[8] As such, it is barely perceptible, if at all; participants have no conscious awareness of having seen it. Yet an abundance of evidence reveals that it nevertheless changes their response to the subsequent target. The fast appearance of a lexical prime produces measurable effects: we read so quickly that we can read almost without reading. It has long been known that readers skip words while reading, but masked semantic priming demonstrates that reading can occur even with minimal stimulus.

Such rapidity scales up from the word to the sentence. I have already noted that syntactic parsing happens automatically. This parsing can be measured by comprehension. Given the sentence "The child went to the store," you could answer correctly a question like, "Where did the child go?" If asked, "What is the name of the child?," you could recognize that this information is not in the sentence. You did more than just read one word at a time: you comprehended the sentence. Of course, if you are distracted, it is possible to read without comprehending. For example, in a famous moment in *Bleak House* Esther receives a newspaper and comments, "I read the words in the newspaper without know-ing what they meant and found myself reading the same words repeatedly."[9] In psychological terms Esther is decoding without comprehending: she can de-code even though she gets no meaning from what she has decoded. Yet experi-ments like the ones with masked priming suggest that, even when we hardly attend to what we read, reading still has effects not accessible to awareness. If we were to indulge the fantasy of Esther as a participant in an experiment, she would probably have speeded recognition of the material in the newspaper, even if she found herself unable to remember it.

*Automatic* is an adjective that the humanities loves to hate because it keeps company with other disreputable words like *routine* or *stereotyped*. At least as far back as Russian formalism, literary criticism has valued the creative imagi-nation for disrupting mental grooves that have become automatic.[10] Yet in psy-chological terms even the ability to disrupt routinized ways of seeing the world depends on automatic processes. A thin layer of disruption perches on a vast bedrock of automaticity. As Stephanie A. Lai et al. note, "Lack of automaticity at a lower level of processing (e.g., letter level or word level) can impede the rate of higher level processing (e.g., sentence level or text level)."[11]

The value of automaticity arises from a key fact about the brain: cogni-tive resources are limited. We can think only so much at once, so automatic-ity is our workaround. While limitations on cognitive resources characterize not only reading but all mental work, they matter for reading because, un-less lower-level processes are automatized, they may use up the brain's cogni-tive energy. Over time and with much practice processes become automatic. Tedious as acquiring automaticity may be, it has a big payoff: it allows us to work more efficiently despite the brain's limitations. Activities that once took considerable cognitive resources no longer do. They have become effortless, although always liable to disruption under special circumstances. This ac-quired effortlessness frees up resources for what psychologists call controlled processing, which can enable the slow, painstaking interpretation that literary critics prize.[12]

While automaticity enables complex processing, it also has a possible downside. Depending on the situation, it can allow reading to go on autopilot. Readers may do just enough work to reach what feels like a satisfactory level of comprehension, a phenomenon that psychologists call "good-enough process-ing."[13] For the average reading experience, good-enough processing is effective for preventing the brain from being overburdened. Yet it can have some strange effects. For example, participants in an experiment by Barton and Sanford read the following passage:

> There was a tourist flight traveling from Vienna to Barcelona. On the last leg of the journey, it developed engine trouble. Over the Pyrenees, the pilot started to lose control. The plane eventually crashed right on the border. Wreckage was equally strewn in France and Spain. The authorities were trying to decide where to bury the survivors.[14]

Readers were asked, "What should the authorities do?" and a majority (59 percent) did not notice that the passage contained a trick: survivors do not need to be buried. The general situation described made sense to these readers, and they assumed that the question would be relevant to what they had read. The combination of habit, easily accessible background knowledge, and pragmatic assumptions about relevance were enough to override the actual words on the page. Even though readers physically perceived "survivors," they perceived it without perceiving it: its meaning did not become part of their mental representation. Their mistake was a result of the good-enough processing that characterizes much everyday reading.

The participants in this experiment were undergraduate students, and one might hope that academics would be less susceptible to such errors. But they, too, are capable of minimal processing, not only in reading but also in the even more effortful activity of writing. For example, here are a series of excerpts from academic book reviews:

> This thoroughly readable handbook *fills a much-needed gap* in the public health nurse's instruction.

> Concise and lucid, this volume *fills a much-needed gap* in the literature.

> This special supplement of *Public Health Reports fills a much-needed gap* in research on oral health care for people living with human immunodeficiency virus (HIV).[15]

In each case the author uses the phrase "fills a much-needed gap" as praise, indicating that there has been a gap in existing knowledge, and the book under review fills it. Yet that is not what "fills a much-needed gap" means: if the gap is much needed, it is not a good idea to fill it. Nevertheless, the phrase has become a formula in academic reviewing. As of this writing, JSTOR lists more than one hundred uses in reviews, from 1929 to 2015, and most (though not all) treat it as praise. The collocation of *fills, much-needed,* and *gap* makes it seem that the phrase means what authors want it to mean. It has the right words, and it does not seem to matter that they are not in the right places. Its familiarity as a formula may further encourage minimal processing. Authors have seen or used it before, so it must make sense.

In explaining good-enough processing, Hossein Karimi and Fernanda Ferreira posit that linguistic comprehension strives to reach cognitive equilibrium. Two potential roots for reaching it work in parallel: a heuristic root, guided by existing semantic knowledge, which "can output a quick overall representation of the information currently under processing" by applying rough rules of thumb; and an algorithmic root, guided by "strict and clear syntactic algorithms to compute precise representations for the given linguistic input."[16] Both systems might be understood as racing against each other to see which can reach cognitive equilibrium first, at which point both systems stop and move on to the next piece of language. If, in language processing, the heuristic route produces cognitive equilibrium first, then the reader may be satisfied, even if, as I have demonstrated, the cost is not quite grasping what has been read. I write "may be satisfied" because some readers, depending on their goals, may not be; not everyone thinks that survivors need burial. Yet good-enough processing is reading's default setting, a way of comprehending that usually works, though it is capable of changing for specific occasions.

As an academic trained to value labor-intensive, time-consuming reading, I can be frustrated by how shallow earlier readers can sometimes seem, at least on the evidence of their surviving accounts. I want to say, "This is all they bothered to record?" Yet what seems to me like shallowness is only a version of what many readers do all the time. Given the circumstances that gave rise to their reading in the first place, they had become experts, through practice, at gauging just how much effort their reading needed, and they put in the right amount for their circumstances. It's not that readers are not capable of perceiving what I regard as deeper, more complex layers in a work; rather, they often have no reason to do so, so they do not use strategies that might have led to such perceptions.

In terms of my earlier distinctions regarding automaticity, good-enough processing fits the category of top-down automaticity, one that is learned and is always subject potentially to interruption. Yet the other category of automaticity, bottom-up automaticity, also has unexpected effects on reading. In a classic experiment D. A. Swinney gave participants a passage like one of the following:

A. Rumor had it that, for years, the government building had been plagued with problems. The man was not surprised when he found several bugs* in the corner of his room. (ambiguous word, no context)

B. Rumor had it that, for years, the government building had been plagued with problems. The man was not surprised when he found several spiders, roaches, and other bugs* in the corner of his room. (ambiguous word, with disambiguating context)

Out of context, *bugs* can mean many things: "a name given to various insects," "diseases," "defects in a machine, plan, or the like," or "concealed microphones." Passage A is written to make two of these meanings, "insects" and "concealed microphones," relevant. Passage B adds four words, "spiders, roaches, and other," to the sentence to disambiguate it, so that only the "insects" meaning is relevant.

Swinney was interested in how readers would access lexical meaning. His hypothesis seems obvious: it should be harder to access both meanings of *bugs* in Passage B than in Passage A because Passage B disambiguates the word. To test the hypothesis, Swinney used a common methodology in experiments, a lexical decision task. Participants listened to the passages until they came to *bugs*. Then, a word appeared on a computer screen, and their task was to decide whether it was a real word or nonsense. Swinney provided four possible words (called "probes") that participants could see: *ant*, *spy*, *sew*, and a nonsense word. In general, participants complete a lexical decision task more quickly if a probe has already been activated in memory. So, for Passage A the assumption would be that responses to *ant* and *spy* should be faster than responses to *sew* because *bugs*, with its ambiguous meanings, should have activated meanings related to insects (*ant*) and to concealed microphones (*spy*). For Passage B the assumption was that, after *bugs* had been disambiguated, only the meaning related to insects (*ant*) should be activated, so only that meaning should have a faster response.

It's important not to get too hung up on the details of a particular example: Swinney gave his participants thirty-six different passages, all following the same format as above. What matters are his results. The average results for passages like Passage A were exactly as expected: participants performed the lexical decision task more quickly when they saw probes related to different possible meanings of a word like *bugs* than they did when the probes were words unrelated to "bugs" or nonsense words. The surprising finding came from the average results for responses to passages like Passage B, which disambiguated *bugs*. As expected, participants quickly responded to *ant* after reading *bugs*. But they responded almost as quickly to *spy*, even after the passage made it clear that the "concealed microphone" meaning was not relevant. (As in Passage A, the unrelated word and the nonsense word received slower responses.)

Here is the point: both possible meanings of *bugs* were active in readers' minds even *after* the word had been disambiguated.[17] This is a strange finding, though one that has been replicated many times, including replications where the participants read the ambiguous sentences rather than just hearing them.[18] Just reading a word with multiple meanings is enough to activate those meanings, even if sentence context makes unmistakable that only one meaning is relevant. Admittedly, such activation does not last long. Subsequent research manipulated how long the probe word appeared after participants read the ambiguous word (in technical terms, the "stimulus offset asynchrony"). If the probe appeared very soon after the ambiguous word, then both possible meanings of the word were activated. But if the probe appeared after only a short delay, readers responded more quickly only to the contextually appropriate associated word.[19]

When a reader confronts an ambiguous word, two actions occur: a spread of activation to all possible semantic associations of that word, followed by a rapid inhibition of contextually inappropriate meanings and a narrowing to the most appropriate meaning.[20] Psychologists argue about exactly how this activation and inhibition happen, but most of their models have common features. Word meanings are stored in memory not as isolated monads but as a network of associations. All meanings have relationships of different strengths to other meanings; these strengths are created by co-occurrence and are constantly shifting. The more strongly a word meaning becomes associated with one set of other meanings, the weaker its associations become to other possible meanings. When you read a word, the most strongly activated meanings are those that, in your experience, have been most associated with that word.[21]

For a literary critic, what may be most striking about this research is its organization in polarities: a meaning is dominant or subordinate; a meaning is ambiguous or not; a possible meaning is inhibited, or it is not; cognitive equilibrium is attained, or it is not. Literary works, especially postromantic lyric poetry, live in spaces between those polarities, where it is not always so easy to tell what meaning is supposed to be dominant and just when (or if) a word has been disambiguated. To take an example from Dickinson:

Through the strait pass of suffering—
The Martyrs—even—trod.
Their feet—upon Temptation—
Their faces—upon God—[22]

If we imagine a reader coming to *pass* in the first line in the way that a reader comes to *bugs* in Swinney's passages, multiple possible meanings might be activated, some more anachronistic than others: "a paper granting permission to travel," "a successful grade," "an abstention," or "a passageway." By the end of the sentence, the verb *trod* points to "passageway" as the meaning most reinforced by other words, but (in terms of the automatic processes of reading) this disambiguation happens long after the word appeared. Although psychological work accounts for inhibiting contextually wrong meanings, it takes so long in Dickinson for the contextually right meaning to appear that inhibition cannot work the way it might in the lab. In addition, *strait* for Dickinson means "narrow," but some readers may assume it is just a misspelled "straight"; even readers who know better may not be able to suppress "unbending" as a meaning for *strait*, especially as it may seem contextually right. Dickinson's poetry thrives by sustaining the lexical ambiguities that we usually inhibit, as responses to Swinney's work demonstrate.

The second line is even more ambiguous because of Dickinson's characteristic ellipsis; it could be parsed as "Even the martyrs trod [through the strait pass]" or "The martyrs trod evenly." *Trod* helps to disambiguate *pass* in line 1 (as does "through the strait"), but *even* could be an adjective modifying "the martyrs," or a reduced form of the adverb *evenly*, modifying *trod*. In the last two lines a word that is not usually ambiguous, *upon*, becomes so because parallel structure sets up what looks like a syntactic repetition. But the *upon* of "Their feet—upon Temptation" is not the *upon* of "Their eyes—upon God": the first *upon* means "on top of," while the second means "toward." Such distinctions are easy to see once the sentence is finished, but, while reading, both meanings may be activated. Syntactic parallelism complicates the context that would usually disambiguate the word by underscoring identity, not difference.

For skilled readers of poetry, what may happen to automatic processes when faced with passages like this one is the controlled inhibition of automatic inhibition. In Dickinson's poetry and lyrics like hers, the factors that should enable inhibition are absent, muted, or delayed. This inhibition of inhibition, a cognitive double negative, prevents or at least slows the usual rapid narrowing of meaning. What happens next depends on the reader. Swinney's experiments and others like it do not show that readers consciously become aware of all the possible word meanings. Activated meanings become explicit only after they have gained enough strength, from successive activations, to rise above a critical threshold. Nothing guarantees that a reader would be aware of the many possible meanings of *pass* that I listed above, for example. Some readers, faced with Dickinson-like ambiguity, might fall back on good-enough processing by piecing together a bare sense, regardless of syntactic or semantic complexities (e.g., "martyrs are walking"). Cognitive equilibrium for such readers may be satisfied with a fuzzier level of comprehension than would be appropriate for other genres.

Others might wrestle with the difficulties and "solve" them by arriving at what they perceive to be a dominant meaning. Still others, especially those with academic expertise in reading lyric poetry, might exploit the spread of activation to multiple meanings and try to capture as many as possible, though such a process would be effortful and time-consuming. The inhibition of inhibition makes available a potential richness of semantic meaning that ordinarily would be just confusing, but readers do not necessarily respond to it explicitly. Yet even if they do not, they may nevertheless be aware of a felt difference in reading poetry, a perception of increased richness in semantic content that does not rise to paraphrasable meaning but lurks at the edge of consciousness as an awareness of language grown unexpectedly dense.

Swinney's experiment focuses on single words, but bottom-up automatic processes can affect narrative comprehension also. Here I turn to the work of Ed O'Brien and his collaborators. They presented participants with stories like the following:

*Introduction.* Bill had always enjoyed walking in the early morning, and this morning was no exception. During his walks, he would stop to talk with some of his neighbors.

*Consistent elaboration.* Bill had just celebrated his twenty-fifth birthday. He felt he was in top condition, and he worked hard to maintain it. In fact, he began doing additional workouts before and after his walks. He could now complete a 3-mile run with hardly any effort.

*Inconsistent elaboration.* Bill had just celebrated his eighty-first birthday. He didn't feel as strong as he was twenty years ago. In fact, Bill began using a cane as he hobbled along on his morning walks. He could not walk around the block without taking numerous breaks.

*Filler.* Today, Bill stopped to talk with Mrs. Jones. They had been friends for quite some time. They were talking about how hot it had been. For the past three months there had been record-breaking high temperatures and no rain. Soon there would be mandatory water rationing. As Bill was talking to Mrs. Jones, he saw a young boy who was lying in the street hurt.

*Target sentences.* He quickly ran and picked the boy up. Bill carried the boy over to the curb.

*Closing.* While Bill helped the boy, Mrs. Jones ran into her house to call the boy's mother and an ambulance. He kept the boy calm and still until help arrived.[23]

Participants read either the consistent or the inconsistent elaboration but not both; all participants read the introduction, filler, target sentences, and conclusion. In the consistent elaboration it comes as no surprise that Bill is able to run quickly to the boy in the street. In the inconsistent elaboration, Bill's ability to run quickly to the boy counters the information we have been given about him. O'Brien et al. found that readers who read the inconsistent elaboration slowed down when they came to the target sentences, and the researchers concluded that this slowdown proved that readers were keeping track of Bill as a character. Knowing that he was old and infirm made it difficult to integrate the information that he ran quickly to help the boy, and readers consequently slowed. Some literary critics might object that the text does not have to be as inconsistent as O'Brien and his collaborators claim: one could imagine that the emergency led Bill to overcome his frailty and manage a burst of speed. Yet even if we grant that option, creating such consistency still needs an extra step by the reader, an inference about Bill's emergency abilities, that requires more reading time.

This finding was not quite as obvious as it might initially seem because of the presence of the filler passage. It guaranteed that the information about Bill's physical condition was no longer in what psychologists call "working memory," defined as "a temporary storage system under attentional control that underpins our capacity for complex thought."[24] Working memory capacity is not large, though it varies from individual to individual; as Marcel Just and Patricia Carpenter have demonstrated, differences in working memory capacity explain major differences in reader behavior with regard to syntactic processing and ambiguity resolution.[25] O'Brien and his collaborators wrote their passages so that when readers reached the target sentences, Bill's physical condition was no longer in focus and would have passed out of immediate working memory. Consequently, the slowdown had to arise from the reactivation of material in long-term memory. It cannot be taken for granted that readers will reactivate relevant textual material from long-term memory (they often do nothing of the sort), so the finding that they did so in the case of an inconsistency was important.[26]

Nevertheless, the finding still seems unexciting, an elaborate setup to prove common sense. But psychologists like to probe what seems obvious. In this case, what exactly does it mean that readers were "keeping track" of Bill? Presumably, it meant that they created a mental model of him as a character, and when they read text that was inconsistent with that model, they found it hard to integrate. So, O'Brien and his colleagues further probed how readers kept track of Bill by adding another condition, which they called the "qualified elaboration" condition. Participants in this condition read the same stories as above, except that instead of the consistent or inconsistent elaboration, they read passages like this:

> *Qualified elaboration.* Bill had just celebrated his eighty-first birthday. He didn't feel as strong as he was twenty years ago. In fact, Bill began using a cane as he hobbled along on his morning walks. He could not walk around the block without taking numerous breaks. Although he was old, he could still engage in feats of strength in emergency situations.

Much of this passage is identical to the inconsistent elaboration passage, in that it stresses Bill's physical weakness. But in the last sentence, this information receives an important qualification: Bill can still move quickly when he has to do so. The inference described above now becomes explicit in the qualified elaboration condition. This information makes Bill's ability to help the child no longer inconsistent, so readers who are keeping track of Bill now ought to have no trouble with the target sentences. The inconsistency that caused the slowdown has been eliminated. Indeed, the description of Bill's ability in emergency situations might lead readers to expect that they will read about just such a situation, in which case they should read the target sentences with no slowdown.

But, as it turns out, readers slow down anyway after reading the qualified elaboration, though not as much as they did for the inconsistent elaboration. Admittedly, differences between the reading times for the target sentences in the consistent, inconsistent, and qualified conditions are small, under three hundred milliseconds. But with processes that happen quickly, such as spread of activation, small differences may have big implications, just as, in traditional close reading, tiny nuances in sound or word order are understood to carry major weight. In this case outdated information about Bill's abilities continued to affect reading, possibly because the text did not encourage readers to outdate it completely. Just as in Swinney's experiment, in which possible meanings of an ambiguous word were activated even after the word had been disambiguated, so in O'Brien's stories (and the story about Bill was only one of many read by participants), material about a character that should no longer matter still slowed reading.

O'Brien and colleagues argue that such results arise from "memory-based processing," which assumes that ordinary memory processes underlie reading comprehension. As Anne Cook and O'Brien note, "Substantial research has provided evidence for three critical characteristics of this activation process; it is passive, dumb, and unrestricted. It is passive in that it occurs without conscious or strategic effort on the part of the reader. It is dumb because information resonates (and is activated) simply on the basis of featural overlap, without regard to whether it is relevant or appropriate with respect to the current discourse model. Finally, the activation mechanism is unrestricted: The signal has the potential to contact related information from either the episodic representation of the text or general world knowledge."[27] In this case the memory processes they are describing start when readers read the target sentences, "He quickly ran and picked the boy up. Bill carried the boy over to the curb." Reading information about Bill running would cause a passive activation of previous information about Bill. It is "dumb" because the information activated is not selective or controlled: it is based solely on featural overlap (how much what you are now reading resembles what you have read or what you know about already) between the description of Bill's current physical state and his previous physical one. And it is "unrestricted" because it draws on information from the text (about Bill) and more general world information, such as knowing that people who are not in good physical shape will probably not run quickly.

After this activation the next stage would be an "integration" stage in which readers would integrate the most strongly activated material into a developing memory representation.[28] In the consistent condition such integration is easy, so readers do not slow down. In the inconsistent condition such integration is difficult, and readers do slow down. In the qualified condition such integration is more difficult than it should be. Even though, according to the narrative, readers have all the information they need to understand how Bill helped the boy, passive, dumb, and unrestricted ordinary memory processes activate outdated information about Bill. It slows down integration, though not as much as inconsistent information does.

Given that memory may retrieve irrelevant information, readers might constantly be overwhelmed by all the irrelevance. Yet boundary conditions govern the strength of activation: featural overlap; how much the existing material has been elaborated (it is easier to activate material discussed at length than material mentioned only in passing); how far away in time the activated material is from what is being read; and the causal relatedness of what is being read to what is activated in memory (the inconsistency effect vanishes if a story gives an explicit cause for inconsistent behavior).[29]

Why should literary scholars care about the finding that outdated textual information affects reading, beyond the explicit control of the reader? This is a traditional question in older literary criticism about narratives focused on character development. Since the criterion for demonstrating that a character was round as opposed to flat was the capacity for change, critics debated how much Emma Woodhouse or David Copperfield really changed. Findings from psychology suggest that the more relevant question is not whether characters can change, but whether readers can. If automatic processes continue to activate outdated information when we read, then no matter how hard a character may work to change, a reader may have trouble fully letting go of earlier phases of a character's development. Those earlier phases may be especially prominent if they have received much elaboration, as they often do in the nineteenth-century realist tradition, and if the causes for the transformation are not compelling.

At times it seems as if authors count on the automatic durability of outdated information. Classic detective fiction, insofar as it elaborates red herring plots and often gives little space to the real solution of the crime, may cause readers to connect characters with guilt even after they are exonerated. Rachel

Verinder in Wilkie Collins's *The Moonstone*, for example, is associated with the theft of the diamond for so long that she never quite escapes blame. Once her ties to possible guilt have surfaced, readers' bottom-up memory processes may reactivate them whenever she reappears. At the same time, as I have noted, various factors may weaken such associations, and activation does not necessarily equal awareness. It may be enough, though, for the automatic influence of outdated information to make it seem as if crime taints multiple characters, even if only one is ultimately guilty.[30]

An experimental variation by Jason Albrecht and Jerome Myers on the inconsistency effect further illuminates the role of automatic memory processes. The basic setup was simple: participants read a story in which Mary needed to make an airline reservation. In the "satisfied goal" version of the story, she made the reservation and then worked on creating an advertisement for her job; in the "unsatisfied goal" version of the story, she was about to make the reservation but suddenly had to work on the advertisement instead. After reading a filler passage about creating the advertisement, participants were tested on how long it took them to read target sentences near the end of the story: "She was tired and decided to go to bed. She put on pajamas and washed her face." Participants in the "unsatisfied" goal version should take longer to read the target sentences if they realized that Mary was going to sleep without having made the reservation.

As it turned out, they did just that—but only in some cases. The intriguing twist in this experiment manipulated Mary's setting. In all versions participants read that Mary, preparing to make her reservation, "sat down on her leather sofa and looked through the telephone book." What differed was a later sentence at the end of the filler, right before the target sentences about Mary getting ready for bed. In one version the sentence read, "Exhausted, Mary sat down on the leather sofa for a moment"; in the other, "Exhausted, Mary sat down for a moment."[31] The first version repeated the phrase "leather sofa" from earlier in the story; the second did not. Participants in the unsatisfied goal condition slowed down on the target sentences *only* when they read the filler with the phrase "leather sofa." Readers reinstated Mary's unsatisfied goal only when the contextual cue "leather sofa" was repeated; without it readers did not notice any problems. Repeating a seemingly trivial detail, "leather sofa," activated other earlier information.

For those interested in the nineteenth-century novel, this experiment is compelling for what it says about metonymy, which Roman Jakobson famously characterized as realism's central figure: "Following the path of contiguous relationships, the Realist author metonymically digresses from the plot to the atmosphere and from the characters to the setting in space and time."[32] Whereas Jakobson emphasized the importance of metonymy for the author, Albrecht and Myers show its importance for readers. On the surface, "leather sofa" barely qualifies as a metonymy for Mary because its role in the story is so small; it looks trivial, exactly the kind of information that most readers would not recall if asked. Yet, whether readers are aware of it or not, "leather sofa" works as a metonymy for Mary because, unimportant though it may be, its mere reappearance can reinstate important information about Mary (whether or not she accomplished her goal).

Rich pile-ups of metonymic details in realistic novels do more than just create descriptive vividness. They enable a continual succession of complex memory cues. The point is not simply a repetition effect (readers recognize the same metonymy that they have seen before). Instead, a metonymy resonates with accumulated associations. These may facilitate readers' quick access to intangible aspects of character that, on the surface, have little to do with the metonymy itself, just as "leather sofa" reinstated Mary's goal of making an airline reservation without telling us much about Mary.

While automatic processes affect the reading of words, as in Swinney's experiment, and stories, as in the inconsistency experiments, they also work at the sublexical level. Brooke Lea and his collaborators (of whom I was one) investigated automatic processing in poetry by examining alliteration: can repeating a phoneme activate earlier text? Lea et al. asked participants to read aloud blank verse passages like the following, adapted from William Carlos Williams's "Spring and All":

... Beyond, the
waste of broad, muddy fields
brown with dried weeds, standing and fallen

patches of standing water
the scattering of tall trees

*Target Lines:*
*No alliteration*: All along the creek-winding road, past Stuart's barn,
*Different alliteration*: All along the raw and rutted road the reddish barn,
*Same alliteration*: All along the way-winding road, wary whispers of the old barn,

. . .

All about them
the cold, familiar wind—
Now the grass, tomorrow
the wooden willowy warp of wildcarrot ∧ leaf {recognition probe: BARN}

Readers read only one version of the target line per poem but, over the course of the whole experiment, would have read an equal number of no alliteration, different alliteration, and same alliteration lines across all the poems. In this example the word that readers are asked to recognize is *BARN*, which appeared onscreen after the word *wildcarrot* in a line that alliterates prominently on /w/. The word *barn* appears in all the target lines, but the "no alliteration" line does not alliterate; the "different alliteration" line alliterates on /r/, not /w/; and only the "same alliteration" line alliterates on /w/, the same phoneme as the line containing the recognition probe task. A few important notes about this experiment: this example was only one of many texts that readers read, and they also read several filler texts that did not contain any alliteration to mask the purpose of the experiment. Moreover, the probe word did not always appear near the end of the line, as it does in the example. Poems were counterbalanced so that the probes were either in the first, middle, or final third of the line, so activation did not depend on where in the line they appeared.

Readers recognized that *barn* had appeared earlier in the poem more quickly when alliterations matched. Lea et al. reproduced these findings when participants read the poems silently, so effects did not depend on hearing, and also when the alliterating lines appeared in prose, so the effects did not depend on possible extra effort used to read poetry. Once again, low-level, automatic effects of which readers have no conscious awareness produced measurable differences in response. What is most striking about these findings is that the probe word (*barn*) did not share the alliteration on /w/ between the target line and the cue line. It's easy to believe that alliteration helps memory because of a repeated sound. But Lea et al. showed that alliteration spreads activation to a bigger neighborhood of words.[33] Alliteration functioned in a roughly analogous way to "leather sofa" in the metonymy experiment.

Lea at al. extended this investigation to look at the mnemonic effects of rhyme. Participants read poetry in rhyming couplets. As in the alliteration experiment, they stopped at a certain point to verify if a particular word (the probe) had appeared earlier. The probe task appeared after the subjects had read a couplet rhyming on a particular phoneme. The varying conditions were a different-rhyme condition and a same-rhyme one. As in the alliteration experiment, participants recognized the probe word more quickly when it appeared in a couplet that rhymed on the same phoneme as the couplet in which the recognition task appeared.

In an interesting twist, Lea et al. varied where the probe appeared: before or after the rhyming word. Novice readers (undergraduates) recognized the probe word more quickly only when it appeared after the rhyming couplet and only if that couplet matched the rhyme of the earlier couplet with the probe word. Expert readers (MFA students, practicing poets, and rap artists), however, had a different result. They recognized the probe word more quickly when it appeared before or after the completion of the rhyming couplet. Anticipation of rhyme was enough to facilitate activation of previous words, even before the couplet was complete.[34]

Automatic memory processes thus matter even on a sublexical level. While this finding may seem interesting to psychologists who care about memory and language, how does it matter to literary scholars? As I have stressed, memory activation is necessary but not sufficient for awareness. It is tempting, but wrong, to believe that alliteration and rhyme make readers conscious of words in previously alliterating or rhyming lines. In the example above, readers would not become aware of *barn* unless they were probed for it. Moreover, conditions favoring activation in these experiments are odd: two alliterating lines in poems otherwise devoid of salient alliteration and, slightly less unusual, two couplets rhyming on the same phoneme that are close but not adjacent.

Nevertheless, the effects detected by Lea et al. are suggestive more about poetry as experience than as meaning. Increased activation from these schemes adds a potential layer of memory activity to ordinary reading. Such activity could create a heightened textural density in reading, a sensation that does not produce paraphrasable meaning but a phenomenological feeling. In his famous essay on Tennyson, Arthur Henry Hallam describes this experience when he likens poetry to magic: "We are therefore decidedly of the opinion that the heights and depths of art are most within the reach of those who have received from Nature the 'fearful and wonderful' constitution we have described, whose poetry is a sort of magic, producing a number of impressions, too multiplied, too minute, and too diversified to allow of our tracing them to their causes, because just such was the effect, even so boundless and so bewildering, produced on their imaginations by the real appearance of Nature."[35] I am most struck by Hallam's association of poetry's magic with "impressions too multiplied, too minute, and too diversified to allow of our tracing them to their causes." Although Hallam uses *impressions*, which has a technical history in British empiricism, and I use *activation*, which has an equally technical history in psychology, we are both battling the linearity of writing to capture the nonlinear, weblike experience of reading. This may be why poetry that avoids such devices can feel comparatively barren, however difficult its words or syntax may be. An implicit hum of mental activity fueled by automatic memory processes fades to silence without the stimulation of familiar poetic schemes.

No one wants writing like Hallam's in academic discourse anymore because it seems too vague. Yet his account captures something important about the aesthetic feel of poetry not available to better disciplined critics. The scientific findings I have discussed illuminate such intuitive feelings in ways that more academically respectable readings do not. A long-standing objection to science is that its cold, emotionless tools do not capture the lived experience of art. Yet, at least for reading, the opposite may be true. Disciplined literary criticism, for all its elevation of subtlety and inflection, has more difficulty encompassing Hallam's "sort of magic" than does the science of memory.

Thus far I have argued that automatic, implicit operations of memory activate even more material than we realize. Yet another research stream paints a different image, in which reading fiction can make readers uncertain about what they have known for years.[36] Participants took an online survey of sixty-four short-answer questions about general world knowledge. Experimenters then manipulated thirty-two items from these and inserted them in two stories that participants read, two weeks after they completed the survey. Of the thirty-two, they invented sixteen false statements based on them, and put eight in each story. For example, for the question "What is the largest ocean in the world?" the corresponding false statement mentioned the Indian Ocean as the largest ocean in the world rather than the Pacific. The experiments used the other sixteen items to create neutral references, such as mentioning "the largest ocean in the world" (without naming a particular ocean). Each story also had eight true statements unrelated to the previous survey, so each story had eight false, eight neutral, and eight true statements. Before reading the stories, participants were told that the stories were fictional and might contain inaccurate information. After reading the stories, participants completed a brief filler task and then took another survey of general knowledge. In it, thirty-two questions were new and thirty-two repeated the questions that had been used to create the incorrect and neutral statements in the stories.

Experimenters found that "reading stories containing misinformation led participants to reproduce factual inaccuracies that contradicted their previously demonstrated knowledge."[37] After reading two very short stories (fourteen hundred words each), readers answered incorrectly questions about facts that, two weeks before, they had gotten right. Many similar experiments have shown that this "misinformation effect" is stubborn.[38] Readers use information that they have learned in fiction to complete later, unrelated tasks, including problem solving and decision making, and they use this information whether or not it is correct.[39]

If the prior experiments discussed in this chapter have demonstrated memory's durability, these experiments do the opposite. In them, memory seems fragile in the face of fiction's seductions because fiction so easily leads participants to counter what they already know. Even worse, as David Rapp argues, this fragility is "an ordinary consequence of the mechanisms that underlie memory, problem-solving, and comprehension": readers rely on easily accessed memories; encoded information is usually not completely overwritten by new information; and readers often do not connect a piece of information to the reliability of its source.[40]

For those interested in nineteenth-century literature, such work sheds light on the otherwise mystifying investment in factual accuracy by the period's authors and reviewers. For example, in the preface to *Bleak House*, Dickens, out of all possible topics he could have discussed, insists on the truth of his depictions of Chancery and spontaneous combustion.[41] For academic readers this preface is a letdown because the truth of spontaneous combustion feels irrelevant. Krook's death fits with the novel's images of inner rot and decay so well that its conformity to fact hardly matters. But its truthfulness mattered for Dickens, and he and other Victorians may deserve more credit than we have given them. Dickensian caricature can take care of itself, but he worries about the danger that readers might be led astray by the fiction's ability to present a false knowledge as if it were true. Getting facts right matters as much to writers like Dickens as conveying larger messages because of an ethical sensitivity to fiction's possible effectiveness as a vehicle for untruth.

The story I have told has two sides. Memory holds on to information and reactivates it quickly, but it can also give up easily on what it should retain. Both possibilities stem from the same phenomenon: ease of access. In the case of the Bill story, information about Bill, relevant or not, is reactivated by Bill's reappearance in the narrative and is enough to slow readers, even after it has been outdated. With false facts the task changes how memory works. Rather than doing word-recognition tasks or having reading times recorded, participants perform a (comparatively) effortful memory search on a test. They retrieve the material in the story because they read it recently, and the ease of this retrieval trumps long-term knowledge of correct facts.

The bigger point: much of what happens during reading is not accessible to consciousness, and that is a good thing. If it were, we would not finish a paragraph. Yet inaccessibility to consciousness does not make automaticity irrelevant. On the contrary, only when we recognize it as a default mode do the disruptions on which literariness are supposed to depend make sense: we notice these disruptions automatically, though how and if we choose to make sense of them belong to conscious awareness. Rather than prize disruptions as the core of literariness, as literary critics since Shklovsky have done, I would rather notice the constant modulations of attention that literary reading assumes, modulations so practiced that they occur under the threshold.[42]

Only through automaticity can readers enter literary time, when they may spend hours, days, and weeks in the company of an author or set of characters. During that time, automatic processes often run well, even in the most difficult of texts. We make necessary connections with background knowledge, inhibit irrelevant associations, differentially allocate attention, and balance reading's demands against multiple, incessant other demands that even the quietest of environments make on our easily distracted minds. Even more, automaticity gives us memory activations in our vast semantic network for free, even though most of them are quickly inhibited.

Although literary scholars like to imagine literature as an encounter with the new and unfamiliar, that encounter presupposes the smooth working of the old and habitual. The cost of that smoothness is that it can work too well: we miss much that we later realize is important, misunderstand passages entirely, uncritically accept information that we ought to doubt. Yet automaticity's pitfalls might also have benefits: concentrating on some passages as being especially dense or provocative requires the ability to pass over others with less effort.[43] As we read, we are hindered and helped by our memory, missing or even misunderstanding much of what we read as we, almost without effort, turn the linear presentation of text into a thick web of felt experience.

# CHAPTER 2

# THREE READERS READING

**WHEN LITERARY CRITICS** talk about reading, they usually do not mean just reading. "Just reading" is what noncritics do or what historical readers did or what critics do in their spare time; but real critics interpret. As one notes, "In college . . . we quickly become aware that though we can 'just read' newspapers and magazines and the fiction sold on drugstore paperback racks, there is a third-order code operating in literature courses, a 'close reading' almost as difficult to master as reading and speech, with as many seemingly arbitrary rules."[1] Close reading belongs in "literature courses," while "just reading" hangs out with "the fiction sold on drugstore paperback racks."

While critics may admit that nonacademic modes of reading exist, they do not want to talk about them: "I can accept the distinction . . . between *interpreting* (critically) and merely *using* a text. To critically interpret a text means to read it in order to discover, along with our reactions to it, something about its nature. To use a text means to start from it in order to get something else, even accepting the risk of misinterpreting it from the semantic point of view."[2] Why discovering something about a text's "nature" forbids using it and why using a text forbids discovering its nature are not clear. What is clear is the scorn of this author (Umberto Eco) for those who "merely" use a text. That scorn trumps the need for a logically rigorous distinction, so long as interpretation remains shielded from utilitarianism. Even reader-response critics treat interpretation as the goal, although doing so goes against their description of the reading process. They care about reading if it is literary reading, usually of hard works studied in school.

While scholars of historical readers and the sociology of reading know that not all readers read the way that literary critics do, or read the same canon, they prefer literary texts to nonliterary ones. Business contracts, words on coins, epitaphic inscriptions, and legal writs deserve study but rarely show up in histories of reading.[3] While this book is not about nonliterary reading either, it does argue that reading literary and nonliterary texts have more in common than scholars admit: the automatic processes described in the previous chapter, for example, operate regardless. The material that you are reading, literary or not, is not necessarily the most important part of the reading process. Texts have received more attention than they deserve because they are (comparatively) durable, and readers are not. We can read medieval manuscripts of *The Canterbury Tales*; we cannot talk to medieval readers of Chaucer. Yet the mere durability of text can make it seem to matter more for reading than it should.

Although *Nicholas Nickleby* and my favorite recipes differ, differences between reading them are not absolute. Reading requires integrating visual perceptions, short and long-term memory, letter and word recognition, social expectations and norms, emotions, spatial and temporal settings, background knowledge, embodied responses, autobiographical data, decision making, expertise, and much else. In narrowing reading to literary works, scholars concentrate on a specialized subset of this integration. By not recognizing how the work of reading belongs to a bigger pool of possible mental actions, it is easy to misunderstand just what reading involves, since most of these actions are not specific to reading. Instead, reading adapts cognitive actions that have many other, often more frequent, uses, such as making judgments, inferring traits from behavior, and validating propositions; and it adds them to the visual and linguistic facets of decoding.

We read with the same mind whether we are reading Henry James or a stop sign. The mind does not dredge up self-sufficient literary-reading skills, although for some readers, some strategies for reading literature may have become highly practiced and even routinized. Reading James and reading a stop sign are not identical, but, different as they are, they overlap because they draw on shared mental activities. The assumption that literary reading differs in kind from all other reading not only makes it difficult for literary scholars to understand reactions of nonacademic readers; it also masks aspects of literary reading by screening out much of what happens during it.

This claim may seem counterintuitive because scholars prize reading literature for its felt specialness: "Reading, then, is the act in which the subjective principle which I call *I*, is modified in such a way that I no longer have the right, strictly speaking, to consider it as my *I*. I am on loan to another, and this other thinks, feels, suffers, and acts within me. The phenomenon appears in its most obvious and even naivest form in the sort of spell brought about by certain cheap kinds of reading, such as thrillers, of which I say 'It gripped me.' "[4] This reader, Georges Poulet, is possessed. His *I* vanishes as the self surrenders to the fictional other, who "thinks, feels, suffers, and acts" within his mind. Alone of all human activities, reading in this account overcomes Yeats's "perpetual virginity of the soul."[5]

Poulet's fantasy overlooks how hard readers have to work to believe that they do nothing and that the author makes it all happen. Part of that work, as described in the previous chapter, is automatic. But much of it is conscious, and this self-aware work is the subject of this chapter. This work has three prongs, as described by Arthur C. Graesser, Murray Singer, and Tom Trabasso: (1) readers read with goals; (2) readers read for coherence; and (3) readers read to explain.[6] The first seems obvious but tends to be sidestepped by critics who assume a bubble of aesthetic self-sufficiency. Reading may be an end in itself at times, but, more frequently, readers read with multiple goals. While poststructuralism emphasized the plurality of the text, I care more about the plurality of the reader: if all readers have different goals, then it seems impossible to generalize about them. But psychology is helpful when facing such multiplicity. The discipline is founded on the ability to generalize about mental behavior in the face of individual differences, and this chapter demonstrates how to make such generalizations about readers.

The second prong of readers' work, reading for coherence, is a good example of language that may irritate critics. For psychologists, coherence works at local and global levels. While local coherence involves "structures and processes that organize elements, constituents, and referents of adjacent clauses or short sequences of clauses," global coherence occurs when "local chunks of information are organized and interrelated into higher order chunks."[7] Any reader confronts an onslaught of perceptual and cognitive data: sounds, words, phrases, sentences, inferences, background knowledge, emotions, metacognitive comments, evaluations, and much else. Rather than seeing the reader as passive in the face of such an onslaught, psychologists argue that readers organize this mass of cues and signals to create meaning. At local and global levels they connect the pieces that seem to be related; they inhibit what seems to be irrelevant; they draw on what they know to explain what needs explaining. Readers meaningfully organize the barrage.

Yet "coherence" and "meaningful organization" may feel like naive concepts to literary scholars because they seem to assume that reading filters out inconsistencies, ambiguities, or puzzles and leaves behind a hard crystal of certainty. In relation to serious literature, such a description feels boring because it leaves out what makes literature worth reading in the first place. Yet, from a psychological standpoint, recognizing inconsistencies, ambiguities, and puzzles allows readers to create coherence: such recognition connects different parts of a work, even if the connections turn out to lead to poststructuralist aporia. Typically, in the face of resistant works, literary scholars create a second-order mental representation in which resistance is meaningful. Rather than rejecting coherence, such a representation relocates it at a different level of interpretation. A truly incoherent mental representation leads not to global meaning but to incomprehension: at lower levels of reading it can cause mistakes in tracking setting, time, characters, goals, or motivations; at higher levels of reading it can create conscious bafflement. An incoherent mental representation is not what literary critics produce when faced with tough postmodern poetry, but they may end up with one when reading a specialized academic article in a remote field.

A famous experiment by John Bransford and Marcia Johnson clarifies how coherence works in relation to linguistic comprehension, although in this case it was oral rather than written language. Participants heard the following text:

> The procedure is actually quite simple. First you arrange things into different groups depending on their makeup. Of course, one pile may be sufficient depending on how much there is to do. If you have to go somewhere else due to lack of facilities that is the next step, otherwise you are pretty well set. It is important not to overdo any particular endeavor. That is, it is better to do too few things at once than too many. In the short run this may not seem important, but complications from doing too many can easily arise. A mistake can be expensive as well. The manipulation of the appropriate mechanisms should be self-explanatory, and we need not dwell on it here. At first the whole procedure will seem complicated. Soon, however, it will become just another facet of life. It is difficult to foresee any end to the necessity for this task in the immediate future, but then one never can tell.[8]

The experimenters judged comprehension of this passage through recall: did hearers understand the text, and how much did they remember? Most hearers rated this a difficult text, even though, sentence by sentence, it has no challenging vocabulary, syntax, or obscure references. But the sentences do not hang together. Trying to create sense from the passage was bewildering, and this bewilderment surfaced in participants' comprehension ratings and poor memory of it.

But Bransford and Johnson also presented the same passage to other participants—with an important change. They prefaced the passage with the statement, "The paragraph you will hear will be about washing clothes." These participants rated their comprehension as much higher, and they remembered much more. Their background knowledge about laundry allowed them to create connections missing for the other group. They built a coherent mental representation, while the other participants did not, and this difference changed their perceptions of comprehension and their recall. The statement about washing clothes helped listeners understand only when it preceded the passage; presenting it afterward did not increase coherence.

The coherence that readers strive to create does not have to be accurate or elaborate. All it requires is that readers do more than focus on the immediate text they are reading: they try to link it to what they have already read and know. Such links are not "in" the text, although certain lexical cues, such as causal words and connectives, can encourage them. As such, they can be difficult to visualize: although it is not controversial to claim that readers make links between pieces of text, exactly what such linking needs is more mysterious. The key involves the mind's ability to store information not as separate items but as an interconnected web, a process I discuss in more detail in the next chapter. The more strongly readers can integrate what they read, moment by moment, with what they have already read in the same work and what they already know, the better chance they have of remembering and understanding it. One of the most immediately apparent distinctions between skilled and less skilled readers is that skilled readers make such connections and less skilled do not.[9]

Graesser, Singer, and Trabasso's third assumption is that readers explain. This assumption is implicit in their second assumption about coherence because readers create coherence in part by explaining. How much explaining readers routinely do is a topic of much debate in psychology: readers who explain too little rarely comprehend well, but overexplaining can also be a problem because readers become overwhelmed. Despite the debate, the bigger point is that successful readers do not expect a text to do all the work. Danielle McNamara's work on the "reverse cohesion" effect has shown that some readers can experience a text as too coherent; this excess causes readers with substantial background on a particular topic to lose interest and consequently understand less well than when they receive a text that gives them some work to do.[10]

Readers become most self-conscious of the three prongs discussed above (goals, efforts at coherence, and explanations) when reading resists them, either because of the social setting in which the readers read, the goals they hope to accomplish, or the difficulty of the material. At such moments good-enough processing is not enough. To demonstrate how readers employ self-aware top-down comprehension strategies in the face of perceived resistance, I turn to three readers as case studies. The first is a fictional character, Mr. Knightley, in Jane Austen's *Emma*; the second, the most famous reader-response critic, Stanley Fish; the third, an anonymous participant from an experiment that I undertook with my colleagues. These readers describe in detail how they read; their descriptions make accessible the self-conscious work of reading. All three have much in common, in spite of differences of period, age, educational level, and ontological status. By examining them, I provide literary critics with a framework for describing aspects of reading that persist across differences.[11]

I turn to Austen's *Emma* both because it is hypercanonical and because it contains a scene of reading, late in the novel, after Frank Churchill writes to Mrs. Weston. In his letter he apologizes for his secret engagement to Jane Fairfax and for using Emma as a decoy. It occupies most of chapter 50 (or volume 3, chapter 14) and ends with his signature. The next chapter opens with Emma's characteristic response: "Every line relating to herself was interesting."[12] Having read it, she gives it to Mr. Knightley, to whom she is almost engaged, because she hopes to soften his harsh opinion of Frank. He reads the letter, but Austen makes an interesting choice in describing how he does so. Rather than having the narrator describe his reactions, as happened with Emma, Austen has him speak his reactions aloud, thereby providing a moment-by-moment account of his reading.

In so setting up her narrative, Austen assumes a reader who remembers Frank's letter well. Without a detailed memory of it, Mr. Knightley's commentary makes no sense, much like the passage used by Bransford and Johnson without its title. Readers who take a break of even a few minutes between chapters will forget many, if not all, of Frank's words. Mr. Knightley's commentary has cues to help them remember, but not all of them may work. Readers may drift in and out of following what Mr. Knightley says, with some parts making more sense and some less, depending on the reader's memory.

I have rearranged Austen in Appendix 1 (following this chapter) to make Frank's letter and Mr. Knightley's responses copresent. The awkwardness of my setup reveals part of Austen's point. Mr. Knightley does not just read Frank's letter closely; he reads it in a "comically nitpicking" way.[13] This comedy arises from a basic but often-overlooked aspect of reading: reading occurs as a passing moment embedded in ongoing social interactions. Graesser, Singer, and Trabasso note that readers read to accomplish goals, and Austen shows just what that often means: sustaining relationships with other people. While literary scholars treat reading as an ideal parenthesis in time, Austen suggests that reading rarely, if ever, occupies such a vacuum. Instead, choices in reading are overdetermined by how others will respond to them.

For Mr. Knightley, his goal is less to interpret the letter qua letter than to judge Frank. But he is also performing for Emma, so he walks a fine line between condemning Frank and pleasing her. Rather than representing a spontaneous overflow of powerful feelings, his comments are carefully calculated. Seeing in Frank a potential rival for Emma, he makes clear to Emma that he regards Frank, or men like Frank, as foolish. At the same time, Emma has a soft spot for Frank, and, as she reminds Mr. Knightley, to condemn him too harshly would disappoint her. He has to condemn Frank but with just a little less venom than he might otherwise. Part of Austen's genius is that we feel the uncensored Mr. Knightley snarling behind his moments of tepid not-quite-praise.

In terms of reading strategy, Mr. Knightley creates coherence by dividing Frank's letter into more and less comment-worthy parts. His responses vary: at times he speaks after almost every sentence; at other times chunks of text go by silently. The lack of commentary does not mean that he is not reading carefully or is indifferent, but it does mean, in light of his audience and goals, that he privileges some parts over others. He signals what is worth discussing by repeating a word or phrase and commenting on it: Frank writes "for my temptation," and Mr. Knightley responds, "He trifles here . . . as to the temptation"; Frank writes, "I did not come till Miss Fairfax was in Highbury," and Mr. Knightley responds, "He did not come till Miss Fairfax was here"; Frank writes, "I behaved shamefully," and Mr. Knightley responds, "You did behave very shamefully" (adding the crushing adverb). In astonishment he repeats Jane Fairfax's words breaking off her engagement, as if taking time to digest them: he recognizes surprising material and slows down to register why it is important and to update his understanding.

Closely bound up with repetitions is his most frequent activity, explicit evaluative judgment: "Bad.—He ought not to have formed the engagement"; "He is unjust to his father"; "Very bad—though it might have been worse": "Ah!

That was the act of a very, very young man." His evaluations have a pattern: a local response to Frank expands to general reflections: "Mystery; Finesse—how they pervert the understanding! My Emma, does not every thing serve to prove more and more the beauty of truth and sincerity in all our dealings with each other?" (Emma is strategically silent.) Eventually, Emma has had enough, and tells him, "I wish you would read it with a kinder spirit towards him." Whatever his actual opinions may be, he is less scathing after her remark; Austen demonstrates how readers can shift strategies in midstream in response to actual (or imagined) audiences.

To evaluate Frank, Mr. Knightley draws on not only his moral opinions but also his personal knowledge. It can lead him to disagree with Frank, as when he rebuts the account of Mr. Weston: "Mr. Weston's sanguine temper was a blessing on all his upright and honourable exertions; but Mr. Weston earned every present comfort before he endeavoured to gain it." But it can also lead him to agree with Frank, as in his comment on the Eltons: "There is no saying much for the delicacy of our good friends, the Eltons." It is not enough to claim that readers draw on "what they know" to understand what they read. It marks Mr. Knightley's skill as a reader that he knows what knowledge to draw on, and when.

Beyond what he knows about Frank, Mr. Knightley also uses generic expectations of letters. First and last impressions have special weight for him: "Humph! a fine complimentary opening: But it is his way"; "a fine ending." Using this genre knowledge helps him to work around his scorn for Frank. If he cannot approve of his conduct, he can almost approve of his prose (at least the opening and closing). He applies this knowledge strategically: after Emma has asked him to judge Frank more gently, he trades moralizing inferences for genre-based ones, which temper his edge.

Beyond knowing what background knowledge to apply, Mr. Knightley monitors his own comprehension: " 'Smallridge!'—What does this mean? What is all this?" Because Frank wrote to Mrs. Weston, his letter has facts that she would know but Mr. Knightley would not. Psychologists call questions like Mr. Knightley's a moment of "metacognition," in which readers reflect on their own reading strategies.[14] Admitting that he is lost, Mr. Knightley fills the gap by asking Emma to explain. Used to being a master-reader, he is offended that Frank's letter refers to facts that he does not know, both because they make him have to stop reading and ask for help and because they mean that he has been left out of the loop. Austen turns the dry act of metacognition into a mini-drama of social inclusion and exclusion.

At the letter's end Mr. Knightley reflects: he has finished reading but not finished comprehending. In light of the whole letter he finds a new coherence to it that leads him to predict Frank's future. For Mr. Knightley, Frank "had great faults," but, because he is "really attached to Miss Fairfax" and has "the advantage of being constantly with her," "his character will improve." He has become as reconciled to Frank as he will ever be. In the end such a reconciliation was the point of reading the letter in the first place: not to judge Frank but to allow Emma to judge him.

I have focused on what Mr. Knightley does, but Austen's representation is also remarkable for what he does not do. First, he more or less reads the letter straight through. When Emma wonders "how Mrs. Elton bears the disappointment" that Jane will not become a governess, Mr. Knightley admits the temptation to let his attention wander: "Say nothing, my dear Emma, while you oblige me to read—not even of Mrs. Elton." Only in scholarly fantasy does reading happen without distraction. Austen knows that one can spot real readers because they are always on the verge of doing something else. In this case Mr. Knightley knows that Emma and the letter compete for attention. He politely avoids distraction by asking Emma to let him concentrate, though he implies that he would love to hear her demolish Mrs. Elton.

Beyond avoiding distraction, he also avoids several other choices. He never connects earlier text to later text, nor does he free associate by conjuring up miscellaneous autobiographical information. Austen avoids such acts because Mr. Knightley is not a real reader but a fictional character: if within the frame of the text his reading is designed for Emma, outside of that frame it is designed for Austen's reader. For example, although I have treated his repetitions of words from the letter as a purely personal response, Austen, by including such repetitions, does her reader a favor by making it easier to follow which part of the letter he discusses. Mr. Knightley notes, "It will be natural for me . . . to speak my opinion aloud as I read," but his action is less "natural" than he claims. It nods to the novel's artificiality, its obligation to respect the reader's needs. Unless he spoke his opinion aloud, there would be no drama because we would not know what he thought. When Mr. Knightley does not repeat Frank's words, Austen leaves open exactly what part of the letter he responds to: are we supposed to guess (as I do in my appendix's double-column arrangement) or to know that pinning down his responses to a particular moment is not worth the trouble? Austen anticipates her readers' needs but only to a degree: for her, readers should not have too much handed to them.

Yet even as Austen highlights the mechanics underlying her treatment of Mr. Knightley, her passage foregrounds aspects of reading that reader-response critics have seen but not seen. Behaviors that critics have often bypassed include

— reading as a node in a chain of social action;

— reading's embeddedness in relation to specific people;

— the primacy of goals in directing reader attention;

— the ability to make inferences spontaneously based on different knowledges;

— metacognition;

— attention manipulation to suppress distraction.

Focusing on an idealized scene of literary reading has made these acts of reading vanish, though some are more prominent in discussions of historical readers and sociological analysis.[15] Bringing psychology to the table alerts us to processes that undergird all forms of reading, from the simplest to the most complex.

I have not yet addressed the strangest aspect of the scene. All Mr. Knightley's virtuosity as a reader looks like a somewhat embarrassed compensation for a basic awkwardness: he judges Frank on the basis of a letter he should not have read. Frank wrote to Mrs. Weston, and we have no idea if Frank has consented for the letter to be read by others, although his words assume that Mr. Weston will also read it. Since he addresses Emma openly in the letter, he may assume that Mrs. Weston will let Emma know what is in it, but Mr. Knightley is another story. Mr. Knightley reads it anyway, at Emma's request. As he does so, Austen turns the flat building blocks of what Graesser, Singer, and Trabasso describe as explicit reading processes (goals, coherence, explanation) into a guilty pleasure: Mr. Knightley judges Frank's problematic morality when he himself is overstepping boundaries. The coherence of his final mental representation of Frank depends on the convenient absence of Frank himself, who cannot rebut any of his judgments.

Austen hints that a reader's ability to complete goals, find coherence, and produce satisfactory explanations may depend on a certain distance from the action being described: comprehending letters written to other people may be easier than comprehending those to oneself. As such, reading a text differs from reading a person. Austen dramatizes this difference in the split between Mr. Knightley's reactions to Frank's letters and his reactions to Emma. For example, when he reaches the section of the letter about the Box Hill episode, she notes his "one momentary glance at [Emma], instantly withdrawn, in the fear of giving pain." He has no such qualms about Frank, in part because Frank is not around to hear him. Complex as reading is for Mr. Knightley, it is safer for him, and for Austen, than the delicate world of person-to-person interactions.

Going from *Emma* to Stanley Fish's "Literature in the Reader" in *Is There a Text in This Class?* means trading one fiction for another. Fish wants to capture "the idea of *meaning as an event,* something that is happening between the words and in the reader's mind."[16] This quotation reveals some nervousness: on the basis of Fish's argument, he should have written "something that is happening between the words and the reader's mind." Instead, he writes, "between the words and in the reader's mind," locating "something that is happening" in two places at once: the page ("between the words") and the reader ("in the reader's mind"). Fish skirts the question of exactly how to connect page and reader, and that avoidance troubles the close readings that should demonstrate the connection.

Fish, for example, plucks one sentence from Pater's famous "Conclusion" to *The Renaissance* and then analyzes it:

> And if we continue to dwell in thought on this world, not of objects
> in the solidity with which language invests them, but of impressions,
> unstable, flickering, inconsistent, which burn and are extinguished with
> our consciousness of them, it contracts still further.

. . . The least forceful word in its first two clauses is "not," which is literally overwhelmed by the words that surround it—"world," "objects," "solidity," "language"; and by the time the reader reaches the "but" in "but of impressions," he finds himself inhabiting (dwelling in) a "world" of fixed and "solid" objects. It is of course a world made up of words, constructed in large part by the reader himself as he performs grammatical actions which reinforce the stability of its phenomena. By referring backwards from "them" to "objects," the reader accords "objects" a place in the sentence (whatever can be referred back to must be somewhere) and in his mind. In the second half of the sentence, however, the same world is unbuilt. There is still a backward dependence to the reading experience, but the point of reference is the word "impressions"; and the series which follows it—"unstable," "flickering," "inconsistent"—serves only to accentuate its *in*stability. . . . Pater perpetrates the very deception he is warning against, but this is only one part of his strategy. The other is to break down (extinguish) the coherence of the illusion he has created. Each successive stage of the sentence is less exact . . . than its predecessors, because at each successive stage the reader is given less and less to hold on to; and when the corporeality of "this world" has wasted away to an "it" ("it contracts still further"), he is left with nothing at all.[17]

We have come a long way from Mr. Knightley. Fish's assumptions, goals, outcome, and tone are so different that he and Mr. Knightley seem hardly to be doing the same thing. Even if one admits that there may have to be some initial perceptual similarities (both Mr. Knightley, in the fiction of *Emma*, and Fish, wherever he was when he read this sentence, had to see written symbols and translate them mentally), these early stage similarities hardly matter next to late-stage differences. Mr. Knightley reads an entire letter; Fish reads a single sentence. Mr. Knightley judges Frank; Fish judges the effect of one sentence on an ideal reader who exists only to experience it. Mr. Knightley ends by creating a story about Frank; Fish, a story about a presumed experience.

Nevertheless, counterintuitive as it may seem, Mr. Knightley and Fish have much in common. Most obviously, they are very close readers, although the comic nitpicking of Mr. Knightley has become Fish's virtuosic professionalism. For both, larger goals drive this close reading. Whereas Mr. Knightley reads to court Emma, Fish reads as part of an essay designed for scholars. The ideal reader he envisions in the passage has no goals other than to experience Pater, but that ideal reader helps Fish the academic reach his goal of demonstrating his theory of reading. Although Fish's audience is not present, as Emma is for Mr. Knightley, it nevertheless affects his choices. More precisely, it affects how he writes: what we see is less Fish reading than "Fish the writer" narrating what supposedly happened to an ideal "Fish the reader" before writing.

Beyond their goals, both Fish and Mr. Knightley create coherence by sorting what they read into parts that are more and less deserving of commentary. Not everything in Frank's letter earns Mr. Knightley's judgments. More spectacularly, Fish omits almost all *The Renaissance* to zero in on one sentence (he does discuss other bits of Pater elsewhere). Even here, however, he looks at some parts and not others: for example, he prefers nouns and adjectives to verbs. Although Fish claims that his method is designed to "*slow down* the reading experience," it slows differentially.[18] Even at its most patient, it still skips what, for a different reader, might be important. For him, as for Mr. Knightley, coherence depends on disintegrating the text, moving some of it to the foreground and shunting other parts out of sight.

Also, like Mr. Knightley, Fish the reader explains what he reads, often at a local level signaled by word repetition. Whereas Mr. Knightley's repetitions had an edge of impatience or astonishment, Fish repeats to provide evidence for his ideal reader's explanatory inferences: "The series which follows it [*impressions*]—'unstable,' 'flickering,' 'inconsistent'—serves only to accentuate its instability." Both Fish and Mr. Knightley likewise use background knowledge to explain what they read. When Fish notes, "Pater perpetrates the very deception he is warning against, but this is only one part of his strategy," he is not describing the historical Walter Pater. Instead, he uses a literary critical convention, the implied author, to whom agency can be attributed post hoc (I discuss the implied author more fully in the next chapter). Similarly, to describe the ideal reader's experience, Fish employs a familiar literary critical flourish: embodying the reader, as if reading a sentence were like experiencing a space. Fish imagines Pater's sentence as putting the reader in a rapidly vanishing physical world. Different as Mr. Knightley and Fish are, they both supplement the words on the page with relevant knowledge, retrieved from long-term memory and integrated with the text.

Mr. Knightley does more than just use background knowledge: he also evaluates. Fish refrains from overtly praising or blaming Pater; his stance as critic removes him from the network of personal relations that Mr. Knightley inhabits. Although Fish participates in the social relations that partly constitute an academic discipline, conventions of academic criticism keep them invisible. Yet he, like Mr. Knightley, projects a personality for the text's author and, also like Mr. Knightley, accuses that personality of deceiving: "Pater perpetrates the very deception he is warning against: but this is only one part of his strategy." This sentence shifts agency to Pater, who, until this moment, has not appeared in the analysis. Suddenly, Fish retrieves Pater as author and infers authorial intention, even at the risk of abandoning his fiction of an ideal reader who is supposed to create meaning. The bigger point is that, although Fish puts his background knowledge to different uses than Mr. Knightley does, they both go beyond the text to draw on general world knowledge, genre-specific knowledge, and evaluative inferences to explain what they read.

Fish and Mr. Knightley are also both highly self-aware. Fish never acknowledges that a reader, even of a text as difficult as Pater's, might stoop to good-enough processing as discussed in the previous chapter. Instead, Fish's ideal reader aims for "too good processing": analysis so slow as to be useless in most situations. Fish's ideal reader is supposed to know, first, that Pater's sentence asks him or her to build up a mental world and, second, that the sentence then takes it away: "at each successive stage the reader is given less and less to hold on to." This reader is so aware of reading processes that syntax is felt as drama. Fish's reader's memory is so good that when the second half arrives, the reader remembers enough of the first half to know that it is being unbuilt.

Fish's ideal reader, like Mr. Knightley, is highly disciplined: both avoid distractions and random associations that float up from memory. Whether or not such associations occurred to the biographical Fish while he read the sentence, his post hoc procedure of writing in an academic context filters out such material. Instead, Fish, like Mr. Knightley, produces a coherent representation in the form of a causally connected story. Where Mr. Knightley creates a minibiography of Frank, Fish creates an ideal plot, not for Pater's sentence but for the reader's experience: "At each successive stage the reader is given less and less to hold on to" so that by the end "he is left with nothing at all." Fish's reader notices the things that a good critic is supposed to notice and avoids the distractions, mistakes, and meanderings that might characterize a less disciplined reader.

Yet, as in the case of Mr. Knightley, the coherence of Fish's ideal reader shows some strain because that reader competes with two other agents: Walter Pater ("Pater perpetrates the very deception he is warning against") and Fish the critic as engaged narrator of Fish the reader ("by the time the reader reaches the 'but' in 'but of impression')." This competition has an odd effect: Fish the reader keeps disappearing from the paragraph that should describe his activities. Although, to make sense in Fish's larger argument, the paragraph ought to be about the reader's temporal experience, Pater the implied author and Fish the critic all but push Fish the reader off the stage. The coherence of the reader's experience takes second place to the coherence of the critic's essay: ultimately, Fish is more interested in making a point about Pater than about reading, and he lets his reader appear only long enough to characterize his understanding of Pater's sentence.

For both Mr. Knightley and Fish the critic, the resistance that they face is that their reading confronts an experience that is not really theirs. Mr. Knightley reads a letter by someone else written for someone else: he is the wrong audience for the letter and struggles at points to understand it. Fish imagines a reader who has had a reading experience that Fish himself may or may not have had: Fish pretends that his experience aligns with that of his ideal reader but only insofar as that experience leads to a tidy reading of Pater's sentence. For both Mr. Knightley and Fish, their ingenuity faces an uncomfortable pretense: Mr. Knightley reads as if it is proper for him to read a letter not intended for him, and Fish writes as if he actually experienced what his imagined reader experiences.

For both, the resistances that they face as readers constitute unusual disruptions of their usual skill. For my third and final reader in this chapter, I turn to a more common experience of resistance while reading: confronting a text that does not make sense. I collected this reader's reactions in a think-aloud protocol, the outcome of a method in which participants speak their thoughts while reading. This may initially appear like a strange, unconvincing way to learn about reading. Having one's reading interrupted creates an artificial context that may not reflect customary reading practices. For readers used to imagining themselves immersed in a text, being constantly stopped to talk seems as if it would upset concentrated effort. At the same time, literary scholars, when reading carefully, may find themselves stopping to ponder word choice, relevant context, links to other literature, and other topics, so that the stop-and-start rhythm of think-aloud experiments may not be as alien as it initially seems. The difference is that, in the experiment, the experimenter imposes the rhythm from the outside, to guarantee that the reader stops to reflect.

As Michael Pressley and Peter Afflerbach note in *Verbal Protocols of Reading*, coming into a lab to participate in an experiment removes readers from everyday experience, even if experimenters do their best to put participants at ease.[19] In addition, no experimental measure of reading will tell researchers all they need to know; any measure has a mix of pros and cons. In the case of think-aloud protocols the goal is not to access every aspect of reading but to learn about the facets over which readers have the most conscious control. The more automatic a task is, the less helpful self-reports are because participants perform it with no explicit thought. The artificiality of the think-aloud procedure, in contrast, guarantees that participants' self-reports represent aspects of reading of which they are most aware.

According to Pressley and Afflerbach, "One characteristic of controlled processes compared to automatic processes is that they tend to occur sequentially, one step at a time. Thus, their structure is well matched to the structure of verbalization, which can only report processes in sequence, one at a time."[20] In terms of validity, Pressley and Afflerbach stress the procedures that researchers should follow to capture valid self-reports. Participants should report the first thing that comes to mind so that reports reflect the contents of short-term memory; they should not be asked to describe or explain their acts because doing so can affect future reading. Moreover, readers should not be discouraged from reporting even if their reports seem incoherent: whatever they say counts as valid evidence. Researchers should intervene only if readers forget to provide reports, which sometimes happens inadvertently as readers become more involved with texts, especially longer ones. Since readers sometimes begin by reporting their short-term memory and then continue by interpreting it, researchers should recognize that the beginnings of self-reports will best represent short-term memory.[21]

The downside of the think-aloud procedure is that it encourages participants to focus on the particular chunk of the text that they have just read rather than on bigger connections. Its benefits are that it guarantees that readers pay attention to the text and, having generated their own responses, are more likely to remember them. Knowing that readers process the text more carefully than they might otherwise counterbalances the artificiality of the experience.

This particular reader, a college student whom I will call H, received Leane Zugsmith's short story "The Three Veterans" (1935) to read. (H was part of a large body of participants in an experiment at my university; to protect anonymity, I arbitrarily assign feminine pronouns to H, but H's gender may have been male or female.) The story appeared in segments on note cards. After each segment, H thought aloud; those thoughts were recorded and transcribed. After finishing the story, H recalled out loud as much of the story as possible and then interpreted the meaning of the story. In Appendix 2 (following this chapter), I present Zugsmith's story in the left-hand column and H's responses in the right-hand one.

In terms of goals, all H has been asked to do is to read and understand. To accomplish this goal, H, like Mr. Knightley and Fish, strives to create coherence and develop explanations. Doing so, once again, involves filtering the story into levels of importance; using background knowledge; inhibiting distractions; repeating and expanding on language in the story; and connecting textual material, inferences, and background knowledge. H frequently paraphrases what has just been read, sometimes echoing the story (Zainer: "with their old, high-veined legs stiff ahead of them"/H: "their old high veined legs"; Zainer: "she had only a little two-inch scratch"/H: "she has just a little tiny scratch"; Zainer: "'How would you girls like to dance in my chorus Friday night?'"/H: "They're thinking about dancing in his chorus on Friday night"), and at other times, rephrasing it at a higher level of generality: Zainer: "Each showed gaps in her front teeth when she broke into her cackle, each had yellow-gray hair wisping from beneath a moldy hat; each wore stained, shapeless outer garments; and each had the same kind of bad leg" / H: "So um they look very much alike and have the same kind of clothing and the same kind of characteristics and the same bad leg."

Typically, H infers important information to explain what is happening, as in many comments about character motives. H reads, "When the pale young woman with the fretful infant came in, relinquishing her numbered green ticket for Room 4, and sat opposite them, Mrs. Betz crooked her soiled finger. 'Gutsie-goo,' she said to the baby," and comments, "Um so she's trying Mrs. Betz one of the three women is trying to entertain the baby and make it happier and they're in room four that's like the room." H filters out details and explains Mrs. Betz's actions in terms of motivations not explicit in the text: she recognizes that Mrs. Betz is trying to entertain the fretful baby. H makes other inferences more rarely, but they still appear, such as when H recognizes that the remedies that the three women suggest are not standard medical practice or when H predicts that we will learn more about the peroxide-blonde woman's abrasion.

Yet what distinguishes H from Mr. Knightley and Fish is that her reading experience is much more difficult: "I'm not sure really what's going on"; "I thought it was kinda confusing I just kept getting confused." As I noted above, it is tempting but wrong to blame H's troubles on the think-aloud procedure itself, as if H would have had an easier time if she had read the story straight through, without breaks. Notably, H does not blame comprehension problems on the procedure. Instead, H knows that her comprehension process has not worked quite well enough for her to understand the story. Although her representation is not completely incoherent, H is like the listeners of Bransford and Johnson's untitled laundry passage: she has trouble integrating story elements, inferences, and background knowledge into a coherent representation.

When psychologists describe low-skilled readers, they often focus on those who do little more than paraphrase the text or who make irrelevant or incorrect inferences. H is interesting instead as an average reader, neither an expert nor a failure. While literary critics assume hypercompetent readers, psychologists often split readers into high- and low-skilled groups, leaving the average out of the picture. Yet, arguably, the bulk of readers are neither especially high- nor especially low-skilled; instead, they are like H, who admits to confusions yet still comes to a conjectural, if uncertain, sense of meaning.

Why do H's problems occur, and how does she react to them? The local challenges she confronts may arise from a lack of background knowledge. Not recognizing that the setting is a clinic for the poor during the Depression, H has trouble understanding the behavior of the three women: "Um, so I think he's telling this to the patient but I'm not sure really what's going on" after reading the passage, "He [the doctor] whispered to the nurse and then, without looking into Mrs. Gaffney's submissive eyes, said, 'You better quit staying out dancing all night, or that'll never get right.' The three old women cackled with delight." H confuses patient and nurse by taking the three women to be nurses. This misunderstanding goes back to her comment about the passage, "Together, they would question newcomers and advise them on their ills, but once The Doctor was in the room, they would remain respectfully silent unless he made one of his lame jokes or scolded them." H notes, "So, they work together and um the doctor is kind of a little overbearing and they want to be quiet and respectful of him they'll laugh at his jokes." H does not remember previous indications that Miss Riordan is the nurse (mentioned in the first sentence) and the three old women are patients (inferred from the description of their varicose veins). Instead, H holds on to the fact that this is a medical setting and notices that the women question "newcomers" and advise "them on their ills"; from this she assumes that they are nurses, despite evidence to the contrary. She even incorrectly updates information on the basis of her assumption: "So um Miss Riordan is not part of these three women I guess and maybe she's like a receptionist more than the nurses."

H maintains her misconception that the old women are nurses during the passage in which they talk to the mother with the sick infant and recommend home remedies. Although she knows that they do not offer medically sound remedies, she still clings to her misconception because changing a knowledge structure is hard (as I discussed in Chapter 1, even after successful updating, outdated information can still interfere with comprehension). Not until the old women receive treatment as patients does H realize that her understanding has gone awry, and she uses "patient" to describe them, although she never states that she has corrected her misconception.

After H recognizes that she is having trouble, the nature of her think-alouds changes because she makes fewer, more limited inferences. When H reads, "'Well, Madam, you can tell your lawyer that anyone who's so careless as to trip on the stairs deserves more than the little scratch you have there.' The three old women lowered their heads, their soiled fingers at their mouths to curb the explosions of laughter," H comments, "So he's telling her not to sue because it was her fault basically." Unlike her earlier paraphrases, H here leaves out material. She omits the old women's reaction and simplifies the doctor's comment, which blames the blonde woman and suggests the woman should have been hurt even more. H's inferences become more tentative, as indicated by the *maybe*. We can see in real time how H's top-down processing changes: in response to recognizing a mistake, H plays it safe by limiting inferential exploration.

Yet the strategy that H adopts to rescue her comprehension becomes a problem, because she avoids making inferences crucial to the story. She takes literally the specialist doctor's request for the women to "dance in his chorus." In addition, H may not know that doctors at this period routinely used live patients in teaching. H does not recognize that the doctor's "chorus" on "Friday night" refers to his "Friday night lecture." Nothing in the story enables H to fix her mistake. The result is that H does not fully understand the story's climax, in which the women, remembering the peroxide blonde, rebel against the authority of the doctors.

Yet in H's final interpretation she grasps more of the story than we might have suspected: "I felt like women power maybe because like a feminist kind of view but maybe that's just how I'm reading it because like the doctor is the overbearing one the three women just like to and they don't want to dance in the chorus and the women with the peroxide hair like says that we have to be treated like human beings too."[22] Although H lacks adequate background knowledge in moment-to-moment processing, when she looks over the story as a whole, she retrieves a different source of background knowledge, feminism, that lets her create a degree of global coherence. Despite misconceptions while reading, H is able to use her understanding of feminism to recognize a power struggle between male and female characters, and that allows her to create an integrated representation.

At a broad level H does much that Mr. Knightley and Fish do. Like them, she reads slowly enough that we can track her mental processes. Also like them, she has a goal, works for coherence, and explains what she reads; to do so, she draws on background knowledge, makes inferences, creates causal connections, monitors comprehension, and paraphrases. Her domain knowledge in one area (feminism) makes up for lack of background knowledge in another area (historical context). Even though she recognizes that she does not understand everything in the story, she still uses her knowledge of interpretation (from a "feminist kind of view") to come to a meaning, though tentatively.

Barthes says, "To read is to find meanings, and to find meanings is to name them," but his description is too broad.[23] Readers engage in two activities at once: understanding the immediate text that they read (the microstructure) and updating a larger model (the macrostructure). For the microstructure readers parse the immediate text, make inferences, connect earlier and later parts of the text, notice and maybe correct errors, and inhibit distractions. For the macrostructure readers choose the most relevant pieces of information and fit them together to meet a goal. This double process characterizes readers across a range of abilities and purposes. Moreover, although it might seem that the macrostructure should be developed as more microstructure becomes available, for the readers in this chapter the macrostructure does not become available until after reading. Mr. Knightley delivers his final evaluation of Frank only after reading the whole letter; Fish, despite the fiction that he describes reading as it happens, projects a post hoc understanding backward, as if it were happening moment by moment; H also does not articulate a global understanding of the story until after it is over, in response to an experimental prompt. As these readers demonstrate, full comprehension and reading do not co-occur, which is why literary scholars should hesitate more than they do to make "reading" synonymous with "interpretation."

The experience of all three readers in this chapter turns the bland psychological assumptions of having a goal, creating coherence, and making explanations into a tense drama against resistant circumstances. To link microstructure and macrostructure, each reader confronts difficulties and overcomes them with varying degrees of success. The difficulties may lie in the social circumstances of the reading event, as for Mr. Knightley; the relation between goal and experience, as for Fish; and inadequate background knowledge and inferring, as for H. When comprehension is not automatic, the reader has to negotiate difficulties that require developing new skills on the fly, such as coping with what is felt to be inadequate or partial understanding.

For psychologists these examples expand how they might conceive of problems with reading. As the field is now structured, memory researchers assume that reading problems arise from problems with memory; attention researchers, from problems with attention; inference researchers, from problems with inferring; and so on. Yet representations of real and fictional readers remind us that these cognitive factors matter in a specific reading context. In particular, research into reading comprehension tends to treat readers as either getting a text right or wrong; either readers create a coherent and useful mental representation, or they do not. The examples in this chapter demonstrate that it may be important to do better research on imperfect comprehension, circumstances in which readers develop links between macro- and microstructure that are almost adequate but not quite. Doing so would provide a more accurate representation of the many readers who are neither novices nor experts but somewhere in between.

For literary critics these examples are meant to point in two directions at once: (1) to general reading processes used across situations and (2) to the particularities of reading in light of varying goals. Reader goals remain understudied in literary scholarship because they are presumed to be so various as to defeat meaningful generalization. But without an explicit account of such goals, interpreters let one of the chief determiners of literary experience vanish. Works of art may or may not belong to an autonomous aesthetic realm, but acts of reading do not.

Acknowledging reading goals is part of what Walter Kintsch meant when he called his classic work on reading comprehension a "paradigm for cognition." The activities he describes are not exclusive to reading but belong to the tool kit of general cognition.[24] Literary scholars assume that characters are not real people and that the questions appropriate to ask about them are not the same ones that we might ask about real people. Yet no matter how often we stress such a point, both students in literature classes and many critics find that it never fully takes hold. For all our efforts, readers persist in treating literary characters as if they were people they had met. This chapter offers an alternative to treating such responses as mere naiveté. Readers respond to literature as if it is real life because many activities that go into understanding literature are the same ones required to understand daily events.

Having discussed both automatic and explicit aspects of reading, I turn to bringing both together in the study of historical readers. What can findings and vocabularies from the empirical study of reading tell us about earlier readers? Whereas historians have devoted much effort to examining the physical evidence of actual books, and understanding how readers accessed and afforded them, the history of reading has had more difficulty in tracking just what happens when readers read. While the evidentiary problems in analyzing historical readers are enormous, I will nevertheless argue that we can understand much about historical readers if we focus not on what, but on how, they read.

## Appendix 1: From Austen's *Emma*

*Frank Churchill's Letter*

Windsor—July.

My dear Madam,
"If I made myself intelligible yesterday, this letter will be expected; but expected or not, I know it will be read with candour and indulgence.—

You are all goodness, and I believe there will be need of even all your goodness to allow for some parts of my past conduct.—

But I have been forgiven by one who had still more to resent. My courage rises while I write. It is very difficult for the prosperous to be humble. I have already met with such success in two applications for pardon, that I may be in danger of thinking myself too sure of your's, and of those among your friends who have had any ground of offence.—

*Mr. Knightley's Responses*

He began—

stopping, however, almost directly to say, "Had I been offered the sight of one of this gentleman's letters to his mother-in-law a few months ago, Emma, it would not have been taken with such indifference."

He proceeded a little farther, reading to himself;

and then, with a smile, observed, "Humph!—a fine complimentary opening:—But it is his way. One man's style must not be the rule of another's. We will not be severe."

"It will be natural for me," he added shortly afterwards, "to speak my opinion aloud as I read. By doing it, I shall feel that I am near you. It will not be so great a loss of time: but if you dislike it—"

[Emma speaking.] "Not at all. I should wish it."

Mr. Knightley returned to his reading with greater alacrity.

You must all endeavour to comprehend the exact nature of my situation when I first arrived at Randalls; you must consider me as having a secret which was to be kept at all hazards. This was the fact. My right to place myself in a situation requiring such concealment, is another question. I shall not discuss it here. For my temptation to *think* it a right, I refer every caviller to a brick house, sashed windows below, and casements above, in Highbury.

"He trifles here," said he, "as to the temptation. He knows he is wrong, and has nothing rational to urge.—

I dared not address her openly; my difficulties in the then state of Enscombe must be too well known to require definition; and I was fortunate enough to prevail, before we parted at Weymouth, and to induce the most upright female mind in the creation to stoop in charity to a secret engagement.—

Bad.—He ought not to have formed the engagement.—

Had she refused, I should have gone mad.—But you will be ready to say, what was your hope in doing this?—What did you look forward to?—To any thing, every thing—to time, chance, circumstance, slow effects, sudden bursts, perseverance and weariness, health and sickness. Every possibility of good was before me, and the first of blessings secured, in obtaining her promises of faith and correspondence. If you need farther explanation, I have the honour, my dear madam, of being your husband's son, and the advantage of inheriting a disposition to hope for good, which no inheritance of houses or lands can ever equal the value of.—

'His father's disposition':—he is unjust, however, to his father. Mr. Weston's sanguine temper was a blessing on all his upright and honourable exertions; but Mr. Weston earned every present comfort before he endeavoured to gain it.—

See me, then, under these circumstances, arriving on my first visit to Randalls;—and here I am conscious of wrong, for that visit might have been sooner paid. You will look back and see that I did not come till Miss Fairfax was in Highbury;

Very true; he did not come till Miss Fairfax was here."

"And I have not forgotten," said Emma, "how sure you were that he might have come sooner if he would. You pass it over very handsomely—but you were perfectly right."

"I was not quite impartial in my judgment, Emma:—but yet, I think—had you not been in the case—I should still have distrusted him."

and as you were the person slighted, you will forgive me instantly; but I must work on my father's compassion, by reminding him, that so long as I absented myself from his house, so long I lost the blessing of knowing you. My behaviour, during the very happy fortnight which I spent with you, did not, I hope, lay me open to reprehension, excepting on one point. And now I come to the principal, the only important part of my conduct while belonging to you, which excites my own anxiety, or requires very solicitous explanation. With the greatest respect, and the warmest friendship, do I mention Miss Woodhouse;

When he came to Miss Woodhouse, he was obliged to read the whole of it aloud—all that related to her, with a smile;

my father perhaps will think I ought to add, with the deepest humiliation.—

a look;

A few words which dropped from him yesterday spoke his opinion, and some censure I acknowledge myself liable to.—

a shake of the head;

My behaviour to Miss Woodhouse indicated, I believe, more than it ought.—

a word or two of assent,

In order to assist a concealment so essential to me, I was led on to make more than an allowable use of the sort of intimacy into which we were immediately thrown.—

or disapprobation;

I cannot deny that Miss Woodhouse was my ostensible object—but I am sure you will believe the declaration, that had I not been convinced of her indifference,

I would not have been induced by any selfish views to go on.—Amiable and delightful as Miss Woodhouse is, she never gave me the idea of a young woman likely to be attached; and that she was perfectly free from any tendency to being attached to me, was as much my conviction as my wish.—

or merely of love, as the subject required;

She received my attentions with an easy, friendly, goodhumoured playfulness, which exactly suited me. We seemed to understand each other. From our relative situation, those attentions were her due, and were felt to be so.—Whether Miss Woodhouse began really to understand me before the expiration of that fortnight, I cannot say;—when I called to take leave of her, I remember that I was within a moment of confessing the truth, and I then fancied she was not without suspicion; but I have no doubt of her having since detected me, at least in some degree.—She may not have surmised the whole, but her quickness must have penetrated a part. I cannot doubt it. You will find, whenever the subject becomes freed from its present restraints, that it did not take her wholly by surprise. She frequently gave me hints of it. I remember her telling me at the ball, that I owed Mrs. Elton gratitude for her attentions to Miss Fairfax.—I hope this history of my conduct towards her will be admitted by you and my father as great extenuation of what you saw amiss. While you considered me as having sinned against Emma Woodhouse, I could deserve nothing from either. Acquit me here, and procure for me, when it is allowable, the acquittal and good wishes of that said Emma Woodhouse, whom I regard with so much brotherly affection, as to long to have her as deeply and as happily in love as myself.—

concluding, however, seriously, and, after steady reflection, thus—

"Very bad—though it might have been worse.—Playing a most dangerous game. Too much indebted to the event for his acquittal.—No judge of his own manners by you.—Always deceived in fact by his own wishes, and regardless of little besides his own convenience.—Fancying you to have fathomed his secret. Natural enough!—his own mind full of intrigue, that he should suspect it in others.— Mystery; Finesse—how they pervert the understanding! My Emma, does not every thing serve to prove more and more the beauty of truth and sincerity in all our dealings with each other?"

Emma agreed to it, and with a blush of sensibility on Harriet's account, which she could not give any sincere explanation of.

"You had better go on," said she.

He did so,

Whatever strange things I said or did during that fortnight, you have now a key to. My heart was in Highbury, and my business was to get my body thither as often as might be, and with the least suspicion. If you remember any queernesses, set them all to the right account.—Of the pianoforté so much talked of, I feel it only necessary to say, that its being ordered was absolutely unknown to Miss F—, who would never have allowed me to send it, had any choice been given her.—

The delicacy of her mind throughout the whole engagement, my dear madam, is much beyond my power of doing justice to. You will soon, I earnestly hope, know her thoroughly yourself.—No description can describe her. She must tell you herself what she is—yet not by word, for never was there a human creature who would so designedly suppress her own merit.—Since I began this letter, which will be longer than I foresaw, I have heard from her.—She gives a good account of her own health; but as she never complains, I dare not depend. I want to have your opinion of her looks. I know you will soon call on her; she is living in dread of the visit. Perhaps it is paid already. Let me hear from you without delay; I am impatient for a thousand particulars. Remember how few minutes I was at Randalls,

but very soon stopt again to say, "the pianoforté! Ah! That was the act of a very, very young man, one too young to consider whether the inconvenience of it might not very much exceed the pleasure. A boyish scheme, indeed!—I cannot comprehend a man's wishing to give a woman any proof of affection which he knows she would rather dispense with; and he did know that she would have prevented the instrument's coming if she could."

After this, he made some progress without any pause.

and in how bewildered, how mad a state: and I am not much better yet; still insane either from happiness or misery. When I think of the kindness and favour I have met with, of her excellence and patience, and my uncle's generosity, I am mad with joy: but when I recollect all the uneasiness I occasioned her, and how little I deserve to be forgiven, I am mad with anger. If I could but see her again!—But I must not propose it yet. My uncle has been too good for me to encroach.—I must still add to this long letter. You have not heard all that you ought to hear. I could not give any connected detail yesterday; but the suddenness, and, in one light, the unseasonableness with which the affair burst out, needs explanation; for though the event of the 26th ult., as you will conclude, immediately opened to me the happiest prospects, I should not have presumed on such early measures, but from the very particular circumstances, which left me not an hour to lose. I should myself have shrunk from any thing so hasty, and she would have felt every scruple of mine with multiplied strength and refinement.—But I had no choice. The hasty engagement she had entered into with that woman— Here, my dear madam, I was obliged to leave off abruptly, to recollect and compose myself.—I have been walking over the country, and am now, I hope, rational enough to make the rest of my letter what it ought to be.—It is, in fact, a most mortifying retrospect for me. I behaved shamefully.

Frank Churchill's confession of having behaved shamefully was the first thing to call for more than a word in passing.

"I perfectly agree with you, sir,"—was then his remark. "You did behave very shamefully. You never wrote a truer line."

And here I can admit, that my manners to Miss W., in being unpleasant to Miss F., were highly blameable. *She* disapproved them, which ought to have been enough.—My plea of concealing the truth she did not think sufficient.—She was displeased; I thought unreasonably so: I thought her, on a thousand occasions, unnecessarily scrupulous and cautious: I thought her even cold. But she was always right. If I had followed her judgment, and subdued my spirits to the level of what she deemed proper, I should have escaped the greatest unhappiness I have ever known.—

And having gone through what immediately followed of the basis of their disagreement, and his persisting to act in direct opposition to Jane Fairfax's sense of right, he made a fuller pause to say, "This is very bad.—He had induced her to place herself, for his sake, in a situation of extreme difficulty and uneasiness, and it should have been his first object to prevent her from suffering unnecessarily.— She must have had much more to contend with, in carrying on the correspondence, than he could. He should have respected even unreasonable scruples, had there been such; but hers were all reasonable. We must look to her one fault, and remember that she had done a wrong thing in consenting to the engagement, to bear that she should have been in such a state of punishment."

We quarrelled.—Do you remember the morning spent at Donwell?—*There* every little dissatisfaction that had occurred before came to a crisis. I was late; I met her walking home by herself, and wanted to walk with her, but she would not suffer it. She absolutely refused to allow me, which I then thought most unreasonable. Now, however, I see nothing in it but a very natural and consistent degree of discretion. While I, to blind the world to our engagement, was behaving one hour with objectionable particularity to another woman, was she to be consenting the next to a proposal which might have made every previous caution useless?—Had we been met walking together between Donwell and Highbury, the truth must have been suspected.—I was mad enough, however, to resent.—I doubted her affection.

Emma knew that he was now getting to the Box-Hill party, and grew uncomfortable. Her own behaviour had been so very improper! She was deeply ashamed, and a little afraid of his next look. It was all read, however, steadily, attentively, and without the smallest remark;

I doubted it more the next day on Box-Hill; when, provoked by such conduct on my side, such shameful, insolent neglect of her, and such apparent devotion to Miss W., as it would have been impossible for any woman of sense to endure, she spoke her resentment in a form of words perfectly intelligible to me.—In short, my dear madam, it was a quarrel blameless on her side, abominable on mine; and I returned the same evening to Richmond, though I might have staid with you till the next morning, merely because I would be as angry with her as possible. Even then, I was not such a fool as not to mean to be reconciled in time; but I was the injured person, injured by her coldness, and I went away determined that she should make the first advances.—I shall always congratulate myself that you were not of the Box-Hill party. Had you witnessed my behaviour there, I can hardly suppose you would ever have thought well of me again.

and, excepting one momentary glance at her, instantly withdrawn, in the fear of giving pain—no remembrance of Box Hill seemed to exist.

Its effect upon her appears in the immediate resolution it produced: as soon as she found I was really gone from Randalls, she closed with the offer of that officious Mrs Elton; the whole system of whose treatment of her, by the bye, has ever filled me with indignation and hatred. I must not quarrel with a spirit of forbearance which has been so richly extended towards myself; but, otherwise, I should loudly protest against the share of it which that woman has known.—'Jane,' indeed!—You will observe that I have not yet indulged myself in calling her by that name, even to you. Think, then, what I must have endured in hearing it bandied between the Eltons with all the vulgarity of needless repetition, and all the insolence of imaginary superiority.

"There is no saying much for the delicacy of our good friends, the Eltons," was his next observation.—"His feelings are natural.—

Have patience with me, I shall soon have done.—She closed with this offer, resolving to break with me entirely, and wrote the next day to tell me that we never were to meet again.—

What! actually resolve to break with him entirely!—

*She felt the engagement to be a source of repentance and misery to each: she dissolved it.—*

She felt the engagement to be a source of repentance and misery to each—she dissolved it.—What a view this gives of her sense of his behaviour!—Well, he must be a most extraordinary—"

"Nay, nay, read on.—You will find how very much he suffers."

"I hope he does," replied Mr. Knightley coolly, and resuming the letter.—

This letter reached me on the very morning of my poor aunt's death. I answered it within an hour; but from the confusion of my mind, and the multiplicity of business falling on me at once, my answer, instead of being sent with all the many other letters of that day, was locked up in my writing-desk; and I, trusting that I had written enough, though but a few lines, to satisfy her, remained without any uneasiness.—I was rather disappointed that I did not hear from her again speedily; but I made excuses for her, and was too busy, and—may I add?—too cheerful in my views to be captious.—We removed to Windsor; and two days afterwards I received a parcel from her, my own letters all returned!—and a few lines at the same time by the post, stating her extreme surprise at not having had the smallest reply to her last; and adding, that as silence on such a point could not be misconstrued, and as it must be equally desirable to both to have every subordinate arrangement concluded as soon as possible, she now sent me, by a safe conveyance, all my letters, and requested, that if I could not directly command hers, so as to send them to Highbury within a week, I would forward them after that period to her at—: in short, the full direction to Mr Smallridge's, near Bristol, stared me in the face.

"'Smallridge!'—What does this mean? What is all this?"

"She had engaged to go as governess to Mrs Smallridge's children—a dear friend of Mrs Elton's—a neighbour of Maple Grove; and, by the bye, I wonder how Mrs Elton bears the disappointment?"

"Say nothing, my dear Emma, while you oblige me to read—not even of Mrs Elton. Only one page more. I shall soon have done. What a letter the man writes!"

"I wish you would read it with a kinder spirit towards him."

I knew the name, the place, I knew all about it, and instantly saw what she had been doing. It was perfectly accordant with that resolution of character which I

knew her to possess; and the secrecy she
had maintained, as to any such design
in her former letter, was equally descriptive of its anxious delicacy. For the world
would not she have seemed to threaten
me.—Imagine the shock; imagine how,
till I had actually detected my own blun-
der, I raved at the blunders of the post.—
What was to be done?—One thing only.—
I must speak to my uncle. Without his
sanction I could not hope to be listened
to again.—I spoke; circumstances were
in my favour; the late event had softened
away his pride, and he was, earlier than I
could have anticipated, wholly reconciled
and complying; and could say at last, poor
man! with a deep sigh, that he wished I
might find as much happiness in the marriage state as he had done.—I felt that it
would be of a different sort.—Are you dis-
posed to pity me for what I must have suffered in opening the cause to him, for my
suspense while all was at stake?—No; do
not pity me till I reached Highbury, and
saw how ill I had made her. Do not pity
me till I saw her wan, sick looks.—

"Well, there *is* feeling here.—He does
seem to have suffered in finding her ill.—
Certainly, I can have no doubt of his being fond of her.

I reached Highbury at the time of day
when, from my knowledge of their late
breakfast hour, I was certain of a good
chance of finding her alone.—I was not
disappointed; and at last I was not disappointed either in the object of my journey.
A great deal of very reasonable, very just

displeasure I had to persuade away. But it is done; we are reconciled, dearer, much dearer, than ever,

'Dearer, much dearer than ever.' I hope he may long continue to feel all the value of such a reconciliation.—

and no moment's uneasiness can ever occur between us again. Now, my dear madam, I will release you; but I could not conclude before. A thousand and a thousand thanks for all the kindness you have ever shewn me, and ten thousand for the attentions your heart will dictate towards her.—

He is a very liberal thanker, with his thousands and tens of thousands.—

If you think me in a way to be happier than I deserve,

'Happier than I deserve.' Come, he knows himself there.

I am quite of your opinion.—
Miss W. calls me the child of good fortune.

'Miss Woodhouse calls me the child of good fortune.'—Those were Miss Woodhouse's words, were they?—

I hope she is right.—In one respect, my good fortune is undoubted, that of being able to subscribe myself,
Your obliged and affectionate Son,
F. C. Weston Churchill.[25]

And a fine ending—and there is the letter. The child of good fortune! That was your name for him, was it?"

"You do not appear so well satisfied with his letter as I am; but still you must, at least I hope you must, think the better of him for it. I hope it does him some service with you."

"Yes, certainly it does. He has had great faults, faults of inconsideration and thoughtlessness; and I am very much of his opinion in thinking him likely to be happier than he deserves: but still as he is, beyond a doubt, really attached to Miss Fairfax, and will soon, it may be hoped, have the advantage of being constantly with her, I am very ready to believe his character will improve, and acquire from hers the steadiness and delicacy of principle that it wants."[26]

## Appendix 2: "The Three Veterans"

*by Leane Zugsmith*

1. As far back as the memory of Miss Riordan, which was three months, for she had been the attending nurse in the clinic for that long, the three old women regularly appeared twice a week.

2. Only when they managed to sit together on the bench, with their old, high-veined legs stiff ahead of them, was she able to distinguish one from the other. Otherwise, Mrs. Farrell could be mistaken for Mrs. Gaffney, or either of the two for Mrs. Betz.

3. Each showed gaps in her front teeth when she broke into her cackle, each had yellow-gray hair wisping from beneath a moldy hat; each wore stained, shapeless outer garments; and each had the same kind of bad leg.

*H's Responses*

So there's three old women, so they're probably the veterans um miss Rio-Riordan um can only remember three months back and she is a nurse.

So I guess they look probably kind of alike um I guessing their old high veined legs so they're old people um and their legs look different maybe their clothing.

So um they look very much alike and have the same kind of clothing and the same kind of characteristics and the same bad leg.

4. Outside the dispensary, the three old women did not lay eyes on one another from one clinic day to the next, but inside they formed a sisterhood.

So maybe outside they're not like they're not friends, but inside, it's kind of like when you have an in class friend, but you don't really talk to them outside of school.

5. Together, they would question newcomers and advise them on their ills, but once The Doctor was in the room, they would remain respectfully silent unless he made one of his lame jokes or scolded them.

So, they work together and um the doctor is kind of a little overbearing and they want to be quiet and respectful of him they'll laugh at his jokes.

6. Promptly then, they would cackle. Anything The Doctor said was a signal for their ingratiating brays of laughter.

The first three to enter Room 4 this morning, they sat together on the long bench, eyes alert on the door as Miss Riordan called to the patients outside, "Number 6 and 7 for Room 4."

So um Miss Riordan is not part of these three women I guess and maybe she's like a receptionist more than the nurses.

7. When the pale young woman with the fretful infant came in, relinquishing her numbered green ticket for Room 4, and sat opposite them, Mrs. Betz crooked her soiled finger. "Gutsie-goo," she said to the baby.

Um so she's trying Mrs. Betz one of the three women is trying to entertain the baby and make it happier and they're in room four that's like the room.

8. Then she addressed the mother. "Something wrong with it?" Mrs. Farrell and Mrs. Gaffney turned professional eyes on the child.

"She had an infected arm, and now she don't eat." The young woman jogged the whimpering infant with her knee.

Um so something's wrong with the child and they're probably gonna help fix it.

9. "Only your first?" asked Mrs. Farrell, who had borne nine.

"Yes," said the young mother.

The three old women smiled knowingly at one another. Mrs. Gaffney flapped her hand down from the wrist.

So maybe she thinks that like she knows Mrs. Farrell and Ms. Gaffney know more about um children because this is only the woman's first child.

10. "Sure, you're always worrying your poor head off about the first. Isn't it the truth?" Mrs. Farrell and Mrs. Betz vigorously nodded their heads, and their moldy hats gave off a little puff of dust.

So they're saying that even though Ms. Farrell um and probably Ms. Betz had more kids than one, they always worried about their first child a little more and there are moldy hats, so they're kinda old.

11. "When it don't eat, you want to pull ten hairs from the right side of your head, and braid them and twist them around its little toe," said Mrs. Betz.

"Give it honey and tea," said Mrs. Gaffney.

So they're using like different remedies than just medical suggestions.

12. "It's always that way with the first of them," said Mrs. Farrell. "You'll be wanting to . . ."

"Who's in attendance around here? You or me?" It was The Doctor, his voice hard, his face red.

So um he's kind of overbearing I think and maybe he wanted to like to give them the women medical advice instead of other remedies.

13. Mrs. Gaffney and Mrs. Betz nudged Mrs. Farrell, who left her mouth open to giggle quickly with them."Just let me know when you want to take my job," he said, and stalked to the end of the room to visit the patients behind the screens.

So he seems kind of upset that they were giving any kind of advice in the first place and Ms. Gaffney, Ms. Betz, and Ms. Farrell maybe seem intimidated by him or something.

14. The old women held their forefingers against their simpering lips. Now they would not even look at the ailing baby. "Anyone else for Room 4?" called Miss Riordan, out the corridor.

Um I wonder if like patients share rooms here or maybe they're just telling the woman with the ailing baby to leave I don't really know.

15. The eyes of the three old women frogged at the sight of the beautiful peroxide-blonde lady in a beautiful imitation-fur jacket. Everything about her seemed sweet and ripe as she handed over her green ticket and sat on the bench beside them.

So, they're probably wondering why this beautiful woman is coming in and yeah and she probably needs some medical advice.

16. The three old women watched her pull down her silk stocking; she had only a little two-inch scratch on her silk stocking; she had only a little two-inch scratch on her fine, shapely leg and her skin was whiter than milk.

So she's fair in skin color, and she's shapely, and she just has a little tiny scratch, so they're probably wondering what's up.

17. But Mrs. Gaffney could no longer stare at her, for now The Doctor was pressing his finger into her highest vein and she must keep her eyes submissive on his face.

So, she just has to look at him instead of looking at the patient because she doesn't have the authority to give advice any longer.

18. He whispered to the nurse and then, without looking into Mrs. Gaffney's submissive eyes, said, "You better quit staying out dancing all night, or that'll never get right."
The three old women cackled with delight.

Um, so I think he's telling this to the patient but I'm not sure really what's going on.

19. Mrs. Betz kept a meek smile on her face as The Doctor examined her leg. When he came to Mrs. Farrell, he wrinkled up his nose. "Suppose you wash your leg off yourself," he said.

So, he's talking to the patient here the doctor is and telling the patient to wash her leg.

20. "Give the poor nurse a break. Just rub it up and down with *soap* and *water*. Ever heard of it?"
This time the brays of laughter from the three old women were wilder than ever.

So, the doctor's kind of having like a change of heart and saying the nurse doesn't have to do this, you can just do it yourself and making them laugh.

21. Seeing him turn to the baby, all three of the old women tried to retard Miss Riordan's manipulations of their legs so that they could remain to watch The Doctor and the beautiful peroxide-blonde lady in the beautiful imitation-fur jacket.

So um the women just want to see how the interaction is between the doctor and the beautiful woman.

22. Mrs. Gaffney elbowed Mrs. Betz as The Doctor stood before the lady.
"What's wrong with you?" he said.
She smiled invitingly up at him. "I tripped on the stairs—my landlord doesn't know enough to have safe stairs in his house—and it's been bothering me."

Um it probably doesn't seem like that big of a deal to them at this point cause the ailing baby and stuff like that um.

23. She pointed a tapering white finger at the abrasion.
He looked at it carefully before whispering his orders to Miss Riordan. Mrs. Gaffney started to edge out of her seat, disappointed, when the beautiful lady said, "Is it serious, Doctor?"

Um we don't really know what the abrasion looks like at this point so we're probably going to see how serious it is.

24. "It hurt you, didn't it?" he said, sarcastically.
At the familiar tone, Mrs. Gaffney, Mrs. Farrell, and Mrs. Betz chuckled, but softly for fear of being sent away, now that their legs were wrapped.

Ok I don't really know why their legs are wrapped um maybe one of them had the scratch on their leg? I'm not sure.

25. "Yes," said the beautiful lady, "but I want to know what to tell my lawyer, in case—"
"Oh, your lawyer?" said The Doctor, witheringly. "I see. You want to bring suit.

So her leg must be pretty bad if she wants to sue her landlord.

26. Well, Madam, you can tell your law-yer that anyone who's so careless as to trip on the stairs deserves more than the little scratch you have there."

The three old women lowered their heads, their soiled fingers at their mouths to curb the explosions of laughter.

So he's telling her not to sue because it was her fault basically.

27. The beautiful lady's eyes flashed. "I don't see why you have to use that tone of voice!" she exclaimed with resentment. "Just because it's free is no reason why we can't be treated like human beings!"

So she's talking about the clinic being free I'm guessing and she's outraged because he's telling her it's not a big deal.

28. The three old women waited breath-lessly, their lips ready to stretch at his sally. Their waiting ears were met by si-lence. Their rheumy eyes saw The Doctor turn his back and regard the table of oint-ments and bandages.

So he's looking to see if there's anything he can do maybe just to help like calm her down.

29. As he stood there, whistling softly, the three old women found themselves staring at one another, and not one was smiling. With gray, tired faces, they rose together. At the door, their way was blocked by the man in white whom they called The Specialist Doctor.

So they're leaving the room um because the doctor's done with her . . . done with the women but the specialist doctor obvi-ously is a specialist in some kind of medi-cal field.

30. "Just the old friends I may want!" he cried in his ringing tones. He turned to The Doctor. "Are they varicose?"

"All three, Chief," said The Doctor.

"Are they interesting? Good enough for my Friday-night lecture?"

So they're talking about their legs and having varicose veins um so that's proba-bly what he's a specialist for or something like that.

31. "I'll show you their charts," said The Doctor.

The Specialist Doctor rubbed his hands. "How would you girls like to dance in my chorus Friday night?" he boomed cheerfully.

The three old women looked at one another.

Um so I think the three women are the ones that he's talking with the varicose veins um and they're thinking about dancing in his chorus on Friday night the specialist doctor's chorus.

32. The beautiful peroxide-blonde lady clack-clacked her high heels across the floor.

"No," said Mrs. Betz, heavily.

"No," said Mrs. Farrell, without looking up.

Um so they don't want to participate in his chorus.

33. "No," said Mrs. Gaffney, plucking at the edge of her stained wrap. "Just because it's free don't mean we aren't human beings."

Then, with lowered heads and somber faces, the three old women trudged out.[27]

So she's saying just like the woman the woman with the peroxide blonde hair said um and they obviously feel degraded maybe um because they lower their heads somber and trudge out of the room.

*Recall*: OK so in the beginning it starts off in a clinic type area like a hospital and there's three women who look exactly alike except their legs um that's the only way you can tell them apart they both have the same hair, the same face the same teeth the same laugh and um they're in room four and then this woman with a little baby comes in and the baby is having troubles ah I don't remember what the troubles are and they say like the first one you always worry about the first baby the most and the three women their names are like Mrs. Betz Mrs. Gaffney and Mrs. Farrell um and they tell her like to pluck off ten hairs from the side of your head and tie it around the baby's toe and the doctor gets kind of mad and is like "so you guys want to take my job?" and then this beautiful peroxide haired woman comes in and has a little scratch on her leg and at this point the three women are bandaged ah their legs are bandaged um and then the doctor kind of makes fun of the woman and tells her that like it's just a little scratch and that she can't really sue anyone over it and the women try not to laugh and then when they're and then they get up to leave room four and this um spec doc specialist of varicose comes in and he asks if they want to dance in his chorus that night and they all say no and somberly leave.

*Interpretation:* Um well I thought it was kinda confusing I just kept getting confused, but um um so there were like three women I felt like women power maybe because like a feminist kind of view but maybe that's just how I'm reading it because like the doctor is the overbearing one the three women just like to and they don't want to dance in the chorus and the woman with the peroxide hair like says that we have to be treated like human beings too.

# CHAPTER 3

# READING ON- AND OFFLINE

**HAVING DESCRIBED** implicit and explicit reading processes in the previous chapters, I now put them together to describe how they work in reading. To do so, I explore the distinction between "online" and "offline" reading processes. A standard and much debated polarity in literary criticism is the one between "the literary fact (or the author's text) and the interpretive act (or the reader's construction)."[1] Psychologists split the second of these into online and offline processes. Online processes, such as inferring, elaborating, and integrating information, may be automatic or strategic. They take place during the act of reading and lead to, or fail to lead to, a coherent memory representation. Offline processes, which occur after reading, modify this representation: for example, any recall of a work may modify its subsequent mental representation because parts that have been remembered may become more easily retrieved than those that have not.

Psychologists developed the online/offline distinction to study the difference between what readers do spontaneously versus what they do when facing experimental prompts after having read material. For example, imagine an experimenter interested in learning how readers respond to an ambiguous sentence in a text. An online measure might check how long it takes readers to read the ambiguous sentence versus how long it takes them to read the rest of the text (psychologists standardize reading times by measuring the syllable or character, since sentences have different numbers of words). An offline measure might ask them to judge, after reading, if certain sentences had appeared in the text; the experimenter might see if readers are better or worse at recognizing the ambiguous sentence versus the others. Outside the lab, in ordinary settings, the exact combination of online and offline processes will vary according to what readers consider important, given different goals, levels of motivation, abilities, background knowledge, and standards.[2]

Psychologists agree that a reader's memory representation resembles a network of "nodes that depict the individual text elements" and the connections among them.[3] To imagine how readers form such a network, researchers have generated various models that, in some cases, can be adapted as computer programs and then tested for their ability to predict actual human performance. Such models are deliberately reductive placeholders for neuroanatomical activities that we are not yet able to describe; they provide a continuous metaphor for how the brain processes textual information.[4] As George Box famously said about statistical models, "All models are wrong, but some are useful."[5] While psychologists agree about the value of generating such models, there is no consensus about the most useful one. I will describe one of the better known and most flexible, the "landscape model," because of its ability to describe how online processes lead to an offline representation.

Literary critics might think of the landscape model as an architecture rather than as a theory.[6] It incorporates assumptions about reading but has enough flexibility to accommodate different theories about what mental representations might result. As an empirical tool it provides a conceptual framework in which researchers can test how various aspects of the reading process will influence a final memory representation. As a computer program it even produces a visual model of readers' activities, which looks like a landscape in constant motion. Its value to humanists is that it provides a detailed breakdown not of interpretation but of cognitive processes that precede interpretation.

At the core of the landscape model are the assumptions that the reader's mental network consists of concepts and the connections among them, that different concepts and connections are more or less strongly activated during the reading process, and that degrees of activation fluctuate. What counts as a concept and what kinds of relations might be formed among concepts will vary depending on the organization of the text, as well as on a reader's goals, abilities, and strategies. Psychologists using the landscape model have tended to work with fairly reductive realizations of these terms: concepts tend to be equated with content words, such as nouns and action verbs; connections among them are understood to arise chiefly from causal and referential coherence.[7] Using this model with a complex literary work would demand considerable expansion of how concepts and connections were defined, although both would need to be identified in some form.

The landscape model also incorporates assumptions about the relation between reading and memory. Arthur Graesser, Keith Millis, and Rolf Zwaan note that many models assume three levels of memory: "short-term memory," which holds "the most recent clause comprehended"; "working memory," which provides resources for processing information; and "long-term memory," which can be a permanent store for information.[8] Researchers in text comprehension have focused especially on the second of these three, working memory. It is the mental faculty allowing readers to store, process, and manipulate recently read textual input through the strategies discussed in the previous chapter, such as comparing current text to previously read text, retrieving relevant background knowledge, and creating forward and backward inferences.[9]

Different operations require different effort. According to Graesser, Millis, and Zwaan, "repetition increases the speed of accessing a knowledge structure and the nodes within the structure. Thus, familiar words are processed faster than unfamiliar words. The nodes in an automatized package of world knowledge are holistically accessed and used at little cost to the resources in WM (working memory)."[10] The differences between more and less effortful processes matter because of a fundamental truth about working memory: it is not infinite. On the contrary, it is highly limited, though its capacity varies from individual to individual.[11] Scientists typically measure working memory capacity through a reading-span test, in which participants read sentences and then recall the last word from each of them.[12] A participant's reading span depends less on amount of mental storage space than on "the ability to control attention" so that the reader can "maintain information in an active, quickly retrievable state."[13] Experts in a domain have usually developed good strategies for retrieving information.[14] Yet even for expert readers, if more attention is engaged with one process, less is available for others. As a result, "at any given point during reading [a reader] can only attend to a small subset of all elements that are relevant."[15] As the discussion of good-enough processing in chapter 1 reveals, readers often attend to the smallest possible subset, just enough to get bare sense.

This finding is a striking one for literary critics, who value the ability to find interpretive significance in a full range of detail. The literary critical effort at comprehensive interpretation is an offline one, existing in tension with online memory processes that filter out most of the text. For example, Stanley Fish's reading of Pater, discussed in the previous chapter, is less what happens online than an offline fantasy of what would happen online if a reader had an infinite working memory capacity. Psychologists have coined the memorable phrase "promiscuous inference generation" for such reading.[16] While I encourage literary scholars to live up to it, even the most skilled readers generate relatively few inferences online. Moreover, for inferences to aid comprehension, they need to be not promiscuous but relevant and valid. Although Fish wants to portray reading as experience, what he offers is not experience but a powerful mirage that would actually overwhelm most readers' working-memory capacity.

In light of constraints on working memory the landscape model assumes four sources through which readers activate concepts. First, and most obvious, is the text being read, typically understood as a clause or line; reading this unit is called a cycle. For example, the first chapter of George Eliot's *Middlemarch* begins, after an epigraph, with the sentences, "Miss Brooke had that kind of beauty which seems to be thrown into relief by poor dress. Her hand and wrist were so finely formed that she could wear sleeves not less bare of style than those in which the Blessed Virgin appeared to Italian painters."[17] Depending on the reader, concepts in the first cycle might include "Miss Brooke," "had," "that kind," "beauty," "seems to be thrown," "relief," "poor," and "dress"; in the second cycle, "her hand," "her . . . wrist," "were . . . formed," "so finely," "she," "could wear," "sleeves," and so on to the end of the sentence. English syntax and function words connect these concepts, so that "Miss Brooke" is the subject of the first sentence, "had" is the main verb, and "that kind of beauty" is the direct object. Depending on such factors as the reader's attention, degree of experience with English, and skill at reading, such syntactic connections would be made more or less automatically and would not strain an experienced reader's working-memory capacity.

Second, concept activation may arise from the cycle immediately preceding the current one. When readers come to the second cycle in *Middlemarch*, some concepts from the first will still be present in working memory; how many can be retrieved will depend on the individual reader. During the second cycle, if a concept "is already part of the text representation and is reactivated, its trace is strengthened"; coactivation of concepts establishes or strengthens a connection between them.[18] For example, because *her* and *she* in the second cycle refer back to "Miss Brooke," the connection between the pronouns and their antecedent may heighten the concept activation around "Miss Brooke." When a reader comes to "finely formed," its activation may simultaneously heighten the activation around the memory representation of "kind of beauty." Simultaneous activation connects two concepts so that they become a larger joint concept. The strength of such connections increases or decreases continuously during reading.

Third, as a reader proceeds in a text and builds up a network of connections, these form a constantly fluctuating "episodic memory representation." This representation in turn will influence how a reader processes new information. In *Middlemarch* a reader who has read Eliot's "Prelude" and the epigraph to chapter 1 may already have developed a network of concepts around the potential heroine of the novel, such as the tragic Saint Theresa paradigm. When Miss Brooke is introduced, some of these associations may be updated to become part of the reader's memory representation of Dorothea, depending on their potential relevance to the individual reader and the reader's skill at retrieving them from long-term memory.

Fourth, concepts can come from the reader's background knowledge. As I described in the chapter on automaticity, the mere appearance of a word is enough to activate all meanings associated with that word in memory, although most activations undergo an almost instantaneous decrease in strength. Those successively activated during several cycles of reading, however, are more likely to enter explicit consciousness and may become part of a memory representation.

To understand the opening of *Middlemarch*, for example, the reader may draw on a host of prior associations to create "Miss Brooke"; these come not from *Middlemarch* but from whatever comes to mind and stays there long enough to enter explicit awareness. Such concepts from background knowledge connect with concepts from the text to become part of a developing memory representation. Their activation and the strength of their connections fluctuate during reading according to perceived relevance. Whereas Mikhail Bakhtin saw novelistic discourse as defined by its "diversity of social speech types," which disrupted the supposed unity of poetic genres, in cognitive psychology the reader's background knowledge renders any text other to itself.[19] The reader's heterogeneous knowledge inevitably becomes part of his or her memory representation, though the results it produces will vary widely. Consequently, taking seriously reader response means that much in the text will not be part of readers' memories, and much that is not in the text will be.

Readers access these last two sources of activation (episodic memory representation and background knowledge) through two mechanisms. The first is "cohort activation." Cohort activation presupposes that, as described above, any encountered concept is not freestanding but has been linked to many other concepts, whether from earlier in the text or from background knowledge. These previous concepts are called up rapidly and automatically from memory during reading. For example, in *Middlemarch* the concept "Brooke" may automatically call up images of actual brooks that readers have encountered. These images are part of the "cohort" activated by the concept "Brooke." For some readers these images, even if they passed a key threshold and entered explicit awareness, may not be useful in constructing an image of Dorothea and would be suppressed; for others these may be an invaluable means of understanding her and would remain a part of the cohort around her mental representation.

In contrast, what psychologists call "coherence-based retrieval" occurs when readers confront a prominent gap, or "coherence break," in their ability to create a mental representation of a text and when this gap consequently impedes their understanding. Such gaps are not in the text: they are part of the reader's effort to represent a text; hence, they vary from reader to reader. Readers who know little about art history might find themselves baffled by Eliot's reference to the bare sleeves of the Blessed Virgin in Italian painters. Faced with such gaps, readers begin a "strategic and deliberate retrieval of information" to help them create coherence.[20] This retrieval may consist of reinstating earlier material, which could come from concepts read earlier in the text still present in working memory or could be retrieved from long-term memory. Readers may also turn back to earlier sentences or chapters to see if they have missed something that might help; they may see if their background knowledge contains facts or interpretive guidelines that could make sense of the text, such as knowledge of generic conventions; they could consult other sources, such as dictionaries or the thoughts of others; or they could decide that the information is not important to them and that they will skip it, either temporarily or permanently.[21] Such "strategic and deliberate retrieval" was the topic of much of the previous chapter, as when Mr. Knightley asks Emma to explain material in Frank's letter or when H used prior knowledge about feminism to understand "The Three Veterans."

Unlike cohort activation, coherence-based retrieval is understood as comparatively slow and resource-demanding. Psychologists assume that readers want to read as quickly as is compatible with their working-memory spans, goals, and abilities, so anything that slows them down and increases reading time deserves notice. Typically, concepts that recur frequently receive a high and sustained degree of activation, such as "Dorothea" in *Middlemarch*. Yet mere repetition is not the only source of heightened activation. In narrative, for example, across a wide variety of reading goals and abilities, concepts associated with causality are often highly activated, even if particular words associated with them are not repeated.[22] Eliot notes that Dorothea is "enamoured of intensity and greatness, and rash in embracing whatever seemed to her to have those aspects."[23] Since several of the concepts in this sentence explain the motivation for many of Dorothea's later actions, they are likely to be included prominently in a reader's memory representation. Depending on the reader, emotional sympathy with certain concepts or the ability to connect concepts to personal experience may also increase activation.[24]

Although the landscape model is useful in linking automatic and strategic processes and predicting which aspects of a text are likely to receive the most activation, it seems less useful in thinking about historical readers. Historical distance seems to render useless the procedures of psychological research, which depend on participants who can be tested in controlled environments. Yet this distance is an advantage as well. As psychologists are well aware, the procedures necessary to create valid evidence occur at the cost of highly artificial reading tasks, such as reading sentence by sentence on a computer screen or wearing optical apparatuses to track eye movements. Moving to historical literacy presents records of actual reading situations, although the interpretation of such records can never be transparent.

The concept that I want to use in translating scientific vocabulary to historical reading situations is one described by Tracy Linderholm and her coauthors as "standards of coherence."[25] These standards "reflect the degree of comprehension that a reader attempts to attain during the reading of a text" and arise from such factors as the reader's purpose, background knowledge, skill level, alertness, sense of the text's difficulty, and relation to internal or external distractions.[26] Although psychologists tend to see these standards in terms of individual choice and ability, they are a border between psychology and sociology. Standards of coherence are the site at which a history of culture intersects cognitive processes of reading. Any, though not all, of the factors listed by Linderholm and her coauthors as shaping standards of coherence are affected by larger cultural imperatives that influence the individual reader. A reader's purpose is not simply an individual choice: it is a choice conditioned by the same cultural expectations as any literacy event. It is potentially overdetermined by any number of sociological factors, including race, class, gender, region, religion, profession, and education. To assume that a given human purpose can be met by reading is already to engage a highly specific set of circumstances about the availability of information, the social distribution of literacy, and the effects of education.[27]

Likewise, although psychologists discussing standards of coherence tend to use "background knowledge" to mean simply how much a reader knows about a topic, background knowledge, like purpose, comes weighted with a reader's historical setting. If readers are reading for information, as when reading a newspaper, an entire social network lies behind their ability to decide if they have relevant background knowledge, are truly being informed, or know what counts as information. Research in the history of literacy by historians and literary critics has been particularly sensitive to such issues. As a result the concept of standards of coherence provides a valuable juncture between the cognitive operations of the individual reader and the evidence of history. Although we may not be able to reconstruct the eye tracking or reading time per word of historical readers, we can use available evidence to reconstruct certain aspects of their standards of coherence and to interpret their local reading strategies. We can also recognize when their standards of coherence broke down and examine how they responded to the resulting challenges.

The success of recreating historical standards of coherence depends on the availability of evidence. Sometimes evidence represents online processes, as in some marginalia or records of reading times, but most historical evidence represents offline processes, as in comments about reading that appear in diary entries, letters, and reviews. Since, as the landscape model reveals, such offline evidence is partly the product of online processes, it provides clues about online reading.

The Victorian reception of Robert Browning offers a useful test case in the applicability of cognitive models to the history of audience because of the richness of the surviving offline evidence from his critics. He was widely acknowledged by his contemporaries to be the most difficult writer of the age. As such, the resistance created by his poems, as with the texts in the previous chapter, spurred useful representations of reading because the violation of expectations made visible what expectations were. Grappling with a difficult text can lead

readers to foreground metacognition, the self-awareness of goals and strategies during reading.[28] This high level of metacognitive discussion in reviews of
Browning enables close attention to the microprocesses underlying differing
standards of coherence.

I focus on four readers who reviewed Browning's masterpiece, *Men and
Women*: Margaret Oliphant, Thomas McNicoll, George Brimley, and William
Morris. These reviewers were not equivalent to the average reader because their
goals demanded reading Browning with enough attention that they could write
detailed analyses of him, for which they were paid as professional critics. They
read so that they could acquaint the public with Browning's chief characteristics, his relation to other contemporary poets, and his aesthetic faults and
successes. Like most Victorian reviewers, the four shaped their opinions to
accommodate the moral, religious, and political outlooks of the journals for
which they wrote.[29] While Browning's *Men and Women* announced no straightforward political program, it belonged to a well-established tradition of liberal
aesthetics, which biased Browning's reviewers even when they did not respond
explicitly to his political sympathies.[30] It was to be expected, for example, that
George Brimley, a conservative, pro-Tennysonian reviewer at Trinity College,
Cambridge, writing in the conservative journal *Fraser's*, would dislike Browning, whereas William Morris, in the circle of Browning's young, radical admir-
ers at Oxford, would praise him.[31]

Yet my goal is not to unmask the reviewers' ideological biases but to analyze how their aesthetic positions affected their reading. Since they all understood enough to write their reviews, their comprehension was successful. Yet
Oliphant's, McNicoll's, and Brimley's reviews bear witness to a prior online
reading moment, in which their goal was to get meaning out of Browning in
a way comparable with their experience with other poets: here their standards
of coherence broke down and resulted in anger and frustration. In contrast,
Browning offered Morris a different experience. Unusual among contemporary
reviewers, he claimed to understand Browning, and doing so involved for him
generating new standards of coherence and new reading strategies.

Oliphant, writing for the traditionally Tory journal *Blackwood's*, adopts one
of the oldest and most familiar standards of coherence for poetry: transportation. For Oliphant, good poets, like those who achieve the Longinian sublime, "arrest and overpower their audience as the Ancient Mariner fascinated
the wedding guest; and we all know how helplessly, and with what complete
submission, we have followed in the train of these enchanters, wheresoever

it pleased them to turn their wayward footsteps."[32] As the previous chapters have suggested, reading never really involves "complete submission" to the work. Rather, in terms of the psychological framework that I have developed, Oliphant's transportation assumes a work that allows its reader to rely heavily on automatic processes; if readers need to do more strategic processing, they draw on information that is easy to access.[33]

While automaticity may underlie transported reading, what the reader experiences, as Oliphant stresses, is far from automatic. Instead, automatized comprehension frees up cognitive resources for emotional sympathy. Oliphant reserves her highest praise for the Psalms, because they create sympathy by portraying "the overflow of the grand primal human emotions to which every living heart resounds" (126). Whereas Wordsworth imagined such "overflow" as a prerequisite for the successful writer of poetry, Oliphant finds it central instead for the reader. Such emotion arises from autobiographical inferences, in which the emotion described in a work activates situations in autobiographical episodic memory. The greater the emotional weight attached to memory, the greater the potential for an emotional reaction to the work that activates it.

Oliphant finds that Browning's poetry inhibits emotional inferences because parsing his syntax requires so much attention: "It is very hard to make out what he would be at with those marvellous convolutions of words; but, after all, he really seems to mean something, which is a comfort in its way" (137). Syntactic difficulty is not an intrinsic barrier to comprehension, since the effort needed to create coherence might for some readers increase engagement with the material. Yet, because working memory capacity is limited, too much mental effort devoted to syntax limits the cognitive resources that might enable the re-creation of emotions "to which every living heart resounds." The only Browning poem that Oliphant likes, "Andrea del Sarto," is one that her experience (of the artistic compromises involved in sustaining family relationships) allows her to sympathize with.[34] Unable to create such online connections with most of Browning's poetry, she rescues her standard of coherence through what the landscape model calls coherence-based retrieval. She transforms her incomprehension by retrieving from her background knowledge an image of the poet as an artist struggling genuinely, if not successfully, for expression: "There is an unmistakable enjoyment in this wild sport of his. He likes it, though we are puzzled; and sometimes he works like the old primitive painters, with little command of his tools, but something genuine in his mind, which comes out in spite of the stubborn brushes and pigments, marvellous ugly, yet somehow true ("Modern Light Literature" 137).

This coherence-based retrieval occurs only after Oliphant is finished reading. She claims that her online experience of reading Browning is confusion: "we are puzzled." Her offline experience, aided partly by writing her review, depends on imagining Browning the author as conforming to her image of "old primitive painters." She then can sympathize with this image in a way that she did not sympathize with the actual poetry; the poet-painter's work is "marvellous ugly, yet somehow true." This image of Browning preserves her standard of coherence, though at the cost of having to admit that most of the individual poems are, to her, little more than "marvellous convolutions."

At first glance, McNicoll, writing in the *London Quarterly Review*, seems to concur with Oliphant's standard of transportation: "True poetry has no equivalent; we are borne along with it notwithstanding, it does not leave us where we were, but carries us whithersoever it will."[35] Yet McNicoll reveals that transportation may have differing causes. Because Victorians typically associated transportation with feminized, degraded reading, reviewers like McNicoll revised their standards of coherence in new, implicitly more masculine directions. Although McNicoll values transportation, its key for him is not emotion but intellection. While he expects to be "borne along" by poetry, he praises Tennyson, for example, because "his verse has gradually become the pure transparent medium of his thoughts" (496). Mapping thought, not emotion, guides his reading of Browning.

Although McNicoll is willing to expend the online effort to create a memory representation based on tracking thought, he finds that Browning makes doing so impossible: "He disdains to take a little pains to put the reader at a similar advantage with himself,—to give a preparatory statement which may help to make his subsequent effusion plain and logical. He scorns the good old style of beginning at the beginning. He starts from any point and speaks in any tense he pleases; is never simple or literal for a moment; leaves out (or out of sight) a link here and another there of that which forms the inevitable chain of truth, making a hint or a word supply its place" (498).

Whereas Browning's syntax overloaded Oliphant's working-memory capacity, McNicoll's difficulty is the absence of adequate background knowledge, as in the passage about laundry discussed in the previous chapter. Admitting that his own background is insufficient, McNicoll complains that Browning does not provide a "preparatory statement" to make his poems "plain and logical." He turns to two microprocesses to enable coherence-based retrieval: connecting inferences, which explain a passage in terms of immediately preceding material (the "link" that forms the "chain of truth"); and reinstatement inferences, which use material even earlier in the work (the desired "preparatory statement") to explain the content. Through such inferences, the parts of the poem that do not seem to make sense might become more comprehensible. Without them, breaks in coherence overwhelm McNicoll's ability to create meaning. As he admits, Browning's work is not intrinsically unreadable, but it is written for "the student, and not the reader." The student who could, for example, undertake substantial library research might be able to understand Browning. But such offline efforts would be at odds with McNicoll's desired online experience, which depends on being "borne along" by poetic thoughts. A reader like McNicoll hoping for such an experience will find only "impatience and fatigue" in reading Browning (499).

Yet not all reviewers assumed, with Oliphant and McNicoll, that reading should produce transportation; some adopted other standards of coherence, though not necessarily more successful ones. Brimley, the reviewer for *Fraser's*, might seem to be the model student reader called for by McNicoll. As the librarian of Trinity College, Cambridge, Brimley was supposed to have had an unusual degree of time to devote to "careful study and elaborate analysis" of the works that he reviewed.[36] He produced, for example, one of the longest and most insightful essays on Tennyson written during the poet's life.[37] Not surprisingly, given Trinity College's long-standing association with Coleridgean thought, Brimley's aesthetics valorizes what, in his essay on Tennyson, he calls the ideal of a "whole composition" that is "grouped and coloured by a dominant idea."[38] Whereas Oliphant and McNicoll looked for transportation, Brimley adopted a newer, more elite standard of coherence: Coleridgean organic unity.

If, according to Brimley, all details of a work should be understood in the light of the "whole composition" and a "dominant idea," then virtually all textual input would create unremitting coherence breaks, which would have to be constantly repaired through reference to background knowledge or prior textual information. Like Stanley Fish, he rejects good-enough processing for a standard of coherence that downplays automatized comprehension. While the landscape model assumes that concept activation fluctuates during reading and that most concepts have little activation, Brimley's reading strategy forces the reader to keep many concepts highly activated so that new ones can be linked to previous ones, in accordance with the standard of a "whole composition."

Nothing could be further from the transportation described by Oliphant and McNicoll, in which readers are carried away. Brimley's standard would almost immediately overwhelm most readers' working-memory capacity and would thus demand considerable rereading.

Starting from this standard of coherence, Brimley finds Browning frustrating. He complains of Browning's "favourite plan of writing a poem that, so to speak, leads to nothing, has no end, is but a fragment of versified talk, as if the very essence of art was not to present things completely from a particular point of view."[39] For Brimley, Browning's words lead to "nothing": Browning frustrates the desire to attain global coherence because nothing is presented "completely."[40] Brimley chooses "Childe Roland to the Dark Tower Came" to demonstrate Browning's difficulty. He searches his background knowledge for a literary genre traditionally associated with difficulty and comes up with allegory. With this knowledge he plans to make predictive inferences, which anticipate what will happen next. Whereas McNicoll's connecting and reinstatement inferences look backward, connecting present material with text that came before, Brimley's predictive inferences look forward, building up expectations of what will come. Yet during his online reading process, Brimley is unable to make these inferences because he can "discover no hint as to what the allegory means": we "find only description preparatory to some adventure which is to disclose the symbol of the 'dark tower' . . . but the adventure never comes off in the poem" (110). Having kept the poem's descriptive information active in memory to link it causally with the dark tower, Brimley finds that his genre-based predictive inferences lead to no meaningful connections, and his comprehension fails. Brimley's standards encourage him to read for allegorical global coherence, but Browning proves too much for him.

Given the frustrations of these reviewers when faced with Browning, William Morris's reading standards, which led to a happier assessment, deserve attention. The success of his standards has two sides. The first is focus. Whereas the reading strategies of Oliphant, McNicoll, and especially Brimley are overwhelmed by the sheer amount of material in Browning, Morris chooses a standard of coherence that filters out large parts of Browning's text by treating the poems as character sketches, of the kind perfected by a writer like Charles Lamb. For Morris, what matters in the poems is information directly relevant to creating an image of the protagonist. All else can be given a low degree of activation, such as the mass of descriptive material in "Childe Roland" that defeats Brimley. This strategy significantly lessens demand on working-memory capacity. While avoiding mere good-enough comprehension, it controls the onslaught of Browning's language and allows Morris to manipulate the material he notices more effectively.

Second, rather than treating character sketches as isolated monads, Morris links them to each other through comparison and contrast. Browning's volume includes no such explicit comparison and contrast, except possibly in the final poem "One Word More," and he generally arranged his book to avoid contiguous thematic sequences. To enable such comparison and contrast, Morris works against Browning's arrangement: he locates common topics in the poems and groups them so that he can understand the poems in light of each other. As he says about Browning in the first sentence of his review, "The poems do fall naturally into some order, or rather some of them go pretty much together."[41] In a way his critical approach to Browning might be seen as prefiguring his later work as an artist, especially in his wallpaper, in which a particular design becomes most meaningful when seen as part of a larger network of patterns.

Through this strategy of seeing the individual item as part of a network, Morris develops a new source of background knowledge and a new source of information for coherence-based retrieval. He decides, for example, that "An Epistle . . . of Karshish" and "Cleon" are both about "the desires and doubts of men out of Christianity" and that the characters in the poems are meant as a contrast: "The Arab is the more genial of the two, less selfish, somewhat deeper too, I think; Cleon, with his intense appreciations of beauty . . . is yet intensely selfish" (269). Whereas McNicoll blames Browning for not providing information in a prefatory statement, Morris reconstructs such a statement by treating certain poems as partial prefaces for others.

Morris's moment of triumph comes in his comments on "Childe Roland." He responds directly to Brimley's review and ridicules his failed allegorical reading: "Some reviewer thinks it an allegory, and rates the poet for not having told us what happened to Childe Roland" (275). Morris's standard of coherence, with its privileging of the mental representation of character, inhibits the move to global coherence characteristic of allegory. Instead, he understands "Childe Roland" as belonging to a group that includes "Before," "After," "The Patriot," and "A Light Woman," all describing men committed to bad or hopeless causes, even to the death. Putting "Childe Roland" in this group, Morris creates a new reference for the poem's coherence by moving from one inside the poem to one arising from a connection to other poems that, for him, are similar. This new reference, together with his standard of coherence, allows him to read "Childe Roland" in a way that Brimley cannot: "The poet's real design was to show us a brave man doing his duty, making his way on to his point through all dreadful things. . . . He will be slain certainly . . . yet he can leave all this in God's hands and go forward" (276).

Using this sense of character, Morris reintroduces the emotional sympathy that McNicoll and Brimley exile from their readings. Morris claims to feel deeply for Roland: "Do you not feel, as you read, a strange sympathy for the lonely knight, so very, very lonely, not allowed even the fellowship of kindly memories?" (276). Such emotional bonds seem to return Morris to the sympathy characteristic of Oliphant's standards. Like Oliphant, Morris suggests that his online and offline experiences of reading have been different and that, also like Oliphant, the strong emotional bond happens offline, as he reflects on the model of character that he has developed. Indeed, his offline review seems to enable emotional bonds with the characters that his online reading experience may not have provided. The key difference between Oliphant and Morris lies in when a reader should be entitled to feel an emotional connection. Oliphant desires it online, whereas Morris lets it happen offline, after his detailed construction of a mental model of a character based on expanded background knowledge of Browning's volume.

The terms of these four critics' success and bafflement reveal elements of standards of coherence used by readers more generally. In the nineteenth century perhaps the most widespread was Oliphant's desire for emotional transportation. For those who feared the effects of novels, such intense sympathetic engagement was often treated as no standard at all but as dreamlike passivity: novel reading "throws us into a state of unreal excitement, a trance, or dream, which we should be allowed to dream out, and then be sent back to the atmosphere of reality again, cured by our brief surfeit of the desire to indulge again soon in the same delirium of feverish interest."[42] As Patrick Brantlinger documented in *The Reading Lesson*, such passivity and reverie were believed to open readers to potentially harmful effects, from inflaming the passions to dulling the mind to preventing readers from doing useful work.[43] The vocabulary of cognitive science enables us to rewrite the Victorian dichotomy of the good, active reader versus the bad, passive reader as a contrast between divergent uses of cognitive resources, guided by varying standards of coherence. Cognitively, no comprehension can be literally passive, since even the most automatized reading of even the simplest material demands mind-body work of such complexity that science has only begun to map it. As a standard of coherence, transportation makes high demands, especially in its need to focus and to monitor appropriate background knowledge.[44]

What may have been most threatening about novels for nineteenth-century critics was not that they required so little attention but that they required so much. The seeming passivity of transportation required a great deal more mental labor than other reading goals that might, at first glance, seem more deserving to Victorians, such as reading familiar sermons to reinforce religious sentiments (if we assume comparable text difficulty, reader ability, and motivation). Underneath Victorian critics' contempt for the novel may lie a degree of awe and fear of the brain work that seemed to be increasingly attainable: if so many people could comprehend objects as complex as novels, what kinds of privileged claims could be made for more traditional intellectual pursuits?

While Oliphant's reading strategy was perhaps the most popular during the Victorian period, the strategies of McNicoll and Morris were taken up by readers who wished to perceive themselves as having a more serious, engaged relation to literature. McNicoll's emphasis on tracing thought, for example, had been and would remain a major trait of autodidact culture during the century, as a means by which those cut off from traditional institutions would use literature to compensate for their felt lack of access to "thought." Morris's standard of coherence was already widespread in novel reviews and would also have a significant effect on the Browning societies that spread throughout Britain and America as prominent sites for the serious middlebrow reader.

Brimley's Coleridgean standards would eventually triumph in the academy, not during the Victorian period but in the twentieth century, in the form of New Criticism. To look at another Cambridge-educated critic deeply influenced by Coleridge, I. A. Richards, is to see the continuity between Brimley's standards and those of twentieth-century academic criticism. Richards, like Brimley, values Coleridgean unity in the work of art: "What is much more essential is the increased organization, the heightened power of combining all the several effects of formal elements into a single response, which the poet bestows. . . . It is in such resolution of a welter of disconnected impulses into a single ordered response that in all the arts imagination is most shown."[45] His standard, like Brimley's, imposes on the reader particular cognitive processes. Readers must overactivate textual coherence-based retrieval so that all "disconnected impulses" can be linked to a "single ordered response," in ways that cut against the limitations of working-memory capacity. Readers can counter these limitations with strategies familiar to literary critics, such as slower reading, frequent rereadings, and skilled use of background knowledge (contextual, generic, biographical). Such intensive strategies may inhibit the emotional transportation of the kind valued by Oliphant and Morris, though not necessarily.

Tellingly, however, Richards invites such focus: he condemns the "common mistake of exaggerating personal accidents in the means by which a poem attains its end" (88). Though basic memory priming makes it likely that readers activate at least some autobiographical associations, or "personal accidents," in reading, Richards encourages the disciplined literary critic to avoid them. Academic literary criticism institutionalized and continues to be fostered by many of the specific cognitive strategies and standards demanded by Richards.

For literary critics much of the value of work done by psychologists lies in making reading strategies visible and thereby clarifying the cognitive work that literary criticism demands. The many theoretical approaches used by academic literary criticism mask the relative similarity of the strategies that most of them entail, such as linking of local to global coherence, extensive use of particular kinds of background knowledge (such as the interpretations of previous critics), attention to details that may not have causal significance, and the inhibiting of routinized processes of disambiguation. Readers encountered in historical archives, in the classroom, or in nonacademic settings may sometimes appear naive or reductive in contrast because they do not use these strategies. The differences arise from their varying standards of coherence, which yield different reading strategies.

For example, when a teacher assigns an epic or novel with complex, dense plots to students who have relatively little background in reading such works, the amount of working-memory resources students will need to track characters, create causal links between plot developments, and register major changes in time and space will inhibit their ability to perform tasks basic to contemporary literary criticism. These include creating connections across wide spans of plot that may not be causally linked, noticing unusual details that may not play a major role in the story, and linking content to generic, historical, or ideological background. In a classic paper on "long-term working memory" K. Anders Ericsson and Walter Kintsch demonstrate how expert readers have developed specialized retrieval strategies that allow them to perform such tasks without overwhelming the brain's limited capacity.[46] For students who are still developing such skills, the tasks may be easier for some, especially those with high reading spans and those who have more background knowledge, skills, motivation, and time to read. But for many others the newness of the cognitive tasks may result in what, to the teacher, look merely like shallow readings and basic mistakes.

As students learn, they may strengthen one of the most salient skills of the literary critic: metacognitive awareness. Psychologists describe such awareness as the ability to monitor and evaluate online reading processes and to alter reading strategies quickly in relation to such evaluation; metacognition has been shown repeatedly to be a key element characterizing skilled readers. The discipline of literary criticism fosters metacognitive abilities by engaging with a remarkably wide range of texts, from Anglo-Saxon poetry to postmodern theory, which encourage the development of varied reading strategies. Exposure to such an array improves the reader's ability to recognize when comprehension has broken down and to search for alternative strategies. For example, strong metacognitive skills enable literary critics to respond rapidly to and incorporate insights from other disciplines, as well as to recognize and question their own and others' governing assumptions. These skills may be among the most valuable that we pass on to our students, especially those encouraged to take courses in many periods and modes.

Although the reviewers of Browning's poetry wrote their reviews after reading him, I looked to their offline representations for clues about their online processes. In some cases, as with Morris, full comprehension did not necessarily occur online but only afterward, in light of greater knowledge of the context. I turn now to a more detailed discussion of offline products, the cognitive representation of literary texts after reading has finished; as I have noted, such a representation includes little of the actual words of a text (most of which have been forgotten) and much that is not in the text (from the reader's background knowledge). In so doing, I will complicate the landscape model by introducing concerns that have yet to receive extensive treatment by psychologists. I move back to the eighteenth century and romantic period because a widespread concern of this era was what should happen after one finished reading a work: this concern provides evidence for the psychological work of offline representation.

"A great work always leaves us in a state of musing," wrote Isaac D'Israeli in his book on the literary character.[47] D'Israeli's epigram claimed that the richest experience of a work happens not during it but after. The reward for reading lies in the seconds, minutes, hours, days after the ending. Literary scholars know that works create such an impression but have no good vocabulary for describing it beyond collecting responses of individual readers. Literary critics' traditional tool, close reading, cuts off just before what might matter most, the time after reading, when there is no more text but there are readers dwelling in and on what they have experienced. Paradoxically, the most important parts of reading start when reading stops.

When psychologists examine offline products, they typically ask readers to remember what they have read. Since they are interested in the long-term memory for a text, this seems obviously useful. Yet it focuses readers' efforts on retrieving plot or, if they are not reading a story, expository content. As a result, psychological studies, which are rich about online reading processes, are disappointing about the long-term effect of literary reading (although better work exists about reading for information). In part, conducting well-controlled, long-term studies of reading, especially of dense literary texts, is hard. It is more rewarding to code and analyze memory protocols about what happened in a text than to quantify vaguer, fuzzier memories about how a work made readers feel, what their favorite parts were, which parts felt closest to their own experience, which parts were the most disagreeable, which details stuck in their minds for reasons not easily explained. Yet historical evidence of real readers suggests that these loose associations form as much a part of readers' long-term gist representations as do event summaries, so I turn from psychology to literary history for information about them.

Perhaps surprisingly, British poets of the eighteenth and nineteenth centuries found the phenomenon of what happens after reading to be gripping, deserving poem after poem. Looking only at the romantic period, we find such works as John Scott's "After Reading Akenside's Poems," Caroline Oliphant's "On Reading Lord Byron's *Childe Harold*," Thomas Peacock's "On Reading Her Poems," Henry Kirke White's "On Reading the Poems of Warton," Helen Maria Williams's "On Reading Burns' 'Mountain Daisy,'" Coleridge's "To William Wordsworth," Thomas Moore's "To Mrs. Henry Tighe, on Reading Her 'Psyche,'" John Keats's "After Reading Dante's Episode of Paolo and Francesca," Felicia Hemans's "To Silvio Pellico, on Reading his 'Prigione,'" William Wordsworth's "Composed After Reading a Newspaper of the Day," and many, many others. The sheer abundance is provocative: why so many poems about reading? If you are a poet, describing reading seems a bad choice for a topic because you do not know if your readers will have read what you describe: you run the risk of baffling them. Yet authors wrote such poems anyway, as if the mere spectacle of response justified new poetry.

Earlier literary treatments of the "after-reading" moment usually, though not always, focused on nonliterary texts, as when Shakespeare shows characters reacting to letters. After-reading poems, in contrast, describe reactions to literary works or to modes that produce a quasi-literary response. The rise in these poems coincided with the eighteenth-century "publishing revolution" described by John Brewer in *The Pleasures of the Imagination*, the arrival of a world where "books, print and readers were everywhere."[48] Print was accessible outside of institutions that had once let readers know how they were supposed to respond: court, church, university, the legal office, and the aristocratic social circle. Without such institutions, readers found new guides about just what they should do after reading a literary work. While eighteenth-century periodical reviews, with their long quotations and short comments, offered one option, "after-reading" poems suggest that, however useful the reviews might be, they were not enough.

After-reading poems say little about the work that has just been read. As a literary scholar I was surprised by this absence because I assumed that they would resemble Coleridge's "To William Wordsworth" and give eloquent, if slanted, overviews. As a scholar interested in psychology, I was further surprised because I had read so many experiments that assessed comprehension with offline summary. But in after-reading poems, if authors touch on events in the work, they do so offhandedly, as in Bernard Barton's poem on reading Scott's *Lady of the Lake*:

> Whether thy song commemorate the Graeme,
>   Or prompt for Douglas the relenting sigh;
>   Or royal James, disguis'd in humble name,
>   Or savage Roderick, Alpine's chief be nigh.[49]

Barton's plot summary takes a single stanza, an obligatory gesture before he moves to what matters to him. If you had not read Scott's poem, Barton's summary would not mean much; even if you had, it would tell you little about Barton's experience because it simply lists characters. What Barton cares about is not plot or even evaluation but the chance to beg Scott to write more, and that plea is the bulk of his poem.

Poems like Barton's may say little about the works that inspired them because they want to avoid spoilers. Moreover, as I mentioned, dwelling on details risks losing the audience. Yet beyond these rhetorical concerns with reception lies another, simpler explanation: plot summary may not be what readers remember. After reading, readers forget the words and syntax of most of what they have read. Finishing a work means deciding exactly if, how, and what to remember, in the face of forgetting almost all its verbal texture. As I have argued in relation to Browning, a key to Morris's success was that his standard of coherence allowed him to filter out more and less important textual information. But readers do not always have strategies like Morris's at hand and may look to cultural conventions to help them know what to notice.

For psychologists the fact that readers usually forget most of what they read leads to a puzzle: how do you comprehend something that you have almost entirely forgotten? The answer is that readers remember a simplified version of what they read, which psychologists call a gist representation. Since I have entitled this book *The Gist of Reading*, I mean to mark this term as a vital one for criticism. As I noted in my introduction, my title includes *gist* both in its ordinary meaning of "core" or "essence" and in its specialized, psychological meaning, which I now introduce. Teun van Dijk and Walter Kintsch influentially locate gist representation in a three-stage reading process. First, the reader encounters the actual words on the page as a surface code. Those are translated cognitively into a textbase, a mental representation of the text. Finally, readers develop their gist, which Van Dijk and Kintsch call a situation model. A situation model differs from the textbase because it contains a reader's background knowledge, inferences, emotional reactions, autobiographical links, evaluations, and much else. Most of the surface code will not be in the situation model, and most of the situation model does not come from the surface code. I want to stress this final point because it is so different from how reading is usually understood in literary scholarship, in which fidelity to the text is a paramount value. Human memory is a terrible literary critic: it stubbornly rejects such fidelity. What readers' memories retain may have only the faintest relationship to what they read.

Of these three levels—surface code, textbase, and situation model—the situation model generally lasts longest in readers' memories, although, as I discuss in the final chapter, in certain cases bits of the surface code can have surprisingly long lives in long-term memory. The situation model is a gist, a simplified representation of what the reader regards as most important, supplemented by all that a reader brings to a text.[50] Van den Broek's landscape model, discussed earlier, is an attempt to show how readers create such a gist by linking online processes to a final, offline product.

I agree with psychologists that readers usually retain a gist, not a verbatim memory of a work. I differ from psychologists in what I think dominates a situation model for literary texts. As I have noted, psychologists typically ask for a plot summary, but the "after-reading" poems suggest that readers, offline, direct their attention elsewhere. Long-term memory is more likely to resemble versions of Aaron Hill's "After Reading an Unknown Author's Book":

> Plain, modest, pleasant, deep, distinct, and clear,
> The author's honest *soul* was printed, here;
> His faithful *memory* past scenes surveys,
> His sparkling *fancy*, on their surface, plays:
> Strong understanding adds reflection's weight,
> And *all* draw purpose, from his manly *heart*.[51]

Hill's title registers the pathos of anonymity, as if, had he known the author, he might not have written a poem, or at least not this poem. By not telling us the title of the book, he also avoids suspicion that this poem is just a puff. Since no patronage relations connect him to the work's origin, he, like Keats facing the urn, creates meaning in the absence of context.

He does so by imagining an author accessible only through print, whose "honest *soul* was printed, here": the soul has left its Christian location to emerge as a by-product of mechanical reproduction, as if it did not quite exist until "printed." Defending against suspicions that print might rob the soul's authenticity, Hill stresses that this printed soul is "honest," displaying a "faithful memory," "sparkling fancy," and "strong understanding." Print reveals an implied author more real than the real one.

Saying that the author's soul is in the book masks what actually happened: Hill created a mental representation of the author during and after reading. If the author's writings "draw purpose, from his manly *heart*," that observation comes not from the book but from Hill's work as a reader. Moving from book to implied author denies the self-enclosure of reading by turning it into a fantasy of communication. In *Before Novels* J. Paul Hunter notes that early novels hold on to a fiction of orality, as if the author were talking to listeners gathered to hear the story.[52] Hill's poem likewise uses the fiction of writing as communication to heat up cold print. After-reading poems reinvent the author function as gist to cope with the radically altered status of books. For Hill the originating author passes into his book; Hill honors this book-author hybrid and in turn passes his tribute to his poem's reader.

Other "after-reading" poems resemble Hill's in focusing not on what has been read but on the imagined author. Here are several opening lines: "O god-like Bard, how hast thou roused me"; "Beattie! 'twas thine to charm the feeling heart"; "Naturalist of the mind! Thy bark sailed far"; "Oh, Warton!"; "Sweet Robin Burns, freak Nature's wanton child"; and "Southey! Thy mind has long aspir'd."[53] Such apostrophes call for action, such as more poetry (if the addressee is alive) or more commemoration (if not). Readers of such poems, who may not have read the work of the inspiring author, may at least sympathize with the proposed action.

The unspoken logic behind the after-reading poems is this: when we read, we generate an image of the imagined author, and that image, far more than the work's details, remains with us once we have finished. I follow Eefje Claassen's distinctions to describe the memories that may combine to create this image: (1) the reader's representation of the narrator; (2) the reader's representation of the implied author; and (3) the reader's representation of the biographical author.[54] These are three distinct categories and should not be confused—but "after-reading" poems depend on readers doing just that. As a result, it would be wrong to assume that each makes a distinctive contribution to long-term memory, although in certain cases they may. My claim, instead, is that at least one of these will dominate, and it may or may not be fused with the other two.

The durability in memory of the imagined author, as opposed to the details of the work, arises from ordinary memory processes: repetition effects and schema theory.[55] Whereas an event in the plot happens only once, the presence of the imagined author endures from the first sentence of a work to the last, especially if we recognize that the imagined author is an amalgam of narrator, implied author, and biographical author. The sheer repetition of exposure to the imagined author during the reading experience, as opposed to any event in the plot, increases the strength of the memory trace and makes it easier to access. The more a reader accesses the memory, the more the trace is strengthened, while the plot, which may not be accessed as frequently, fades.

I have listed the biographical author as one of the elements that might be included in a reader's memory representation, but that inclusion happens only in some cases: (1) the reader knows something about the author's biography and (2) the reader believes that using this knowledge can help explain the work (as when a reader perceives parallels between the life of the author and that of the protagonist). If either condition is not met, then the biographical author may not become part of a representation of the imagined author. In terms of what readers know about authors' lives, specialists may know much about the details. More frequently, readers may draw on the small pool of conventions often used to describe authors' lives, most of which are variations on the myth of the romantic genius (tortured childhood, vexed relation to sexuality, social marginality, tendency to addiction, and so forth).[56] The more easily a reader can link such clichés to events in a work, the more likely the biographical author will become part of a gist representation. A reader may even use such clichés to invent a pseudo-biography as a source of explanations (e.g., "This author must have really hated his mother"). The sheer familiarity and accessibility of these schemata of authorial lives may make them more prominent in a reader's memory of a work than the specifics of what happens in it.

In literary history the best representations of the imagined author in long-term memory come from the Victorian period, when critics made such representations the heart of their aesthetic criticism. Several of these appeared in my earlier discussion of critics' responses to Browning. Yet there, my focus was on how critics recreated their online experience of reading; here, I focus on how the imagined author becomes a possible core of long-term gist representation. For example, Algernon Charles Swinburne describes *Wuthering Heights* in ways that are no longer acceptable as academic criticism but that deserve attention for suggesting how one reader did, and others still may, remember Brontë's novel:

> The whole work is not more incomparable in the effect of its atmosphere or landscape than in the peculiar note of its wild and bitter pathos; but most of all is it unique in the special and distinctive character of its passion. The love which devours life itself, which devastates the present and desolates the future with unquenchable and raging fire, has nothing less pure in it than flame or sunlight. And this passionate and ardent chastity is utterly and unmistakably spontaneous and unconscious. Not till the story is ended, not till the effect of it has been thoroughly absorbed and digested, does the reader even perceive the simple and natural absence of any grosser element, any hint or suggestion of a baser alloy in the ingredients of its human emotion than in the splendour of lightning or the roll of a gathered wave. . . . As was the author's life, so is her book in all things: troubled and taintless, with little of rest in it, and nothing of reproach. It may be true that not many will ever take it to their hearts; it is certain that those who do like it will like nothing very much better in the whole world of poetry or prose.[57]

As I have noted, readers remember not all the details of a work but a simplified gist representation. Swinburne enthusiastically embraces such simplification.

He omits not only every character but also every event. It is hard to imagine how he could have left out anything more and still discuss *Wuthering Heights*. Instead, the core of his representation is how the novel mirrors Brontë's life: "As was the author's life, so is her book in all things." What matters to him in her life and book is the "special and distinctive character of its passion." Whereas psychologists might ask readers to remember how this passion arises, what conflicts it encounters, and how it does or does not resolve itself, plot details matter little to Swinburne. Instead, what he remembers is "the love which devours life itself, which devastates the present and desolates the future with unquenchable and raging fire." What is special about this love is its chastity: Cathy and Heathcliff never actually have sex (at least as Swinburne reads the novel).

Such love has a strong causal role in the plot, and Van den Broek's landscape model would predict that it should feature strongly in a reader's long-term situation model. But for Swinburne it becomes virtually the entire situation model because he links it to the life of Emily Brontë. The implied author and the biographical author merge, so the passion that he sees as dominating the novel is understood to arise not from Catherine and Heathcliff but from Brontë's soul. In particular, just as Cathy and Heathcliff never have sex, so Emily Brontë is understood by Swinburne to have been a virgin.[58] What mesmerizes Swinburne is how an author who (supposedly) never experienced physical passion creates an overwhelming sense of passion in a novel that nevertheless remains asexual. The novel's multiple narrators do not become part of his situation model probably because Swinburne does not understand them as versions of Emily Brontë: he cares not about narrative perspective but about the chaste passion that emanates from Brontë herself.

What's particularly strange about Swinburne's gist memory, along with those of many of his contemporaries, is its coherence. Victorian novels, including *Wuthering Heights*, range from farce to satire, from melodrama to picturesque description; authors orchestrate weird, uncomfortable tonalities that rarely settle into a single key. Given this range, how can a reader like Swinburne be so comfortable giving a single tonality to his memories? The answer involves the power of gist to respond to the desire for coherence discussed in chapter 2; Swinburne wipes away everything in the novel except for his sense of its passion. In part, social conventions shaped Victorian retrieval and production, as they do today: readers remembered and wrote about novels within an existing idiom of aesthetics that encouraged a unified impression. Using this idiom proved them to have mastered a valuable sociolect. In addition, despite novels' tonal variety, these readers may have had one impression more often or intensely than others, and this repetition blocked out competitors. A novel's plot and characters are given by the author, but the reader generates the impression; when Victorian readers wrote of Dickens's pathos or sentiment, they meant not Dickens's sentiments but their own impressions as catalyzed by reading Dickens. These lingered in readers' gist memories rather than well-organized records of fictional settings, plot twists, or character development.

For literary scholars trained in the rules of the discipline, Swinburne's analysis may seem weirdly reductive: is this all that he takes away from *Wuthering Heights*? But rather than treating criticism like Swinburne's as woozy sentimentality, I see it as a valuable body of evidence about what readers' long-term memory for complex literary works may look like. Ordinary memory processes make it much more likely that readers' average situation models will resemble something closer to Swinburne's rhapsody, albeit a less eloquent version, than tidy plot summaries.

Once a reader has retrieved the gist memory of an imagined author, that gist may prime memory for more specific details of a work: having remembered what is easily accessible may facilitate remembering other material that is less accessible. Recalling a gist may function as a gateway for recalling more, depending on the needs of a reader. The power of the imagined author in constructing a gist representation helps explain why, even though there are good theoretical reasons to question the truth of the imagined author as the purported origin of a literary work, it is almost impossible to read literary works without creating such a representation.[59] The likelihood of developing one may increase as a reader experiences more works by a given author and develops a better sense of his or her career.

I want to be careful about the generalizability of my claims. In discussing the imagined author as the core of a gist representation, I am not making an argument about all readers' memories in all times and places. Rather, I am describing a mode of gist memory that became especially salient during the nineteenth and twentieth centuries. But it never was the only option: in other occasions readers' situation models could look quite different. For example, Michael Saler's *As If* provides an excellent account of the success of the fictional worlds created by Arthur Conan Doyle (the Sherlock Holmes stories), H. P. Lovecraft (the supernatural stories), and J. R. R. Tolkien (*The Hobbit* and *The Lord of the Rings*). Whereas Byron the author dominated the early nineteenth century, a figure like Sherlock Holmes the character had to arrive to compete by the end of the century. Writing of Holmes, Saler notes, "For the first time, a fictional character entirely supplanted the author who created him. Holmes was said to be real, Conan Doyle was said to be fictional; scholarly monographs and the first journals devoted exclusively to a fictional character were published to prove these ironic claims."[60]

In such a case, what mattered for long-term gist was less the imagined author than the imagined character. For example, readers of Conan Doyle's Sherlock Holmes stories may have retained vivid situation models of Sherlock Holmes and John Watson long after the plots had faded. Again, repetition effects and schema account for this durability: Holmes and Watson appear in story after story, whereas the events of a particular story are encountered only once. In addition, these characters' traits (Holmes's powers of deduction; Watson's role as faithful sidekick) have causal centrality in the stories, so they are likely to be retained beyond particular events. Readers create a general category of "Sherlock Holmes story" that takes over in memory for any single item.

It may seem strange for me to refer to "imagined characters" since Holmes and Watson are actual characters. I do so to distinguish Holmes and Watson as they appear in a Conan Doyle story from a reader's gist memory of Holmes and Watson. The characters in a story are confined to it. The characters as they endure in long-term memory, however, are subject to reader inferences about how they might act in other settings; they acquire a life of the reader's own. Fan fiction in general is notorious for using readers' long-term memory for imagined characters to put them in new and unexpected settings, as when Jane Austen's characters find themselves battling zombies. In other cases long-term gist representation may center not on characters but on place, as in the Victorian reception of the early Rudyard Kipling: the feel of an exotic world mattered more than what happened in Kipling's works.

As a literary scholar I like academic conventions of reading. They provide opportunities to gain knowledge from texts not available in other ways; also, whatever their popular reputation, I think that they can be a source of great pleasure. At the same time, they have been developed partly to separate them from what are perceived to be more ordinary, less expert forms of reading. In examining online and offline reading in this chapter, I want to provide scholars with a way of understanding just why nonacademic readers do what they do, without seeing it as naive or wrong. In some cases, as in Victorian literary criticism, academic dismissal of such modes has been a lost opportunity for understanding how literary works have long-term effects. More generally, it makes the gap between expert and popular reading more dramatic than it should be. I hope that this chapter will provide a step toward transforming these styles of reading from embarrassments to opportunities.

# CHAPTER 4

# HARD READING

**I TURN NOW** from what reading is to what it should be. Rather than preaching a gospel of good reading, I want to understand prescriptive reading, especially of literature. To link prescriptive debates in the next chapters to descriptive accounts in previous ones, I return to Paul van den Broek's concept of standards of coherence, a reader's sense of how much effort is right for a given reading situation. In my experience this phrase has received questioning looks from literary scholars, who dislike both *standards*, because it sounds as if it belongs to bureaucratized educational accountability, and *coherence*, because it seems to assume that texts cohere in a simple way. Yet, as I have noted, these reactions are unnecessary. In a psychological context, *standards* and *coherence* make sense only through individual reader goals. Van den Broek uses the concept to explain why readers use different cognitive processes when they read the same work for different goals (such as studying versus entertainment). In this context *coherence* means meaningful links between parts of what is read: for some readers, finding paradoxes and contradictions may make the text cohere, while for others, the same may block comprehension.

Since readers' standards of coherence come from experience, some of that experience includes how they think about reading. While cognitive psychologists know how important reader attitudes are, they only occasionally explore them because disciplinary borders assign such issues to sociologists and historians, not to cognitive psychologists.[1] Psychological work on the topic has come chiefly from educational psychologists studying, for example, how gender stereotypes affect boys and girls learning to read.[2]

This chapter moves from the psychology of individual readers to social standards of coherence. I add *social* to Van den Broek's phrase because attitudes about appropriate reading arise not from readers in isolation but from readers interacting with norms. No psychologist would deny this interaction, but research in cognitive psychology tends not to explore it. Only at this social level can we address the question not of what makes reading easy or hard but of whether it should be easy or hard in the first place.

Such questions are easier to ask in the sociology of reading, a field that includes sociologists, historians, and literary scholars. As Wendy Griswold and her collaborators note, the sociology of reading asks "who reads what, how people read, and how their reading relates to their other activities."[3] In addition, sociology is far more aware than psychology of what Johannes Fabian calls "relations of power and submission that determine all reading."[4] Of Griswold's questions the issue of "how people read" comes closest to my topic here. In sociology the question of how people read has meant why and where they read; sociologists explore, for example, book clubs and the kinds of personal networks that they sustain.[5] In contrast, I am interested in specific reading behaviors at the level of collective imagination: what do readers think they need to do to be good readers?

The methodology of this chapter and the next should be more familiar to literary scholars than the earlier chapters because it is more about history than psychology. I nevertheless aim to integrate concepts from my earlier chapters, such as gist, into historical analysis to foreground issues about reading strategy invisible in earlier accounts. I look to eighteenth- and nineteenth-century Britain because digitization and copyright laws make sources from this period easy to access and search. Debates about reading in Britain in this period revolved around two topics: effort (should reading be easy or hard?) and ethics (when is reading good, and when is it bad?). Different combinations of effort and ethics created four possible social images of reading:

| Effortful and Positive | Effortful and Negative |
| --- | --- |
| Effortless and Positive | Effortless and Negative |

The two options on the left side represent actual social standards of coherence; the two options on the right indicate what happens when those standards collapse. This chart leaves out the many shades of gray in real reading experiences, which resist binaries. Yet if we move from individual experience to historical writing, much writing about reading places it in one of these four niches.

This chapter looks at the top row (the effortful options). In terms of positive, effortful reading, many readers from this period brag about reading carefully:

A few weeks ago I *read with care and attention* a celebrated "Essay on Taste."[6]

*I have read your play carefully*, and with great pleasure.[7]

During my last year at Cambridge, *I read with care* and profound interest Humboldt's *Personal Narrative*.[8]

*I read, with care*, and with great pleasure, the ecclesiastical polity of Hooker.[9]

I may mention that *I read carefully* the two first chapters and the first section of the third volume of Mitford's *Grecian History*.[10]

For these readers, adverbs like *carefully* and phrases like *with care* come with an implied assumption: the reading that they describe differs from their ordinary reading, which might not need such care. Admittedly, these writers want to impress their audience. Their phrases do not mean that they truly read with care, only that they wanted to seem to have done so. They do show, however, that readers believed "careful reading" to be meaningful and good.

It's harder to know what they did when they read carefully. To find out, I turn in this chapter to the most accessible prescriptive models of effortful reading, those devoted to Bible reading, and to their influence. John Ruskin generalized strategies from these Bible-reading models to literary reading more generally; his influence on teaching in secondary schools gave his model institutional clout. The American high school beatification of George Eliot's *Silas Marner* demonstrates just how deeply Ruskin's ideals permeated a cultural understanding of careful reading. My goal is not to emphasize that reading became important but to analyze what came to count as culturally valuable reading.

Francis Bacon's "Of Studies" stated about reading: "Some books are to be tasted, others to be swallowed, and some few to be chewed and digested; that is, some books are to be read only in parts; others to be read, but not curiously; and some few to be read wholly, and with diligence and attention."[11] Eating gives Bacon a happy metaphor for characterizing differences that are hard to grasp literally. Comparing reading to eating, Bacon understands the book itself as a guide to how to treat it: some books deserve more attention than others. He does not specify how a reader knows what books deserve which treatment. His passive infinitives ("to be tasted," "to be swallowed," "to be chewed and digested") give books intrinsic edibility apart from a reader's goal or motive in reading, so an educated reader should just know.

When John Locke revised Bacon in his much-reprinted "Some Thoughts Concerning Reading and Study for a Gentleman," he made two changes. First, he ignored Bacon's option of lighter reading: in Locke all reading is serious. Second, he replaced metaphors of eating with those of building, as when he writes, "The third and last step therefore, in improving the understanding, is to find out upon what foundation any proposition advanced bottoms; and to observe the connexion of the intermediate ideas, by which it is joined to that foundation, upon which it is erected, or that principle, from which it is derived."[12] For Locke, reading means reading argumentative prose, so readers need to understand arguments. First, they must comprehend what Locke calls "propositions," sequences of ideas. Then, they must understand the "connexion" between those propositions. For Locke, the danger lurks of treating ideas as isolated monads: good readers avoid this by going beyond separate ideas to comprehend a full proposition. "Connexion" in Locke does the work of "coherence" in contemporary psychology: it names the process by which parts come together meaningfully.

Finally, Locke argues that readers go beyond the information presented to make inferences. Specifically, he assumes that any proposition requires assumptions, the "foundation" on which "any proposition advanced bottoms." Readers should see both these assumptions and the "intermediate ideas" by which they lead to the main proposition. Locke does not specify how readers make such inferences, but they presumably arise from logical analysis plus existing knowledge about a proposition. The bigger point is that Locke's construction metaphor, unlike Bacon's eating metaphors, makes readers into hard-working building inspectors, examining the "foundation" on which each proposition "is erected."

As such, Locke's reading is part of a war against reading for the gist. He refuses the distinction between online and offline processing: in his account, if you read carefully enough online, you will retain in memory a representation so precise that it will be even better than a verbatim recollection. In Walter Kintsch's terms Locke's reader will surpass the textbase to create an ideal situation model. Locke skirts the dissolving power of the memory: even the most careful reader will never retain as much as Locke imagines. But Locke creates a cultural fantasy of good reading that refuses the dissolving power of a gist.

Influential as Locke was, his book's scope was limited because it was for gentlemen; his list of appropriate books was accessible only to a few. Far more accessible were the many guides to Bible reading in the eighteenth and nineteenth centuries. For an intensely Protestant country, access to scripture mattered: reading in Britain meant, above all, reading the Bible.[13] Despite changing attitudes toward the Bible in Britain, core advice about reading remained constant over time in these guides. I stress their commonalities over their differences because I am interested not in individual texts but in collective practices: Bible guides are our most visible source for the strategies demanded by serious reading.

Deep contradictions in British Protestantism ruffle all the guides: the Bible's supposed ease and transparency versus the cryptic ancient records of a small Asian religion; stern anti-Catholic rejection of external guides (as stated in Article 6 of the Thirty-Nine Articles) versus their own status as just such guides; and a circular insistence that reading the Bible led to belief, but only for those who already believed. The guides handle such contradictions not by acknowledging them directly but by treating Bible reading as conscious, effortful, and sustained work. An early eighteenth-century writer notes, "As these Books are not penned after an *ordinary* Manner, so they require *more than ordinary* Application to understand them."[14] A mid-Victorian guide expanded on this idea: "We are called upon, in studying the subjects on which God had condescended to address us, to put forth our very best powers; and to spare no pains of thought, investigation, or research, where these will serve us."[15] If readers work hard enough, the tensions I have noted should not matter, even if noticed, because greater benefits will accrue.

In these guides readers' efforts have three stages: creating the right mind-set before and during reading, using specific strategies while reading, and understanding the results. To prepare the mind, the guides recommend prayer, as in the Book of Common Prayer's Collect for the second Sunday of Advent: "Grant us that we may in such wise hear them [the words of the Bible], read, mark, learn, and inwardly digest them, that by patience and comfort of thy holy Word, we may embrace and ever hold fast the blessed hope of everlasting life."[16] The guides expand on the prayer's "in such wise" by telling readers what they must set aside to let good reading begin: "Before opening the Bible, all worldly cares and anxieties should be left at the throne of grace. . . . Watch against vain thoughts, lest they hinder your profit. Do not be restless and impatient, or in haste to go away from your Bible, lest it remain a sealed book; but search it reverently, and thoughtfully, with patient prayer."[17] Such self-regulation requires constant watchfulness: "He must watch all the Motions of his Heart, lest some irregular End should secretly move him."[18]

Insisting on what readers should not do makes Bible reading seem like an ascetic activity that inhibits other, more fun things to do. The goal was to clear a reader's mind to allow exclusive focus on the holy text. Yet inhibiting any "irregular End" actually increased readers' cognitive load: asking readers to block out certain ideas forces them, paradoxically, to pay more attention to those ideas so that they can be blocked. The guides place a heavy cognitive burden on readers because they ask for attention to both the text at hand and the inhibition of distractions.

In terms of what readers must do online (while they are reading), all guides stress building a coherent representation. First, readers need to grasp the meaning of a passage: "Endeavour to ascertain the literal or first sense of a passage, before you look for any other."[19] Doing so requires focusing not only on the immediate passage but also on connections with context, both local and global: "If you are reading Genesis in the evening, go through with it before you begin Exodus. You will thus see the connexion between one part and another."[20] Likewise, any word or phrase needs to be understood in context: "Carefully consult the context, or observe the connection in which the particular word or phrase stands."[21] Readers must make connective inferences so that they constantly link what they are reading to what they have read.

Even focusing on an individual word requires connective inferences: "Choose a text, and think upon it word by word, adding to it such passages of scripture as each word may suggest"; this author shows how short passages, such as "This do in remembrance of me," might be read creating connections to other biblical uses of *remembrance*. He also recommends using a concordance to follow words or subjects (his example is *temptation*).[22] Even those who do not look just at the word should recognize parallel passages (notes in the King James Bible typically provided references, but readers had to look them up themselves). More generally, readers must "compare the quotations from other books," and one author notes, "Part must be compared with part, for elucidation or confirmation."[23] Beyond making connective inferences, readers are also urged to do research: "Use such human helps as God has placed within your reach"; they should make sure that "all available helps be employed," including other books and other people.[24] If readers do not have background knowledge, they should find it.

Good Bible readers constantly update their situation models: "Former ideas must be revived by new impressions, corroborated by kindred ones, and augmented by perpetual accessions, till the whole be got in. These must be excited and enlivened by renewed examination."[25] Despite the Bible's supposed transparency, the guides insist that readers must do much more than just decode. Their online work must connect the bare words of the text to other parts of scripture and to relevant knowledge, and they are responsible for dynamic learning.

Their most serious work comes after reading, when they must use their situation model as a guide to deeds; the reader needs "to order his whole Life and Conduct according to the *Directions* the Word proposeth. . . . [It] will inspire all his Thoughts and Actions, Words and Inclinations, with *Heavenly minded-ness*."[26] Readers should connect abstract moralizations to potential actions, which they then must remember and perform. This may be the only moment in which the Bible guides cede something to gist memory, insofar as acting on the Bible requires generalizing and abstracting from the specifics of what has been read, to apply it to one's own life. As Edward Bickersteth notes, "Seek to apply each part personally, to realize all its truths, and to obey all its instructions."[27] Bible reading should heighten prospective memory, the ability to remember not what you have done in the past but what you need to do in the future.[28] In this case readers need to plan their future actions to embody the truths that they understand first through reading.

With much practice some strategies that the guides recommend may have become automatic for certain readers, such as recognizing parallel passages, but, overall, these guides wanted readers to avoid good-enough processing; instead, they demanded prereading inhibition, online connective and explanatory inferences, and offline prospective memory. The result was a cognitive ethics of reading, the belief that exercising the mind in certain ways was inherently good, and the harder, the better.[29] For a reader who took the advice seriously, the labor of reading would be all-consuming; as in Locke, gist memory is never good enough. It also would be tiring, even with practice, although the guides rarely acknowledge that readers might need a break.

While such standards might seem appropriate for adults, the guides' real challenge came when they faced children. Good Protestant British children were supposed to read the Bible as soon as possible. But given how hard the social standards of coherence were for adult Bible reading, what would be right for children? The answer was that, just as there were guides for adults, another set existed for teachers of children. Such guides loudly distanced their pedagogy from that of the public schools and of classical learning. Generations of schoolboys memorized by rote the rules of Greek and Latin grammar; they translated increasingly difficult passages, also memorized, with great attention to syntactic obscurities and rhetorical figures. In Kintsch's terms, as discussed in the last chapter, their school reading was about comprehending a textbase rather than creating a situation model. While many schoolboys may have comprehended the classics more deeply, cultivating such comprehension was not part of the recognized school curriculum. Given the demands on working-memory capacity required by memorizing and translating difficult Greek and Latin, it is not surprising that little time was spent on much else.

Nineteenth-century Bible guides recognized that such rote learning was all wrong for the Bible: children had to understand, not just read. In the 1840s the first school inspectors in British history were horrified by how badly children understood the Bible: "[The children] learn the words of the propositions, but attach very little, if any, signification to them"; "The misconceptions as to time and place, and the relation of one event to another in the minds, not of children only, are amazing and too ludicrous for me to record them in connexion with so grave a topic."[30] The revelations of poor Bible comprehension created a minicrisis in British education: suddenly, developmental reading comprehension mattered more than it ever had. More accurately, an old consensus about appropriate standards of coherence for school Bible reading came under attack.

This change stemmed from a seemingly unlikely source: Thomas Malthus, the economist who famously argued for the inevitable gap between population and food supply. Confronting the disaster of overpopulation, Malthus recommended "moral restraint" among the poor, which required "training up the rising generation in habits of sobriety, industry, independence, and prudence."[31] Malthus's economics altered the tone around working-class pedagogy from one of Christian charity to one of urgent national security. In light of the population disaster that he saw looming, grilling the working classes in rote catechisms was not enough, because doing so would not necessarily produce sobriety or prudence. The hope was, however, that educating them would lead them to understand their role in a larger economic system and, even more, to restrain their sexual urges to prevent that system from collapsing under the burden of overpopulation. Literacy was the first step in such an education, and textual comprehension suddenly mattered.

Influenced by Malthus's concerns, David Stow, a Glasgow merchant, started the first "infant school" in Britain in 1828 for children from two to seven years old; even more significant, in 1837 he established Britain's first teacher-training school.[32] Stow reformed education radically: boys and girls had the same education in the same classroom; corporal punishment was banished, as were competitions and awards; the playground became central to school architecture; and songs and games appeared. Stow gave unprecedented attention to reading comprehension. Like Victorian inspectors, he knew that existing methods were not working: "Children and untutored persons are too passive in general to draw practical lessons for themselves from the mere reading of a subject. . . . We have only to question children . . . on what they remember of a passage they have just read, or an address to which they have listened . . . to be convinced how little—how extremely little they have gathered for themselves."[33] Stow insisted on a new standard of coherence: "Every lesson ought to pass first into the understanding: that is, the child ought not to commit it to memory, in the first instance, and then afterward have it explained, for the mere words are, to a certain extent, a barrier to the understanding, when got by rote; but reverse the process, and the increased effect is very apparent."[34] In Kintsch's terms Stow wanted children to move backward, to start with a situation model and then move to the textbase and surface code. Only then could their comprehension be guaranteed.

Since children were spending all their time memorizing, they put large demands on their long-term memory and entirely bypassed online processes associated with comprehension. They stored strings of signifiers: recognizing the concepts associated with the signifiers, using strategic recall of background knowledge, and creating connections between concepts became incidental. Such pedagogy, according to Stow, murdered literacy, at least as he understood it, in accordance with the Pauline doctrine that "the letter killeth, but the spirit giveth life" (2 Corinthians 3:6). "The letter" (rote memorization) wiped out "the spirit" (comprehension) of the Bible's teachings. Stow disseminated a new standard, in which children under seven would not memorize, would spend comparatively little time on decoding, but would give great attention to comprehending.

For example, Stow created "Bible Lesson Cards," sent home with children on Friday or Saturday, to be returned on Monday. His sample card about the

lion contains a picture, questions about lions to be answered through references to the Bible, and a rather creepy poem, entitled "The Lion":

> The lion is the king of beasts;
> He noble is and strong;
> His face is broad, his eyes are fierce;
> His mane is rough and long.
>
> We never saw a lion wild,
> But we, though children, know,
> That like one roaring, Satan doth
> Continually go.
>
> O may we, in our infant days,
> Be kept from Satan's power;
> For he is ever trying how
> He may us all devour.[35]

Afterward came questions to teach comprehension. In a virtually unprecedented
piece of textbook design, Stow does not answer most of his questions, though he
does provide some clues. Equally important, his instructions on the card firmly
state that the questions are "to be answered in the Children's own words." Rote
memorization of answers, as in catechisms, had to go.

His questions focus on four major skills: recognizing genre choice, focusing attention, creating causal connections, and recruiting relevant background knowledge. As Kintsch and Van Dijk argue, recognizing genre can
be a critical element of text comprehension, and Stow asks students to see
that this poem is a prayer, not just a description of a lion.[36] Stow also uses his
questions to focus students' attention by suggesting what concepts in their
memory can be inhibited. Specifically, rather than focus on the lion's noble
physical aspects, he asks them to emphasize its threatening biblical links with
Satan. He also focuses on causal links between elements of the poem, especially ones that can be made only by using relevant background knowledge,
such as God's power; God is not mentioned in the poem, so children need to
retrieve knowledge of his power from long-term memory. While these strategies may seem obvious, they were not so when Stow was writing, and they
have been invisible in histories of education, which have treated pedagogy
like Stow's solely as religious indoctrination. Although the religious indoctri-

nation is obvious, I draw attention to the specific steps that Stow took to lead children to deeper textual processing.

Did Stow's methods help? A clear-cut answer is difficult. Compulsory education and standardized educational testing were in the future. Although Stow's reports on his schools included glowing testimonials from parents, in the long run many Scottish parents suspected Stow's methods, preferring the more established routine of rote memorization and decoding. Professionals with more experience in education, however, perceived them as a huge improvement. One Victorian inspector, speaking about schools in Lancashire, noted, "The Master (a Scotch episcopalian [sic] trained under Mr Stow) aided by his sister, was more successful in bringing into action the intellectual faculties of the children than any other paid teacher that I saw in Lancashire."[37] Horace Mann, the most influential educator in nineteenth-century America, wrote of Stow's schools that "they furnish a model worthy of being copied by the world" because of "the thoroughness with which they teach the *intellectual* part of reading."[38] As Mann's example indicates, Stow's school acquired a disproportionately large influence on world education because educators visited it, and its numerous trainees were sent across the globe to found new schools. In England James Kay-Shuttleworth, the first secretary of Britain's Committee of Council of Education, established a teacher-training college at Battersea using three men trained in Stow's school. Even more significant, Kay-Shuttleworth developed the standards whereby Victorian school inspectors evaluated schools.[39] Influenced by Stow, whose school he had visited and helped to fund, he made sure that the inspectors paid careful attention to comprehension of the kind that Stow thought was so important. Through his efforts, schools in English-speaking countries for the first time became accountable for students' ability to understand what they read.

I would like to say that all this attention to reading the Bible carefully had a demonstrable effect on everyday reading. Yet evidence of such is not easy to find. In terms of the Bible, many, many British readers describe reading and reflecting on it.[40] But they read the Bible so often that they usually describe not particular moments of reading but the general habit of doing so. Reading the Bible was so ordinary that it rarely called for detailed commentary. While nineteenth-century divines discuss their Bible reading, it is surprisingly difficult to catch average British readers analyzing a specific moment of Bible reading outside of spiritual autobiographies and publications specifically for Bible reading societies. Just as many literature professors may wonder if the reading strategies that they teach affect students' reading outside of class, it is an open question whether the prescriptions of books and schools altered how ordinary readers read the Bible.

More certain is that significant effort went into persuading readers that such effort in reading ought to matter, whether or not they actually made it. I will look at two influential moments in this effort: John Ruskin's essay "Of Kings' Treasuries" in *Sesame and Lilies* and the American institutionalization of George Eliot's *Silas Marner*, under the influence of Ruskinian ideals. "Of Kings' Treasuries" combined the two traditions of serious reading that I have described—the student-centered tradition of Bacon and Locke and the Bible-centered tradition of the guides and David Stow. This combination is notable, but what earns Ruskin a place in the history of hard reading is that, for him, such reading produces a healthy society. Whereas Malthus hoped that good comprehension could save the lower classes, Ruskin argued that it could save everybody. His elevation of hard reading gave educators the rhetorical ammunition they needed to put it at the center of schooling, as the American reception of *Silas Marner* demonstrates.

John Ruskin's "Of Kings' Treasuries" is the first lecture in *Sesame and Lilies*, a notorious book because of its second lecture, "Of Queens' Gardens," a richly bizarre account of Ruskin's views on women. Next to the debate over "Of Queens' Gardens," "Of Kings' Treasuries" has received less attention. It begins tamely enough, with Ruskin explaining that his title is metaphorical and that he proposes "to bring before you a few simple thoughts about reading."[41] Yet Ruskin's "simple thoughts" turn out to be a catastrophe of national dyslexia: "But, at all events, be assured, we cannot read. No reading is possible for a people with its mind in this state. No sentence of any great writer is intelligible to them. It is simply and sternly impossible for the English public, at this moment, to understand any thoughtful writing—so incapable of thought has it become in its insanity of avarice" (48–49).

Ruskin begins with his staggering generalization, "we cannot read," a proposition refuted by his audience's ability to read it (although his words started as a lecture). As he goes on, that generalization morphs into a provocative criticism. By *reading* he means not decoding but understanding major writing: what cannot be read are the sentences "of any great writer" and any "thoughtful writing." By *cannot* he means not that the English are incapable of reading but that the "insanity of avarice" has so warped their minds that they cannot comprehend. He adds the adverbial phrase "at this moment" to turn a timeless generalization ("we cannot read") into a time-bound phenomenon: when he lectures, circumstances have made real reading impossible. Cumulatively, his modifications make it harder to dismiss him by the end of the paragraph than at the start.

Ruskin defines real reading and then explains why the English cannot do it. His standard of coherence overlaps with that of the Bible guides. Like them, he cautions about projecting personal meanings onto the text. A reader reading great authors needs "first, by a true desire to be taught by them, and to enter into their thoughts. To enter into theirs, observe; not to find your own expressed by them. If the person who wrote the book is not wiser than you, you need not read it; if he be, he will think differently from you in many respects" (34). Like the Bible guides, Ruskin insists that careful reading demands cognitive inhibition, an eradication of the self before the text, of the kind that George Levine has studied in *Dying to Know*.[42] For Ruskin the goal is "annihilating our own personality, and seeking to enter into his, so as to be able assuredly to say, 'Thus Milton thought,' not 'Thus I thought, in misreading Milton'" (43). Yet Ruskin goes further. The Bible guides assumed a hierarchy between author and reader: a good reader should erase a sinful self to understand an omniscient God. Since Ruskin is not writing about the Bible, he asks his reader to venture on a potentially riskier endeavor by requiring them to "enter into" the thoughts of an author who may or may not be worth it. As Ruskin knows, the result is likely to be a surprise: "He will think differently from you in many respects."

The Bible guides insisted that the Bible was accessible to all who read with faith. Attention was more important than interpretation: carefully attending to connections guaranteed good reading. Ruskin, in contrast, requires even more work: "The metal you are in search of being the author's mind or meaning, his words are as the rock which you have to crush and smelt in order to get at it. And your pickaxes are your own care, wit, and learning; your smelting furnace is your own thoughtful soul" (35). Initially, Ruskin asks readers to extinguish their personality to receive the author's wisdom. But when Ruskin describes reading, it looks as if the text, not the reader, is destroyed: "His words are as the rock which you have to crush and smelt in order to get at" authorial meaning. The reader, far from passively receiving meaning, discovers it destructively with the "pickaxes" of "care, wit, and learning" and the "smelting furnace" of a "thoughtful soul." Ruskin renews the Bible guides' hermeneutic circle, whereby reading the Bible bolsters the faith of those who already have faith before they read it. In Ruskin, reading produces "care, wit, and learning" but only for the careful, witty, and learned.

Ruskin provides a case study in what textual mining looks like in his close reading of St. Peter's speech in Milton's "Lycidas." His choice of "Lycidas" mattered because it suggested that poetry, as opposed to science, history, philosophy, theology, or economics, was the right place to read hard. When Locke described reading, he had a different canon in mind, as did the writers who described Bible reading. Ruskin transfers to literary texts the standards of hard reading previously directed at nonfictional texts (or those, like the Bible, believed to be nonfictional). For Ruskin nonliterary works, whose goal was to transmit information, did not ask for the serious effort needed for literary ones: "In Ruskin's account of reading, it was precisely because words were not referential or transparent . . . that the reader had to work. And it was this work . . . that constituted the unique value the Literary work could provide."[43] Ruskin's account is not especially true: the work needed to understand words that are "not referential or transparent" draws on skills found in many other situations aside from reading literature. But, true or not, his argument linked literary reading to a mental discipline supposedly found nowhere else.

Ruskin prefaces his reading of Milton by insisting that a good reader must look "intensely at words" and learn "their meaning, syllable by syllable—nay, letter by letter" (35). Once again, hard readers set themselves against the power of gist and appeal to the fantasy that online processing, if deep enough, can overcome the dissolving power of memory by preserving an exceptionally detailed understanding. But as he proceeds, this vision of one word at a time gives way to his actual procedure, which links each word to its context. Discussing Milton's description of those who "for their bellies' sake / Creep and intrude, and climb into the fold," he takes verbs one by one: "[Milton] needs all the three;—especially those three, and no more than those—'creep,' and 'intrude,' and 'climb'; no other words would or could serve the turn, and no more could be added. For they exhaustively comprehend the three classes, correspondent to the three characters, of men who dishonestly seek ecclesiastical power" (40). Those who "creep" want "secret influence"; those who "intrude" have "natural insolence of heart" and obtain "authority with the common crowd"; and those who "climb" "gain high dignities and authorities" because of their "selfishly exerted . . . ambition." One might object that Milton's verbs describe not three distinct groups but the same men as they approach a flock of the faithful. But Ruskin wants to demonstrate attention to the authorial word, and this goal leads him to chop up the poem so that each word stands for something distinct. While it is no surprise that Ruskin's personality dominates an analysis that is supposed to demonstrate how to annihilate personality in front of a work, more important is his willingness to demonstrate what hard reading entails by transferring traditional methods of Protestant Bible study to English literature.

In his lecture's second part he moves from cognitive processes to emotional ones. Bad reading is not just about poor cognitive skills; it is also an empathic failure: "Alas! it is the narrowness, selfishness, minuteness, of your sensation that you have to deplore in England at this day;—sensation which spends itself in bouquets and speeches: in revellings and junketings; in sham fights and gay puppet shows, while you can look on and see noble nations murdered, man by man, without an effort or a tear" (47). For Ruskin a Victorian version of Wordsworth's "gross and violent stimulants" has withered English feeling. Busy lavishing its sensations on "sham fights and gay puppet shows," it has no compassion for "noble nations murdered, man by man." Ruskin borrows a technique from Matthew Arnold's "The Function of Criticism at the Present Time" by quoting a newspaper article about a tragedy, in this case a worker starving to death, and using it as a metonymy for a wider collapse in care for the needy.

Powerful as Ruskin's indictment of Victorian selfishness may be, it does not seem to have much to do with reading or social standards of coherence; this may be why discussions of his essay, such as those by Mary Poovey and Stephen Arata, focus on literary analysis and say less about social vision. But linking good literary analysis to saving the nation is central to Ruskin's purpose, outrageous as it may seem, and to his later influence. If hard reading, as Ruskin understands it, asks for self-annihilation, then the empathic failure represented by "sham fights and gay puppet shows" dooms it. Although Ruskin hardly annihilated himself in his own reading, he wants hard reading to halt the domination of text by self. A narcissistic reader would be a lazy one, whereas a hard-working reader must respect what is being read. Capitalist selfishness undermines qualities needed for hard reading.

Yet Ruskin does not condemn his audience too harshly:

And the reason that I have allowed all these graver subjects of thought to mix themselves up with an inquiry into methods of reading, is that, the more I see of our national faults or miseries, the more they resolve themselves into conditions of childish illiterateness, and want of education in the most ordinary habits of thought. It is, I repeat, not vice, not selfishness, not dulness of brain, which we have to lament; but an unreachable schoolboy's recklessness, only differing from the true schoolboy's in its incapacity of being helped, because it acknowledges no master. (59)

Although Ruskin has indeed lamented his audience's "vice," "selfishness," and "dulness of brain," he now backtracks. England's failures shrink into "childish illiterateness, and want of education in the most ordinary habits of thought." This is a strange switch, since his previous attack has been devastating. It occurs because Ruskin's return to "an inquiry into methods of reading" allows him to see "all these graver subjects" in a new light. The hope that improving reading methods could model social improvement has a potent rhetorical edge when addressed to readers. The banal fact that his readers can read proves that they have been educated, even as young children. If they have been educated once, they can be educated again. Having learned to read as children, they should now be able to read as adults. What Ruskin laments, therefore, is not original sin ("vice," "selfishness," "dulness of brain") but the persistence of adults in childish behavior, "schoolboy's recklessness."

Ultimately, Ruskin wants his instruction in hard reading to model attending to the state. As I argued in the previous chapter, many cognitive skills required to comprehend literature are not unique to literature: they are skills of general event understanding. Ruskin's desire to transfer literacy skills to politics may be outrageous, but it is not as outrageous as it initially seems. In his peroration he presents a utopian vision of what England might look like if hard reading assumed its rightful role as the nation's lifeblood: "That we should bring up our peasants to a book exercise instead of a bayonet exercise!—organise, drill, maintain with pay, and good generalship, armies of thinkers, instead of armies of stabbers!—find national amusement in reading-rooms as well as rifle-grounds; give prizes for a fair shot at a fact, as well as for a leaden splash on a target. What an absurd idea it seems, put fairly in words, that the wealth of the capitalists of civilised nations should ever come to support literature instead of war!" (63). Once again, Ruskin begins with an extreme claim, only to moderate it as his paragraph progresses. He first calls for the nation to exchange fighters for readers but then moves from a rhetoric of replacement to one of supplement: "in reading-rooms as well as rifle-grounds"; prizes for "a fair shot at a fact, as well as" at a target. Although in the final sentence he admits how absurd it sounds for capitalists to support "literature instead of war," he believes that the inability to read literature indicts both capitalist indifference to art and more basic failures of thinking and feeling. "Of Kings' Treasuries" elevates hard reading to a test of a nation's ability to overcome cognitive and emotional ravages of industrial capitalism.[44]

This elevation may explain why "Of Kings' Treasuries" mattered so much to later teachers. Arata discusses Ruskin's association of reading with hard work and notes that he expected readers to find his idea "unfamiliar"; yet, as Arata also argues, "by the 1880s . . . the idea that reading, properly done, constituted a form of labor had passed into the realm of common sense."[45] Arata traces the proliferation of late Victorian guides to how readers should read, a trend that continued well into the twentieth century. Poovey's chapter "Delimiting Literature" similarly shows how Ruskin's distinction of aesthetic value from commercial value required new protocols for reading literature focused on its connotative, rather than denotative, force.[46] I continue the story that Arata and Poovey tell by examining the migration of Ruskin's hard reading across the Atlantic to high school teaching in the United States. I do so because high school became the most enduring institution for preserving and disseminating Ruskinian hard reading to a wide population, a role that it continues to fulfill to this day.

Evidence for Ruskin's influence on American educators at the turn of the century is plentiful. Blanche Wilder Bellamy and Maud Wilder Goodwin entitled their 1890 school textbook *Open Sesame*, in reference to Ruskin's *Sesame and Lilies*, and quote his essay at the end of their introduction.[47] Angeline Parmenter Carey foregrounds her indebtedness to Ruskin's ideals in her *Guide to the Study of Literary Criticism*, which she designs for the high school English teacher.[48] Superintendent P. W. Horn of the Texas schools in 1915 maintained that "every Texas boy or girl should read about Kings' Treasuries," and L. A. Williams quotes Ruskin's mining metaphor in a 1921 essay on high school reading.[49] Rowena Keith Keyes even recommended "Of Kings' Treasuries" for the third-year Regents Syllabus for New York schools.[50]

Ruskin's popularity with American high school teachers had a pragmatic edge. He let them solve concrete institutional problems in ways that empowered hard reading. American higher education at the end of the nineteenth century faced a crisis: standardizing college admissions. American high schools exploded from forty in 1869 to almost eight hundred in 1889; this number grew even more in the early twentieth century.[51] Before this growth, colleges handled admissions easily: each institution chose who got in and who did not, and institutions were flexible about student quality and remedial instruction. But the increase in high schools meant a corresponding increase in college applicants, and colleges suddenly had to be more selective. High schools, eager to ensure that their students would get into colleges, wanted to know what they needed to succeed.

To handle the new burden, college administrators formed regional groupings to consult about entrance requirements. Initially, they cared less about standardizing admissions than about comparing notes and learning about each other's practices. As soon as they did, a topic that had not been central to admissions suddenly mattered: literary study. Previously, some colleges asked admissions questions about literary reading; others looked only at composition, without expecting background in literature. In a fateful move, early regional conferences on admissions requirements, attended by both high school teachers and college professors, elevated not just composition but also literary knowledge to an admissions requirement. Given Ruskin's argument that hard reading was a prerequisite for social salvation, how could colleges refuse their civic duty? More important, Ruskin had shown that the best site for such skills was literary reading rather than mathematics or science. He had given educators a reason to insist on not merely good writing but also hard reading as a criterion for college admission.

In 1895 the conferences on admissions led to a national joint committee on English entrance requirements, and by 1898 it had created a recommended four-year program for high school English that would prepare students for admission to college. Numerous colleges agreed to abide by its expectations.[52] Next, the College Entrance Examination Board (CEEB) created a standardized test for college admissions, first administered in 1901.[53] Although it never set the texts to be studied, it used lists from the National Conference on Uniform Entrance Requirements in English, made up of representatives from the smaller local boards. The CEEB soon gained authority from the perceived fairness and objectivity of its tests, which replaced those formerly administered by each college or university. Early on, the CEEB split the book list for the test into three categories: books for study, for reading, and for general knowledge. The first were books that students had to know in detail for specific questions; the second, books that they should read but that would not be discussed in the classroom; the third, books to be tested with general questions. In the early decades of the exam the weight of these lists varied, and in time they led to two examinations, a "restricted" exam on specific books and a "comprehensive" exam on reading more generally.[54]

Such tests created a demand for special editions of the literature that students were supposed to know, and editions of required books poured from presses. As the tests varied from year to year, some books fell out of favor, while others received short-term canonization. One book, however, endured like a rock across all variations: George Eliot's *Silas Marner*.

As soon as the list of books "for study" appeared, *Silas Marner* was on it.[55] Even before the CEEB formalized its entrance exam, *Silas Marner* had become de facto required knowledge, to judge from admissions examination topics: "The stealing of Marner's gold and his discovery of Eppie" (Cornell University, June 1896); "Why does George Eliot in *Silas Marner* give detailed descriptions of the scene in the Rainbow, of the scene at Squire Cass's, of the visit to Lantern Yard?" (Vassar College, September 1897).[56] According to J. N. Hook, the novella entered high school classes as early as 1881, only twenty years after its publication.[57] *Silas Marner* remained a CEEB requirement from 1901 to 1914 and from 1920 to 1928. For 1915–19 and 1929–34 *Adam Bede* and *Romola* were permitted substitutes, but, given the lengths of these alternatives, I suspect that teachers and students stayed with *Silas Marner*; like many other required works, it had the virtue of brevity. Test questions about *Silas Marner* on the CEEB exams included "the different stories which are worked together in the plot of *Silas Marner* (2 or more pages)" (1901); "What elements in the character of Godfrey Cass account for his relief at his wife's death and his failure to care for his child; also for his confession to Nancy and resolve to adopt Eppie?" (1905); "Show how Godfrey Cass, in *Silas Marner*, was a worshipper of 'blessed chance' (at least 2 paragraphs)" (1908); "What was life worth to Silas Marner? (150 words or more)" (1914); "In any *one* of these six novels—*A Tale of Two Cities, Silas Marner, Quentin Durward, Treasure Island, Kidnapped, The House of the Seven Gables*—show how the environment affects a leading character."[58]

Beyond specific questions, *Silas Marner* crept into admissions tests in other ways. In 1903 the grammar section included an excerpt from the novella with underlined words to parse. Likewise, it appeared on lists of books that candidates were assumed to have read. One question, for example, asked, "Select four names from the following list and give the name of some woman whom the author associates with each. Briefly characterize each of these women."[59] Ten names followed, including Godfrey Cass. I note this question because it appeared in 1917, when *Silas Marner* had a brief hiatus from being a "book to be studied." Even though it was no longer required, it was still a book to be known, since it could be queried in general essay questions. Likewise, several "general questions" about prose fiction asked candidates to address issues in a range of texts, always including *Silas Marner*.[60]

Given the popularity of *Silas Marner*, editions of it were everywhere. A search of WorldCat for editions between 1895 and 1935 turns up more than 650 entries, most of them reprintings of about twenty high school editions. *Silas Marner* had begun life as a short Victorian novel and continued as part of Eliot's collected works. But it was reborn as a twentieth-century American textbook because editions contained not only Eliot's text but also critical commentary, notes, and assignment recommendations. The editorial apparatus attached hard reading not only to literature but also to the school.

In general, these editions use Eliot's text to argue for reading fiction. It is as if the education that Silas receives by raising Eppie models the education that students might receive from reading. George Armstrong Wauchope's edition notes, "There should be in our system of education a place for aesthetic as well as for strictly scientific studies; for the former, besides possessing a disciplinary value, afford a distinct means of spiritual culture."[61] Wauchope does not specify what "spiritual culture" is, but he recognizes it as an important alternative or supplement to "strictly scientific studies." J. Rose Colby's edition begins with an essay, "The Study of Fiction," before it even mentions Eliot, and it endorses fiction as a guide to life. Literary study creates "the enlargement of life that comes to the student through living so intimately and intelligently in the lives of others." The second, "distinctly inferior," result is "the quickening and strengthening of the critical instinct and the development of the literary judgment."[62] For Colby literature raises social intelligence by increasing students' background knowledge about other people, much as Silas learns about Raveloe while parenting Eppie. Similarly, May McKitrick introduces her edition's "Questions and Suggestions for Study" by stating that she hopes they will help the student "to appreciate the power and truthfulness of the picture of life here presented," because "unless the reading of literature influences the character and life of the pupil, there can be no excuse for its inclusion in the school curriculum."[63] Like the Bible guides, these editions insist that the work of reading is not complete until it affects everyday behavior.

Unsympathetic critics have often reduced such statements to the naive claim that literature makes you a better person, as if reading instilled moral goodness. Some do foreground flat didacticism, as when Emma Miller Bolenius praises *Silas Marner* because it is a "consummate piece of the story-telling art" that contains "some wholesome moral lessons for boys and girls."[64] Yet such moralizing is less frequent than one might expect.[65] Given the indebtedness to Ruskin that fueled the American elevation of literature, these editors might have tried to imitate his close reading of Milton. Yet the status of *Silas Marner* as prose fiction rather than as poetic elegy leads them to find different ways to realize Ruskin's hopes.

They do so by maintaining that the novella's didacticism, and that of fiction generally, works indirectly by augmenting students' interest in the world and giving them "a more intelligent curiosity."[66] As Silas must learn about a different world to be a good father to Eppie, so students must extend themselves to appreciate *Silas Marner*. Gilbert Sykes Blakely notes that "so many important lessons for the beginner may be drawn from the structure of this book, from its teaching, and from its representation of life, that it especially repays thorough study."[67] While Blakely admits that Eliot's "teaching" is important, he pays equal attention to her book's structure and to its "representation of life." In cognitive terms *Silas Marner* matters because it leads students to contemplate a world different from their own, much as Ruskin understood the challenges of hard reading. They have to learn knowledge transfer: how, using their own background knowledge, to understand a different time and place. Hard reading privileges alterity, but in Ruskin that alterity belonged to the mind of the author, in *Silas Marner* to the setting and culture of the novella. Privileging alterity does not sit well with good-enough reading; the school provided the support that students needed to use existing knowledge in a new context.

Editors negotiate a contradiction between reading as a specialized, effortful activity for school and reading as an activity that should transcend the school to become a guide to living life. They manage it by teaching students how to form a good gist representation through aesthetic evaluation. This is the key addition that they make to the standard of hard reading traced in this chapter. Repeatedly, students are asked to link literature to life through their aesthetic responses: "Notice how many of the paragraphs in this chapter are peculiarly touching at the close. How is this appeal to the feelings made?"; "What makes this scene at once so diverting and yet half pathetic, too?"[68] In doing so, editions are repeating the injunction in the Bible guides to apply literature to life, an injunction that requires developing a gist representation.

Other editors similarly emphasize not didacticism but aesthetic effect. Commenting on the line "That habit of looking towards the money and grasping it with a sense of fulfilled effort made a loam that was deep enough for the seeds of desire," one editor refers to the "fine metaphor. Notice that George Eliot's similes are usually so terse that they are almost as forcible as metaphors."[69] Writing of chapter 18, another editor asks, "2. Does this portion of the ending satisfy you? 3. Was the discovery of the manner of Dunstan's death as much of a surprise to you as it was to Godfrey Cass?"[70] Adult readers might object to having an editor bully them into aesthetic evaluation, but Ruskin had stressed that capitalist selfishness had made such evaluation impossible. For high school readers who might not evaluate at all, the editors are at pains to point out what makes Eliot a compelling writer. As such, they fight a constant battle against the indifference that Ruskin had diagnosed.

Aesthetic evaluation is not important either to writers like Bacon or Locke or to the Bible guide readers, and Ruskin assumes greatness as a criterion for serious reading. He does not spend time discussing evaluation in his essay, although he attacks British readers for being incapable of it. But when hard reading enters the school curriculum, editors encourage students to form a gist by evaluating what they like or do not like. Rather than leaving long-term memory of *Silas Marner* up to individual vagaries, they help students shape what the long-term representation of the work could be.

This constant appeal to evaluation contrasts with what John Guillory has analyzed as the New Critical focus on difficulty, its use of the canon as a *Hochsprache* distinguishing educated and uneducated language.[71] While, as I have noted, difficulty mattered to the institutionalization of literature, early editors of works like *Silas Marner* do not want literary study to become so arcane that students stop consulting their own taste. Evaluation prevents editors from severing too sharply studying literature from life outside the school because students are asked to judge one by the standards of the other. As such, schools developed a social standard of coherence that democratized hard reading by recognizing it as a difficult, challenging task, while simultaneously insisting that it directly applied to life.

In the late 1920s the CEEB's new Scholastic Aptitude Test (SAT) changed everything.[72] The test no longer required specific readings, so the justification for *Silas Marner* in high school vanished. Yet *Silas Marner* did not disappear, unlike other required readings. Instead, at least on the evidence of textbooks, it underwent pedagogical ossification. It is striking to contrast student editions of *Silas Marner* from before and after the SAT. The Noble's Comparative Classics series published *Silas Marner* in 1953 together with John Steinbeck's *The Pearl*, a pairing that seems bizarre despite the attempt of the editor, Jay E. Greene, to explain it: "There has been a strong demand for more modern literature in secondary schools; there is at the same time a feeling that no English education is complete without some knowledge of the great classics. The present plan meets both demands."[73]

At first glance Greene's edition looks like the earlier ones: after the novels it has test questions, multiple-choice questions, recommended projects, and sample CEEB questions. Tellingly, however, it lacks the introductory essay justifying literary study found in earlier editions. Such essays marked a discipline trying to use Ruskin's categories to prove social usefulness. By 1953 the discipline had succeeded, yet the price of success was the loss of imaginative urgency. Greene's questions are lackluster and care not at all about the cognitive and aesthetic skills so important to the earlier editions. May McKitrick's 1911 edition asks the following questions about chapter 5:

> Select a passage in the first paragraph that might be omitted without marring the narrative. How many such passages have you already found?
>
> What change has taken place in the character of Silas Marner since his residence in Raveloe? What incidents has the author used to show this?
>
> What good picture has the author given us in this chapter? Why does she dwell on this scene? How does she contrive to paint such a powerful picture?[74]

McKitrick asks students to move beyond the literal level of the plot to understand the text as the product of artistic technique and purpose. Her questions have no simple right-or-wrong answers: they leave considerable room for debate. Moreover, as is typical of these editions, the role of aesthetic response is central: "How does she contrive to paint such a powerful picture?"

In contrast, the questions in Greene's 1953 edition plod:

1. Why had Silas left his home on this night? Why did he leave his beloved gold unprotected?

2. Once certain that his gold was gone, why did Silas welcome the idea that a thief had taken it?

3. What is the meaning of Silas's subsequent thought: "Was it a thief who had taken the bags? Or was it a cruel power that no hands could reach, which had delighted in making him a second time desolate?"[75]

Preparing students for a multiple-choice test, Greene polices basic comprehension. He writes as if he does not trust the students to understand on their own, so they must be pinned down with clunky questions that leave no room for debate and development. In cognitive terms Greene focuses students largely at the level of shallow comprehension: can they paraphrase specific passages? McKitrick, in contrast, cares about deep processing that engages global comprehension, the ability to understand the whole text.

Neither McKitrick's nor Greene's textbook is a transparent window into classroom practice; teachers using either might have excited or bored students. But the difference between them does suggest a routinization in the editing of high school texts, if not in the teaching of them, that may have led to pervasive Marnerphobia in American letters:

> Every high-school pupil throughout the entire breadth of America must be reading *Silas Marner* and analyzing with peculiarly American enthusiasm the character of Godfrey Cass. I found myself repeating Rosalind's question, "Can one have too much of a good thing?"—and answering in the affirmative.[76]

> I strongly question the value . . . of spending four weeks studying "Silas Marner."[77]

> You have a son. You want him to form . . . the reading habit. . . . You wouldn't make him read this unacceptable scenario for a second-rate Shirley Temple movie—this "Silas Marner" . . . unless you wanted to turn him away forever from "great books."[78]

> "Silas Marner" . . . almost made this correspondent a high school dropout. We read it in class, a few pages a day, from September to June, and had to answer a lot of silly questions about character and plot development all along the route. What a terrible way to teach kids to read.[79]

For such writers high school English equaled the remembered hell of *Silas Marner*. Although these writers' vitriol is so strong that it is almost convincing, their accounts cannot be taken at face value. Hatred of *Silas Marner* scores different rhetorical points, depending on the writer: for journalists it bolsters their authority against the school's; for educators it argues for a new curricular design; for autobiographers it asserts continuity between a younger and older self. Across their differences, however, these respondents share a dislike for what they recall as the forced passivity of the child reader. At times, this dislike verges on misogyny, as when "J. H." (1937) claims that the popularity of *Silas Marner* stems from a failure "to prevent the teaching of public school English from becoming an almost exclusively female occupation."[80]

The experiences of actual children may have differed. In a 1912 survey of high school children in seven cities, *Silas Marner* topped the list of favorite required readings.[81] Such findings reappeared in numerous later surveys.[82] For some, positive memories lasted into adulthood. Margaret A. Edwards, speaking for many Marnerphiles, wrote that "I loved *Silas Marner* when we read it in school because I had a teacher who brought it to life for me."[83]

It was easy to cast the novella as a metonymy for a curriculum stuck in a Silas-like narcolepsy, ready to be replaced by a more hip, relevant plan of study. Yet I draw attention to the losses incurred when "more relevant" literature replaced it. Arguments for relevance tend to avoid the question of relevance for whom. That students had to work harder to understand a novella with social settings, norms of behavior, and conversational strategies so different from their own may have encouraged the development of cognitive skills in ways that more immediately relevant material may not. To update Ruskin, the struggle to comprehend difficult material offers an unpleasant experience during the moment of learning but a beneficial one in the long term, because learners can extend their existing reading strategies and develop new ones. Psychologists of learning call this the "desirable difficulties" effect, where, when presented with appropriate supports, challenging material can produce improved learning over easier material. The extra effort that students put into comprehending such an alien world made it more likely that *Silas Marner* would be both memorable and a model for later coping with unfamiliar material and possibly with unfamiliar situations.[84]

When teachers dethroned *Silas Marner* to install supposedly more relevant, often more American, literature, the classroom experience may indeed have become easier and more fun. But the opportunity to learn skills for how to use background knowledge to understand unfamiliar circumstances was lost; instead, teachers chose the simpler option, using background knowledge to understand familiar circumstances. Hard reading became easy reading.

Hard reading survived, though, by migrating to the upper levels of the curriculum, especially as New Critical close reading. While the New Critics originally had a strong sense of social mission, the disciplining of literary studies in time allowed that sense to wither.[85] Instead, hard reading became valued because it was hard. Difficulty as an end became useful for the university because it established hierarchies of literacy: some students handled it better than others. On the basis of their success or failure, the university could credentialize them differently.

For the Bible guides the value of hard reading was self-evident: it made salvation more likely. Ruskin transferred salvation from theology to politics by believing that hard reading counteracted capitalist selfishness: a provocative claim, yet one far less self-evident than that of the Bible guides. When the social mission of English faded after its institutional success, hard reading produced the suspicions of narcissism voiced by Poovey: "If we acknowledge that theoretically informed ingenuity can take marginal fragments of a text and build from them a timeless city of gold, . . . then what would prevent us from simply flaunting our ingenuity without the pretext of any literature at all?"[86] What prevents us is that no one will pay for a class on "Professor Y's Ingenuity," while they will pay for classes on literature. Even if we admit that some classes may be most illuminating to students as displays of professorial ingenuity, that ingenuity still has no institutional support without simultaneously transmitting knowledge about a topic, like literature.

As support for literary studies dwindles in the face of the demands of more lucrative disciplines, it remains an open question if hard reading will survive in any form as a social standard of coherence. Difficult reading will survive, any time a reader confronts texts that assume unfamiliar background knowledge. Yet hard reading in the high Ruskinian sense no longer produces the benefits it once seemed to offer. Our choices are either to show that it indeed has benefits, though they may no longer look like Ruskinian ones, or dispense with it altogether, along with a core justification for studying literature at all.

# CHAPTER 5

# EASY READING

**THE PREVIOUS CHAPTER** traced hard reading as a social standard of coherence, arising from overlapping traditions in educational and religious writing. This tradition found a powerful base in the school, which made any form of reading that did not follow its standards look trivial, pointless, or slack. By the end of the nineteenth century, easy reading could look like intellectual suicide. One American writer notes that "fiction kills the appetite for wisdom and it gives nothing in its place. The reader has had the pleasure, the emotional experience, of the reading; but nothing of any value is left over. Useful reading requires brain-work. We can not expect to acquire knowledge without patient attention and careful thinking. The habit will gradually be formed of reading for profit, and then such reading will become a pleasure."[1] Such descriptions are typical of the heavy artillery aimed at light reading throughout the nineteenth century. Although often directed specifically at the female reader, denunciations of reading fiction were everywhere in the nineteenth century, and as such have received considerable attention from critics.

What has received less attention is that, outside of educational and religious settings, it is not easy to find evidence of ordinary readers who did what they were supposed to do. This absence could mean (1) evidence of readers' hard reading has not survived; (2) such evidence does survive, but I have not found it; or (3) there is no evidence because they did not do it. Before searchable online databases it would have been difficult to decide among these. But on the basis of the evidence from databases, I believe that the third option is most probable because so many diverse reading experiences appear in them that we would expect to find at least some examples of independent hard reading.[2] Its almost complete absence, while not conclusive, suggests that hard reading was a pedagogic ideal more than a lived reality, a model that readers may occasionally have approximated but that was too time-consuming to be practical in most cases. The automatized strategies of good-enough reading described in the first chapter were so useful, so often, that the incentive to surpass them was low. Much like contemporary Americans reading about diet and exercise, nineteenth-century audiences may have liked reading about what they should do more than they liked doing it. Endless denunciations of fiction enabled having one's cake and eating it too: they satisfied a deep mistrust of fiction without stopping anyone from reading it.

Vigorously as educationalists disseminated hard reading, as I demonstrated in my discussion of Eliot's *Silas Marner*, they were not the last word on reading. They competed with a different standard of coherence, which also had a long history, that presented reading in a different light and is the focus of this chapter. In this tradition, reading should be easy: if it is hard, something has gone wrong. The seventeenth-century theologian François de Fénelon offered a classic statement in his *Dialogues on Eloquence* (first translated into English in 1722 and often reprinted): "We should use a simple, exact, easy style, which lays every thing open to the reader, and even prevents his attention. When an author writes for the public, he should take all the pains imaginable, to prevent his readers having any. All the labour should be his own; and he should leave nothing but pleasure and instruction to his readers. They should never be put to the trouble of finding out his meaning. None but those who deal in riddles are allowed to puzzle people."[3]

If a writer does his job correctly, according to Fénelon, readers should breeze through: "They should never be put to the trouble of finding out his meaning." Fénelon believes that an easy style "prevents" the attention of the reader: *prevents* here blends its older meaning of "anticipates" (a good writer should consider all the possible needs of a reader) and its newer meaning of "stops" (a good writer makes a text so easy that a reader does not work at all). Fénelon sidesteps the problem that texts may actually be too easy. Reading *The Iliad* in the style of a grade-school basal reader would prevent attention, as well, but not in the way that Fénelon intends: it would bore mature readers who have automatized basic reading. Motivation to keep reading depends on finding the right balance between too much and too little effort.[4]

More seriously, he sidesteps the problem that no author can predict all readers' background knowledge, reading skills, and motivation. A text that provided the right background knowledge for one reader would bore another. Fénelon's ideal assumes a shared body of knowledge between writers and readers, so writers could know just when to help readers out by providing just enough background and knowledge. Without such common ground, no rules could ever make prose universally easy.

Yet Fénelon's advice is nevertheless appealing because of what I described in Chapter 1 as good-enough processing, which occurs when readers process what they have read just enough to make sense of it. Doing nothing but hard reading would quickly drain cognitive resources, as well as take too much time. Readers settle for good-enough processing because it usually works well enough. Fénelon hopes that good writers can make good-enough processing more than good enough: readers should never have to work harder than they usually do to get by.

Fénelon's advice is not to readers but writers: his image of the effort-free reader is less a goal for readers than a constraint for authors. Whereas the standard of hard reading described in the previous chapter arose from books about reading and study, the standard of easy reading arose partly from books about writing and style. Many of them were, like Fénelon's, aimed at the pulpit, but they addressed themselves to print as well as to speech. Such works argued for an inverse relation between ease in writing and reading, as explained by Edward Young in his second "Epistle to Mr. Pope, on the Authors of the Age":

> Write *not* like *Gentlemen*, with ease exceeding;
> Such easy writing is not easy reading.
> To say things *rare* and *excellent* with ease,
> Not *trite and tasteless*, is the way to please.[5]

Young creates a gentlemanly putdown of gentlemanly writing. To write with "ease exceeding," meaning "with a great deal of ease," should be a gentlemanly virtue, a sign of a well-formed, educated mind. But Young puts another spin on the phrase "ease exceeding"—"with too much ease and too little effort"—and recognizes that "such easy writing is not easy reading." Here, "easy writing" arises only from laziness. Young balances two kinds of ease: easy to produce and easy to consume. The first is worthless; the second is invaluable. His epigram that "easy writing is not easy reading" became a much-repeated motto for the next century and a half to remind writers of the inverse relation between the work of author and reader.

Samuel Johnson agreed with Young and devoted an issue of the *Idler* to defining how poets could make their work easy: "The discriminating character of ease consists principally in the diction; for all true poetry requires that the sentiments be natural. Language suffers violence by harsh or by daring figures, by transposition, by unusual acceptations of words, and by any licence, which would be avoided by a writer of prose."[6] At such moments Johnson sounds like Wordsworth in the "Preface to *Lyrical Ballads*." Both dislike poetic diction, use prose as a standard for poetry, and appeal to "natural" sentiments as poetry's core. Yet for Johnson easy poetry marks a truly aristocratic writer, as opposed to vulgar climbers who affect "harsh" and "daring" figures; for Wordsworth, in contrast, a natural style can be found in the rural peasantry, a notion that Johnson, like Coleridge, found silly.

Young and Johnson wrote about poetry, but their understanding of easy reading appeared in eighteenth-century rhetorics as well, with their exaltation of clarity and rejection of Renaissance *copia*. I argued in *Romanticism and the Rise of English* that the emphasis on clarity enabled a dream of frictionless communication that would make the author's meaning obvious to a reader. As popularized by writers such as Hugh Blair and Lindley Murray, the norm of clarity entrenched itself in the teaching of rhetoric and composition, and has been repeated in textbooks from then until now.[7]

The result: a clash between norms for reading, as discussed in the previous chapter, and norms for writing. According to those who focus on reading, like Ruskin, authors wrote challenging, cryptic works that called on a heroic reader to probe them with loving care. Such reading demanded hard work but promised exceptional rewards. According to authors who focus on writers, in contrast, no reader labor should be needed. Readers should read texts so well written as to make misunderstanding impossible. If writers have done their job, then minimal effort will guarantee a perfect transfer of authorial meaning to readerly understanding.

The reason that no one noticed this clash was that these two different standards of coherence lived in different generic niches. The easy reading of Fénelon and Young became an ideal of nonfictional, expository prose: the language of information. Hard reading, as I have argued, found its home in literature, either in poetry or in prose that could be poeticized. Byron's conversational style in *Beppo* and *Don Juan* represents a late flowering of the easy poetic tradition soon overwhelmed by the difficulties of Wordsworthian simplicity and the complex diction of Keats, Shelley, Tennyson, Browning, and others; easy poetry was relegated to light verse, popular doggerel, and the nursery.[8]

Yet even as Fénelon (in translation) and Young described one mode of easy reading, a different tradition arose alongside it, one often associated with narrative. In this case ease arose not from authorial diction but from a good story. Readers dove so deeply into a work that they lost track of effort and were aware only of the magical pull of literature. While descriptions of aesthetic absorption date back to the classics, for British literature a key statement came from Edward Young's pivotal *Conjectures on Original Composition* (1759): "But if an Original, by being as excellent, as new, adds admiration to surprize [*sic*], then are we at the writer's mercy; on the strong wing of his imagination, we are snatched from Britain to Italy, from climate to climate, from pleasure to pleasure; we have no home, no thought, of our own; till the magician drops his pen: And then falling down into ourselves, we awake to flat realities, lamenting the change, like the beggar who dreamt himself a prince."[9]

For Young, reading is like bad sex, only better: it is a willing rape, as readers, "snatched" from themselves, rapturously surrender to "the writer's mercy" as they fly "from pleasure to pleasure." Young expands the metaphor of "transport" by emphasizing self-abandonment; first we lose our sense of place ("no home") and then our metaconsciousness ("no thought of our own"). He adds a twist by describing "the strong wing" of the writer's imagination, which snatches the reader. He hints at the myth of Ganymede, the beautiful Greek youth, whom Jupiter-as-eagle snatches to heaven to be his cup-bearer (prior writers on the myth repeatedly use Young's verb, *snatch*, to describe Jupiter's rape).[10] Surrendering to the power of a great imaginative writer thrives on hints of juicy, transgressive pederasty. Unfortunately, it is short-lived, as the verticality of reading gives way to the horizontal "flat realities" of everyday life. Yet, Young implies, readers can have such transport whenever they wish.

In the next chapter I will examine the cognitive underpinnings of transportation; this chapter will remain on the surface of easy reading by describing how British readers experienced it. I emphasize readers because I avoid detailed evidence about publication practices, the book trade, and readers' access to books, which have received ample attention from previous scholars.[11] The history of reading has often been treated as a branch of the history of the book: useful as that association has been, I leave aside the book as object for the more ephemeral responses of readers. I focus on scattered, off-the-cuff comments about reading that, for various reasons, happened to survive.

William St. Clair condemns scholars who rely on excerpts from letters, diaries, and biographies like the ones I use because they do not provide a representative view of the reading public.[12] He and others have turned to alternative sources to study reader response, such as publishing records, library catalogues and records of borrowers, and the physical form of books as clues to intended audiences. While I have learned much from this scholarship, I want to defend excerpts from St. Clair's attack because we gain from them information available from no other source. Even though St. Clair is correct that they are unrepresentative, they are too useful to ignore because they describe the mental processes of nineteenth-century readers in ways impossible to determine otherwise.

These comments reveal a history of the relation between readers' online experiences of reading and their offline thoughts about them. Standards of coherence around easy reading in Britain created a tension between these two moments. In a culture suspicious of novel reading, readers found strategies to enjoy novel reading without seeming in retrospect to have enjoyed it too much. They distanced themselves from their own online enjoyment to maintain a general self-image of sophistication and restraint.

For several eighteenth-century readers the sign of this distance was offline irritation that they had given themselves so thoroughly to entertainment so worthless. For example, in 1728 Gertrude Savile wrote in her diary, "Made an end of 'The Adventures of Abdella.' I can find no morrall or design in it. 'Tis a collection of silly but very entertaining Lyes, of Fairies, Enchantments etc. Such books I read as people take Drams, to support for an hour sinking Spirits, and alas! the more is taken, the more is nessasary."[13] For Savile, reading *The Adventures of Abdallah*, an "oriental" fantasy by Bignon, offers a means of forgetting herself: books like it "support for an hour sinking Spirits." The critical phrase is "for an hour." The novel distracts but only temporarily. Even worse, distraction is addictive, so the cure may be worse than the disease: "the more is taken, the more is nessasary." The novel's unsatisfactory distractions become part of its seductiveness so that readers want more and more.[14]

Although many eighteenth- and early nineteenth-century readers responded enthusiastically to their reading, the interesting reactions come from those who express their own versions of Savile's offline disappointment:

> At candlelight D.D., and I read by turns, and what do *you think* has been part of our study?—why truly Peregrine Pickle! We never undertook it before, but *it is wretched stuff*.[15]

> Finished reading that *Emmeline*, a Trumpery novel in four volumes. If I can answer for myself I will never again undertake such a tiresome nonsensical piece of business.[16]

> Read the *Castle of Otranto*; which grievously disappointed my expectations. The tale is, in itself, insipid; and Mrs. Radcliffe, out of possible contingencies, evokes scenes of far more thrilling horror, than are attained by the supernatural and extravagant machinery, which, after all, alone imparts an interest to this Romance.[17]

> Fetched the "Castle of Mowbray" from Lindley's Library; a very silly Love tale.[18]

> *Windermere: A Novel* in 2 vols. This is below Mediocrity; the *title* induced me to read it; and with the title I am satisfied—and disappointed.[19]

We should be careful about taking these readers too literally. If the novels really had been so bad, they could have stopped, and no one mentioned doing so. Instead, like Savile, they complete the novel and then attack it. Novels are a perfect guilty indulgence: the pleasure of absorptive reading followed by that of attack. Although not all eighteenth-century readers experienced similar ambivalence, such reactions are common enough to suggest, at least for the sector of readers whose reactions survive, reading novels combined entertainment with doubts about whether they were worth the time. These doubts were their own pleasure, since they let readers manifest their critical acumen.

Two factors in their reactions have had a long afterlife in reconciling readers to the embarrassing pleasures of a novel: finding redeeming moral value in them and believing that everyone else was reading them. A good moral could make up for dull plotting, as James Beattie suggests in his comments about Samuel Richardson: "I doubt not, if I were now to read 'Clarissa' a second time,

I should find these tedious parts not the least useful. Whoever rails at Mr. Richardson's tediousness should recollect, that his design is more to instruct than to amuse; and that consequently his tediousness is a pardonable fault, as the motive to it is so laudable."[20] Beattie's remarks can be clarified through Kintsch's distinction between global and local coherence: the coherence of the work as a whole versus the coherence of the local episode or event sentence. For Beattie, recognizing the novel's global coherence, that it is meant "more to instruct than to amuse," could carry him through local moments that, though they may be coherent, are tedious. More generally, reviewers of novels routinely evaluated their good or bad moral tendencies, and novels like *Clarissa* worked for some as anthologies of moral sayings.[21] Morality was a useful but never perfect tool for reconciling readers to the novel's suspect value, and online boredom was a high price for offline respectability.

Luckily, morals could be bypassed if enough other people were reading a novel. Especially in London, people read to keep up with the few hundred best families. If a novel was a hit in these circles, then "everyone" made sure to read it, as if reading were a social necessity. In this case readers' standard of coherence required not understanding a novel per se but being able to discuss it with their friends and to show that they were in the know; such reading was a special case of "good-enough processing." In 1726 Lady Mary Wortley Montagu found *Gulliver's Travels* to be a book "that all our people of taste run mad about,"[22] while Lady Luxborough noted in 1753, "I think I must read *Sir C. Grandison* in my own defence; for I hear of him till I am tired. Let us read him here together. I remember I heard so much in *Tom Jones*'s praise; that when I read him, I hated him."[23] The *Gentleman's Magazine* claimed in 1741 that it was "as great a sign of want of curiosity not to have read PAMELA, as not to have seen the French and Italian dancers,"[24] and Elizabeth Carter wrote in 1752 to a friend about Fielding's *Amelia*: "Methinks I long to engage you on the side of this poor unfortunate book, which I am told the fine folks are unanimous in pronouncing to be very sad stuff."[25]

As Carter's comments reveal, part of the fun of reading was sharing reactions with others. Online reading had to produce a stable enough offline representation that it could be compared. Thomas Gray wrote in 1742 to Richard West, "I have myself, upon your recommendation, been reading *Joseph Andrews*. The incidents are ill laid and without invention; but the characters have a great deal of nature, which always pleases even in her lowest shapes."[26] The Bishop of Gloucester noted in 1760, "I pride myself in having warmly recommended 'Tristram Shandy' to all the best company in town."[27] Although reading is sometimes imagined as a withdrawal from social relationships, for many readers reading novels sustained friendships and occasioned new ones.

By the century's end, although antinovel sentiment never slackened, offline embarrassment at novel reading lessened, as Anna Seward suggests when she wrote to Humphry Repton in 1786, "That you have not read the Clarissa does not much excite my wonder. I know the aversion which most sensible people have to novels; and those who, like you, live much in the world, are deterred by the idea of eight volumes closely written. It is but of late years that this work has been considered as amongst the English classics."[28] Seward begins by giving Repton the upper hand, recognizing that "most sensible" people think novels silly, and anyone "much in the world" has no time for *Clarissa*. But her next sentences put him behind the times, since it is "but of late years" that *Clarissa* has been elevated to its place "amongst the English classics." Though Repton may be in the world, he does not know what Seward knows: novels have become classics.

Similarly, when John Davis met a fellow Englishman during his travels in the United States, he found the man's ignorance of novels proof that he was a fool: "*Potpan* informed me that he had subscribed to a Circulating Library in *London*; and asked me very gravely if I had ever read the history of *Tom Jones, a Foundling,* by the author of *Roderic [sic] Random*."[29] During a parliamentary inquiry, the Reverend Lancelot Sharpe claimed, "I conceive it is not at all derogatory to a clergyman, after having labored through the day, in an hour of relaxation to read a good novel."[30] Likewise, Lieutenant General George Vaughan Hart mentioned to a parliamentary committee in 1816 that "Innishowen is not worse than other parts of Donegal; but it has been particularly brought into notice, I believe, by Miss Owenson, in one of her novels."[31] The specifics of his comment are less striking than his ability to mention a novel as if his hearers would know of it. Rather than being shameful, by the beginning of the nineteenth century, knowing at least some novels could be taken for granted, at least among the reading classes.

Easy reading's respectability had two boosts at the beginning of the nineteenth century. Large-scale collections of novels appeared, complete with critical apparatus: first, Anna Barbauld's fifty-volume *The British Novelists* (1810), followed by Walter Scott's *Ballantyne's Novelist's Library* (1821–24).[32] Even more, the success of Scott, the nineteenth-century's most widely read novelist, consolidated the novel's prestige. He lessened the vulgarity still clinging to the novel by combining fiction with the more respectable genre of history. However silly other novels seemed to be, Scott, at least, was safe.[33] By 1849, when a clergyman complained about a church library, "I have found some of the younger subscribers to the library difficult to get to church on Sunday, because they were reading Walter Scott's novels," the response was, "But is it not better that they should read Walter Scott's novels than that they should do something worse?"[34]

According to Richard H. Hutton, Scott himself analyzed his success well: " 'I am sensible,' he says, 'that if there be anything good about my poetry or prose either, it is a hurried frankness of composition, which pleases soldiers, sailors, and young people of bold and active dispositions.' . . . Scott's is almost the only poetry in the English language that not only runs thus in the head of average men, but heats the head in which it runs by the mere force of its hurried frankness of style."[35] Scott transforms the two earlier traditions of easy reading that I have described (easy style and narrative transport) by uniting them. In the tradition of writers like Fénelon he privileges the "hurried frankness" of his composition. His term *frankness* positions him against overt rhetorical display, as if the flowers of rhetoric would slow down his "hurried" narratives. Scott's style draws attention to itself for what it does not do: it does not slow the reader. Describing the other tradition of easy reading, narrative transportation, Hutton notes that Scott's poetry "heats the head in which it runs," and his description is characteristic of tributes to Scott's fascinating powers, which earned him the nickname "the Wizard of the North." Scott's famous merging of history and romance also merged the two traditions of ease: the clarity of nonfictional prose (as formulated by eighteenth-century rhetoric) and the enrapturing power of narrative (as described by Young). After Scott, easy reading belonged to the novel more than to any other genre because he had linked prose that was easy to understand with plots that gripped the imagination.

A sign of easy reading's new status appears in one of the most popular works of Scott's disciple Charles Dickens. In *A Christmas Carol* Dickens did for easy reading what Ruskin did for hard reading: he transformed it into a spectacle so imbued with value that it could induce something like religious conversion. The Ghost of Christmas Past begins to reform Scrooge by letting him see his boyhood self, alone at Christmas, reading at school:

> The Spirit touched him on the arm, and pointed to his younger self, intent upon his reading. Suddenly a man, in foreign garments: wonderfully real and distinct

to look at: stood outside the window, with an axe stuck in his belt, and leading an ass laden with wood by the bridle.

"Why, it's Ali Baba!" Scrooge exclaimed in ecstasy. "It's dear old honest Ali Baba! Yes, yes, I know! One Christmas time, when yonder solitary child was left here all alone, he *did* come, for the first time, just like that. Poor boy! And Valentine," said Scrooge, "and his wild brother, Orson; there they go! And what's his name, who was put down in his drawers, asleep, at the Gate of Damascus; don't you see him! And the Sultan's Groom turned upside-down by the Genii; there he is upon his head! Serve him right. I'm glad of it. What business had *he* to be married to the Princess!"[36]

While the young Scrooge's online processes remain unspoken, Dickens presents the old Scrooge reexperiencing his youthful reading offline but so intensely that he maintains that his young self actually conjured up the characters: "when yonder solitary child was left here all alone, he *did* come." Scrooge should have said "was left there," since he is physically far from "yonder solitary child," but he feels so close to his past self that he says "here" instead. Given this felt closeness, we expect Dickens to let young Scrooge interact with the products of his imagination, to make the point that his reading was so vivid that it was as if he were in the tale himself. But something different happens. Young Scrooge remains blind to the proof of the power of his reading; he never looks out of the window. Old Scrooge claims that Ali Baba did appear, "just like that," but young Scrooge does not notice. Only old Scrooge does, and Dickens underscores the gap between old and young Scrooge with "what's his name": old Scrooge no longer remembers the name of a character whose name might have been vivid to his younger self.

The window splits the young Scrooge's online reading from the old Scrooge's offline fantasy of its intensity, so vivid that Ali Baba is "wonderfully real and distinct to look at." Absorbed by the book, the young Scrooge does not need to look outside the window: online reading suffices. Old Scrooge, no longer fully remembering what he read, recaptures young Scrooge's experience only through a pageant of characters, turning narrative into theater.

In terms of my discussion of gist, Scrooge's memory resembles the kind that I discussed in Chapter 3 that can form around characters like Sherlock Holmes. Rather than remembering the author of the *Arabian Nights*, Scrooge remembers the characters. Although he remembers a few scraps of plot, he does not see the characters enacting what they do in the tales: the core of his long-term memory is simply the characters. This is a very different memory from that privileged by the advocates of hard reading, who want readers to retain, paradoxically, a detailed gist. Instead, Dickens presents an alternative version of gist more appropriate for easy reading: characters who outlive their plots.

Having recaptured something of his original transportation, Scrooge becomes a new man. Motivated by "pity for his former self," he says, "Poor boy," and cries; when the Spirit asks what is the matter, he responds, "There was a boy singing a Christmas Carol at my door last night. I should like to have given him something: that's all."[37] Familiar as this episode is, it's worth pausing over the strange relationship between cause and effect. As Audrey Jaffe notes, "the narrative of the development of fellow feeling offered here makes the two kinds of sympathy (identification and compassion) appear to be continuous, as if the opening up of a space between the self and its representation produces a general desire to identify, which can then be detached from the self and shifted to some other identity."[38] After having viewed his younger self absorbed in reading, we might expect Scrooge to recall how much he liked reading, to pity his younger self, or to assert that the characters compensated for his loneliness. Given Scrooge's crabbiness, we might even expect him to resent the adults and other children who left him all alone. We would not necessarily expect him, solely from what he has seen, to feel like giving money. Scrooge is already self-absorbed: the memory of having been absorbed in reading while a child would seem a likely stimulus for further self-absorption rather than for what Dickens represents as concern for others (setting aside the mix of sympathy and narcissism that a skeptical interpreter might argue makes up ordinary Dickensian charity).

If the point is simply that Scrooge, in pitying his younger self, transfers that sympathy to others, Dickens could have chosen any number of other sad scenarios to stimulate pity. Instead, he foregrounds narrative transportation. So powerful is this scene that the essential action of *A Christmas Carol* is over after it. Far from tracing a gradual thaw and change of heart, Dickens presents Scrooge's transformation as instantaneous: future episodes draw out implications of this scene, but they do not fundamentally alter it. Just as Ruskin argued in "Of Kings' Treasuries" that the nation could be saved by hard reading, so Dickens shows in *A Christmas Carol* that people can be saved by easy reading. More particularly, in the terms I have been developing, Dickens revises the familiar topos of a sinner saved by scripture into the salvific power of recalling narrative gist. He notoriously ejects Christianity from *A Christmas Carol* but keeps the grace-giving power of reading, or, more accurately, of remembering having read with absorption. Recalling the gist of reading heals the soul.

Having used Dickens's novella to argue that it advocates the social value of easy reading, I want to turn in the second half of this chapter to actual nineteenth-century readers to see what their gist memories of easy reading were. To access such accounts, I turned to traces of historical memories accessible in databases like Chadwyck Healey's House of Commons Parliamentary Papers, Gale Cengage's Making of the Modern Law and Nineteenth-Century British Library Newspapers, and Google Books. For my searches I imposed rules. First, only novels: I searched for nineteenth-century responses to imaginative literature, though I did not confine searches only to Victorian novels. Doing so would have created problems, such as omitting the most widely read author in my sample, Scott. Second, no professional reviews: I wanted not professional critics but ordinary, unofficial reactions because I cared less about interpretations or evaluations than memories. Third, only nonfictional sources: letters, diaries, biographies, autobiographies, legal cases, parliamentary reports, newspaper articles. Fourth, as few as possible responses from those who knew the author of the book that they read. Fifth, all readers were eligible within my time frame, 1830–1920: English, Irish, Scottish, Welsh, American, European, and colonial. Sixth, only one response per person: in the case of a writer who recorded numerous reading experiences, I used the first described. And, finally, I grouped together autobiographical memories with biographical accounts of personal memories; I refer to this group as "life memories," and it includes first-person and third-person accounts.

My research assistants and I collected about five hundred responses, and I will describe them quantitatively and qualitatively. Although I refer to readers in this sample as "nineteenth-century readers," I need to specify just what that means. Samples are good or bad depending on how well they represent a population, and only randomization eliminates sample bias. Unfortunately, we can never sample nineteenth-century readers randomly. Instead, we have writings that for miscellaneous reasons happened to become searchable.

My research team used the initial fifty entries to develop coding schemes, and the entries were coded by two independent coders; disagreements were settled by discussion.[39] My sample had 355 men, 87 women, and 59 readers whose gender could not be identified. In terms of age, 63 were between 0 and 20 when the reading experience took place (though they may have been older when they wrote about it); 231 were between 20 and 60; 57 were over 60; and 150 could not be identified in terms of age. In terms of professions, 10.4% were academics, 33.7% were professionals, 31.8% were artists or writers, 4% were businessmen, 1.4% were laborers, 7% were students, 3.6% were women in service, and 8.4% were children. In terms of nation, 41.3% were from the United States, 41.7% from England, 6.6% from Scotland, 3% from Ireland, and 7.4% from another country.

We do not know exactly who was in the nineteenth-century novel reading population, so there's no sure way to know how well this sample represents it. Yet even without exact knowledge I recognize that my sample has obvious problems. I have far less evidence from working-class readers than I do from the upper ranks and the professional classes. Men outnumber women, and it is hard to know how well various age groups are represented. Artists and writers are significantly overrepresented, as are readers from England and America, as opposed to Scotland and Ireland.

Such lopsided representation does not mean that no generalizations are possible, however, only that I need to specify the population to which this sample generalizes.[40] My sample represents not nineteenth-century readers as a whole but a subset: the novel-reading sector, a group that crosses traditional class and gender lines but shares literacy, investment in and access to novels, and the ability to write about experiences or to have their experiences written about. Members of this sector had more in common than they had differences. Past work in nineteenth-century reading has assumed that identity categories, such as gender and class, shape behavior so fundamentally that, for example, women's responses must differ from men's. It's easy to see where this assumption comes from: since many stereotypes floated about the bad female reader, female reading as myth was distinguished from male reading. Yet the assumption that gender (or class, or religion, or sexuality, or region) inevitably produces different reading practices needs evidence to be believable. Did nineteenth-century gender ideology fully constrain the novel reading experience of men versus women? Despite nineteenth-century diatribes distinguishing women's reading from men's, gender did not help predict readers' responses in my sample. The same was true for class. While many, many working-class readers had motivations, opportunities, and settings for reading quite different from those of the middle and upper classes, these differences did not necessarily lead to different reactions in my sample, although, as I have noted, working-class readers are underrepresented. The broad patterns in my evidence emphasize what readers shared more than what separated them. I stress "in my sample" because I am not claiming that all previous scholarly generalizations about the effect of gender or class on nineteenth-century reading are wrong, only that my evidence and approach did not validate them.

My categories for readers' responses arose from distinctions regarding the how, when, and what of memory. The "how" of a given memory trace has three stages: the online stage of encoding, when information enters the brain; and two offline stages, storage and retrieval.[41] Storage describes how information remains in the brain, and retrieval arises, when, in response to a stimulus, some aspect of what was originally encoded comes back to conscious awareness; I write "some aspect" because what is retrieved is not a direct copy of an original experience but a reconstruction shaped in response to present demands.[42] Since I used archival evidence, I added another category, "production": the writing down of a memory. When, as is often the case, nineteenth-century readers mention having read a novel but do not give the title, this absence may indicate (1) that they did not encode the title (unlikely, but possible); (2) they encoded it but could not retrieve it (slightly more possible); or (3) they retrieved it but did not find it relevant to what they were writing and so did not produce it (most probable). Records of reception have usually been treated as "what they thought." But textual memory is not a static mental construct. Real memories, if communicated, are shaped to fit an occasion. They are adaptations, not re-cords, of a preexisting storage, and the nineteenth-century writings I discuss are second-order adaptations: the construction in retrieving a memory trace and transforming it through writing.

So much for the "how" of memory. More interesting, in relation to novels, is the "when." Although most readers do not remember verbatim the beginning of a paragraph by the time they finish it, nobody doubts that we can remember novels—but just what are we remembering? As I have discussed, Walter Kintsch proposed the tripartite model of (1) surface code (registering the actual words of a text); (2) textbase (the translation of surface code into mental language); and (3) situation model, which eliminates most of the textbase, preserves gist representations of important episodes, and incorporates inferences from the reader's background knowledge, emotions, predictions, and experience. Surface code and textbase often disappear rapidly from short-term memory, leaving the situation model as gist to form the basis of offline, long-term memory.

The offline retrievability of long-term situation models may depend on on-line "depth of processing."[43] People give different amounts of attention to what they do; not surprisingly, working harder at encoding something may make it easier to retrieve later. While we do not have firm records of how long it took nineteenth-century readers to read novels, surviving accounts from libraries suggest that they read them quickly. For example, a Parliamentary Inquiry asked this question directly: "682. Have you any means of ascertaining the amount of time usually employed in reading any particular class of books?—That varies entirely as to the class of reading; you seldom get a work on mathematics back under 14 days, and it is sometimes renewed for a further seven days; in the ordinary calculation a three volume novel is devoured in four or five days."[44] Emily B. Todd's work on novel borrowing in the United States reveals a similarly rapid rate of consumption.[45] The speed with which Victorian readers read novels suggests a shallow depth of processing, akin to good-enough processing: they generally gave themselves little time to ponder what they read, at least with novels. Nevertheless, novels demand a reader's skill in strategically allocating attention; if you read a novel too shallowly, you lose track of what is going on. Nineteenth-century readers who left behind reactions to their reading had become expert readers, not as academics but as users with skills that let them track long, messy plots, often in distracting circumstances.

The last set of assumptions I make regards the "what" of memory or just what kind of memory nineteenth-century readers employed. Three of the most prominent memory systems are procedural (how to do things), semantic (general world knowledge), and episodic (events that have occurred to you or others).[46] The bulk of my evidence represents only the last, event memory. Nineteenth-century life memory falls into large categories: (1) readers remember reading "a novel" without providing a title; usually, as I have suggested, this absence seems to represent pragmatic accommodation rather than retrieval failure; (2) they remember reading a named novel at a specified time; (3) they remember themselves or others reading as a customary, repeated event, such as "reading Scott" when they were children.

So, a specific answer to the question of what kind of memory I am describing: nineteenth-century writing is an offline, second-order adaptation of situation models in long-term event memory. This fussy description means that my data do not arise from transparent representations of reading. They capture only what enters long-term event memory and is later retrieved for a particular setting. What readers remember comes not only from different depths of online processing but also from pragmatic relevance, the way that the occasion shapes what readers do. These accounts represent not what people *can* remember, when tasked in a lab, but what they *do* remember in ecologically valid settings.[47]

In addition, since I am describing written accounts rather than direct reading experiences, my sample combines the two kinds of processing described in earlier chapters. For most readers, much of their novel reading depended on automatic processing and easily available upper-level processes: inferences that were easy to make, background knowledge that could be recruited quickly, and minimal metacognition. Yet when they wrote about their experiences, the act of writing imposed effort, since, however practiced these writers were, writing needs more cognitive resources than reading, if only because it takes more motor skills. So these accounts are readers' memories of online easy reading as transformed by the effortful, offline filter of writing.

In my sample, writers remember different things when they write about a novel: 40% remember a specific novel; 35.6% mention an author and title; 15.2% mention only an author; and 9.2% mention reading a novel without providing author or title. The fact that only 35.6% mention an author and a title does not indicate that other readers were incapable of remembering both author and title or had some memory failure. It indicates only that, when they wrote about their experiences, they did not include both author and title in their accounts. From the sample only 170 could be identified in terms of recent versus distant memory: of these, 40% were recent, while 60% were distant. In terms of memory type, 475 could be categorized: of these, 47.8% were memories of a particular reading experience (either biographical or autobiographical); 38.3% were recollections of novels as part of general world knowledge (semantic memory); and 13.9% were memories of a general reading experience (again, either biographical or autobiographical).

In terms of the content, we coded for the presence of the mention of characters, plot, language, setting, and evaluation: 49.5% of readers mentioned characters, 35.3% mentioned the plot, 22.2% mentioned language, 14% commented on the setting, and 67.7% provided some evaluative comment. I want to draw three points from all these statistics. First, the sheer variety of how and what nineteenth-century readers remember is valuable because it complicates our sense of nineteenth-century responses to reading. Even within the novel-reading sector, which represents only a part of the literate population, there is wide variability. Monolithic scholarly statements about how the nineteenth-century novel affected readers need to give way to much more careful and nuanced analysis.

Second, this variety also has implications for how psychologists approach long-term memory for narrative fiction. As I have noted, their primary interest has been in what happens to readers' situation models in long-term memory. The responses of the nineteenth-century readers reveal that, outside the lab, readers are not necessarily interested in sharing their situation model memory. This matters for long-term memory because the more a memory is retrieved, the more easily it will be subsequently accessed. This leads me to my third point: the most striking finding is that, when the nineteenth-century readers remembered novel reading, either their own or that of others, the most common aspect of their gist memory involved whether or not they liked what they read. Evaluation mattered, and, for the most part, readers' evaluations were overwhelmingly positive.

After coding for these variables, we also looked for significant correlations in the data. I am using *correlation* in its statistical sense of two variables that are not probabilistically independent.[48] Put more loosely, variables are correlated if one increases as the other increases, one decreases as the other decreases, or one increases as the other decreases. Since all my data are observational rather than experimental, they do not support causal explanations. But correlations highlight patterns that might not otherwise be visible. I found no correlations between gender or national origin and the content of readers' memories; I did find, as I noted above, that authors and writers were more likely than those in other professions to comment on the language of novels, so such comments may not represent the reactions of the novel-reading sector more generally. Evaluative comments were most common among readers between twenty years old and sixty years old rather than among children or older readers, though this may be an effect mostly of the fact that they were also the largest group.

A significant minority of readers ($n = 195$) included a temporal and/or spatial marker in their memory: they remembered when and/or where they were when they read. We coded these responses so that they fell into two groups: memory of time, and memory of setting or of setting and time. Those who mentioned just time were more likely to mention characters, plot, language, and an evaluation than those who mentioned just setting or setting and time together. But across readers, some element of environmental encoding (encoding the time and/or place where an event happened) is a widespread, though not universal, feature of nineteenth-century gist memory, especially a time marker.

In terms of memory we distinguished among general and specific episodic memories (a general episodic memory recalls having done something repeatedly over time; a specific episodic memory recalls a unique event); for nineteenth-century readers, episodic memories were autobiographical or biographical descriptions of episodes of reading. A third category was semantic memories: memory for facts about the novel that did not arise in the context of autobiographical or biographical events. Discussions of character, plot, and setting were more common among readers who recalled semantic memories; discussions of language more common among those who recalled general episodic memories of reading for themselves or others; while evaluative comments were more common among specific and general episodic memories than among semantic memories. Semantic memory was more associated with aspects of plot summary, whereas episodic memory was more associated with evaluative comments.

Overall, these correlations suggest a basic pattern in the way that novels entered nineteenth-century gist memory, arising from the presence or absence of autobiographical detail. Readers could remember novels as the focus of a specific reading event (by themselves or others) or as an object of knowledge apart from their individual experience. While these two forms of memory are not exclusive, they rarely overlap. Either readers remember a reading event (in which case they say little about the novel's content), or they remember the plot, characters, language, or setting of the novel (in which case they say little about biographical or autobiographical experience). Novels are either an item of knowledge or the object of experience but rarely both at once. This distinction matters for how scholars understand novels' reception: scholars have privileged the first over the second in ways that do not do justice to the surviving evidence or to the place of novels in nineteenth-century experience.

While such quantitative analysis foregrounds large-scale patterns, it does not tell the whole story. I supplement it with a more qualitative account to give a better sense of what readers wrote. Admittedly, readers do not always tell us what we want to know. After having read novels that, in the twentieth century, would spur scholarly hyperactivity, nineteenth-century readers may write comments such as "Spent the day in camp. Read Scott's 'Heart of Midlothian.' Much interested";[49] "Yesterday I went to the Athenaeum, and finished the second volume of 'Shirley.' . . . I like it";[50] "We have had callers as usual both in the afternoon and evening. In the intervals between, I have read 'Adam Bede.'"[51] Just as often, readers do not even say what they were reading: "'I was reading a novel,' said Mr. Elmore to me, 'and the next instant, as it seemed, I found myself suffering great pain in a strange bed, with strange surroundings, in what I afterwards found was a French cottage'";[52] "Read newspapers & a novel nearly all day the

weather being so unsettled that it was not deemed wise to go out";[53] "I am spending a quiet Sunday morning in Birbeck's smoking room—reading a novel."[54]

Yet even these bare comments reveal that, despite the prolific antinovel industry, many readers had the good sense to ignore such advice and enjoy their
novels. I have noted that they often included evaluative comments, and they
liked communicating these evaluations:

> By-the-bye, have you read a novel (though what novel have you not read?)
> called *Vivian Grey*? Pray do, as I wish to give you the best treat of the kind you
> ever had in your life.[55]

> Your mother has been completely carried away with "Jane Eyre." She went out
> yesterday and bought herself a pair of new shoes. After she came home she took
> up "Jane," and read till tea-time; then she read till bed-time. Then I retired, and
> she read till nearly morning, finding, when she went to bed at last, that the toes
> of her new shoes were fairly burnt through, over the dying embers.[56]

> He enjoyed Mrs. Ratcliffe's [*sic*] novels; and in the week before his death, when
> his wife was reading the clerk's ghost-story from "Barnaby Rudge," he listened to
> it with fresh delight, saying as she finished, "Dickens is a man of real genius."[57]

> Have you been reading Disraeli's novel *Lothair*? I have finished it. I do not give
> it high praise when I say that it is incomparably better than the mass of fictions.
> At the same time it is really clever, and very amusing.[58]

> I am greatly indebted to a patient, Mr. Burroughs Lewis, an English gentleman
> who first introduced me to the delights of Anthony Trollope. . . . This was forty-
> five years ago, and I have been reading Trollope ever since. . . . He is not very deep
> or profound . . . yet he knew the people and the times in which he lived, and has
> depicted their salient points so correctly, so vigorously, so charmingly, that one
> seldom tires even under the prolixity of some of his analytical characterizations.[59]

> I was most struck in "Mary Barton," with its fine constructive power, and the
> graceful use that it makes of Lancashire dialect.[60]

> I have finished "Ruth" and "Villette," and several of Sir Walter Scott's, and am
> much struck by the marked difference between the fiction of his day and ours;

the effect produced is very opposite. From those of Scott you rise with a vigorous, healthy tone of feeling; from the others, with that sense of exhaustion and
weakness which comes from feeling stirred up to end in nothing.[61]

"Ouida" . . . had puzzled, baffled, excited, and sometimes terrified me when, as a
young girl, I had read her first serial novel in Colburn's *New Monthly Magazine*.[62]

Even now, long after they were written, the delight that these readers took in
their novels remains vivid. When reading their comments, I feel at least a bond,
if not an identification, with readers who, in a very different time and place,
responded to novels in ways that feel familiar. For a brief instance, historical
distance fades as I imagine that I, too, can know how they felt.

Even evaluations that start critically have a way of turning around: "M. has
been reading 'Wuthering Heights' aloud. I don't recommend any one to read
it, and I hate even to think of it, for it comes near the chief position, in my
opinion, of all the outrageous conceptions ever written down. . . . Yet there are
some moments, certainly one, where it approaches, and perhaps reaches, the
pathos of real tragedy. . . . The style, to my thinking, is admirable, so simple, so
clear, and every now and then illuminated with thrilling words."[63] If this writer
wanted to convince anyone not to read *Wuthering Heights*, he ended up doing
exactly the opposite. Similarly, readers could admit that easy reading let them
put aside their more critical capacities: "I've been reading the first of the three
vols. of Victor Hugo's last novel, 'Quatre vingt-treize.' . . . It may very justly, I
think, be called melodramatic or sensational; but I have a faculty for accepting such a fact as this, and then setting it on one side and continuing to enjoy
all that is full of wonder and beauty in a book."[64] Offline, this reader can acknowledge Hugo's flaws, but, online, those are not enough to stop his pleasure.
Those less admirable aesthetic qualities may even contribute to the "wonder
and beauty" he admires.

Readers love to pay tribute to the power of easy reading. Connop Thirlwall
tells an exemplary story about a man reading *Bleak House*:

The purchaser [of *Bleak House*] immediately set to, but I suppose in a critical
chapter found the envious light [in the train] failing him. . . . He continued to
catch at every gleam of light that permitted him to read another line. . . . While
I was waiting with painful curiosity to see when he would acknowledge that
his visual powers were unequal to their task, he suddenly raised his eyes to the

faint glimmer of the lamps on the opposite side, and instantly sprang up on the seat which was unoccupied, and holding his book close to the glass, remained perched there until we reached Paddington. The most remarkable thing was that when we stopped he observed to me that we had come uncommonly fast—"had never gone a better pace." . . . He was totally unconscious that it was the "Bleak House" that had made the time pass so quick![65]

Thirlwall observes a psychological case study. Reader absorption plays with the sense of time, so that his fellow traveler does not realize that speed owes nothing to the train but everything to his pleasure. The book's transportation accelerates the train's. Reading becomes almost obsessive as the man clings to the last shreds of light in order to read Dickens, with no awareness of the "painful curiosity" that he incites.

Although Thirlwall tells his story with detached amusement, readers shared novelistic transportation across borders of class, gender, and other marks of social identity: "I wrote 11 foolscap pages and then for the last 2 hours buried myself in a novel";[66] "Finished *The Pathfinder; in tears* just think! A novel of a thousand that! for 'making the heart beat' and taking one out of oneself";[67] "Read a most powerful and extraordinary story by R. L. Stevenson: 'Dr. Jekyll and Mr. Hyde.' In the few days which followed, I read the story seven times over, with as much care as when of old preparing for an examination: watching every clause of every sentence, and its bearing";[68] the famous lawyer Sir William Maule "was said to devote himself entirely to novel reading, for he declared that there was nothing so well calculated to air the mind as a good novel."[69]

Other records let us glimpse transportation even among those who left no accounts behind. A dry parliamentary report on boiler explosions notes the sad case of the attendant blown up "neglecting his duties whilst engaged in reading a novel."[70] More happily, an emigrant to New South Wales recollected "the exquisite relish with which a huge and very raw Scotch lad—with a face like a great pumpkin—read Pickwick on our voyage out. In ecstasies of delight he used to roll about the deck, like a young leviathan at play; then, snatching up the book, he would pursue the captain, or whomsoever else he could get to listen to him, saying, 'D'ye hear what Sam said to the fat boy, and what the fat boy said to Sam?' whereupon he used sometimes to get chastised by those he annoyed too frequently."[71] Although Scott was the "Wizard of the North," the sense that a good novel magically took readers away from their present time and place is everywhere in nineteenth-century gist memory.

I noted in my quantitative analysis that a significant minority of readers mentioned setting (time and/or place) in which they read. What numbers alone do not reveal is how vivid these memories could be. Readers may simply note that they read in the evening or before bedtime, but often they provide more detail: "By the way, I may tell you that I fell in with 'Ivanhoe,' at thirteen, on a bright July morning in my midsummer holidays. . . . It was lying conveniently at hand; I looked into it, became absorbed, and spent the whole day in the garden reading it . . . and never stopped till I had finished it!"[72] "Sixty hours after time my ship arrived, and I had to leave a large dinner-party at Government House to go on board. . . . It was frightfully cold, and I huddled myself up in my opossum rug and read Miss E.'s new novel and Disraeli's";[73] "I read Jane Austen for the first time at Land's End, years ago. *Persuasion* was the novel. . . . I remember how, as I read, the Atlantic rains beat against my window, and Cape Cornwall appeared and vanished in the swirling elements";[74] "On a day I can still recall, a still November day, when the mist lay on the halmes and the yellow sunshine touched the crags on the moor, Cooper came to me with 'The Last of the Mohicans,' and almost persuaded me to be an Indian";[75] "Went to bed and read myself to sleep on Dickens' *Great Expectations* and dreamed all night of Pip and Orlick."[76]

Such descriptions accord with a well-known finding in psychology: people encode aspects of the environment as part of a memory trace. As Smith and Vela note, "the environment is processed and represented [in memory] unless efforts to suppress the environment are made to permit conceptual processing."[77] Although the environmental effect is well known, psychologists have overlooked it in their studies of narrative memory. Nineteenth-century readers mention the reading environment even when they do not have to. Environmental encoding is so strong a part of their gist memories that, at retrieval, such readers write about it regardless of relevance. Where and when a novel was read, in their accounts, outweighs what was in it.

Even as novel reading transported some readers beyond themselves, it could become an embodied autobiographical memory, inseparable from the location of its occurrence. The more they left the world behind, the more it stayed with them. Memory for the reading experience blended opposites (remembering one's surroundings versus forgetting them), in ways that are predictable from empirical work on memory but that seem strange nevertheless. Surroundings become most vivid, most prone to deep encoding, when we might expect them to be least important, as readers are interacting not with what's around them but with the words on the page.

In their episodic memories, readers shy away from plot summary, though less so in their semantic ones. To interpret their responses, we can imagine retrieval as occurring on a continuum at different levels of specificity, from the vague to the detailed. Plot summary would fall somewhere in the middle: not necessarily detailed but not too abstract either. Nineteenth-century memories, however, occupy the far ends of the continuum. Readers remember either a generalized gist containing few specifics, or an event, character, setting, or quotation that, for personal reasons, has acquired an outsized importance.

As a result, when readers do write about the plot of novels, they single out particular situations, characters, or quotations, as if those had separated themselves from the larger work to become isolated reference points:

> I wonder if you ever read Mrs. Marsh's novel "Emilia Wyndham"; it must be twenty years since I read it, but it left an indelible impression on my mind, of the misery needlessly caused, when a husband and wife are too proud to open their hearts to each other. I almost forget the story; but the impression has remained as vivid as on the day I read it.[78]

> My aunt, well read in Dickens, whose writings were very real and vivid to her, freely drew from that fiction master's gallery of types, and fitted them to uncle's character. "Don't sit there a-rubbin' your slimy hands like Uriah Heep!" she would exclaim; or, "Yes, there you go, always and ever a-sayin' that something's bound to turn up, you old Micawber, you!" But this literary tailoring was not at all one-sided, for uncle was even better read than his wife, and with great effect he could say, "Yes, there you go, always insinuatin' everlastingly, like Becky Sharp."[79]

> I don't know whether you ever read Dickens' novel entitled *Great Expectations*, in which he depicts the evil effects of living in a state of suspense; but if you have, you will in some measure be able to understand why, wishing to write you, I have from day to day deferred doing so until now.[80]

> In Charles Dickens's *Great Expectations* there is painted a lawyer's clerk of sober, severely legal disposition, who has yet a streak of romance in his constitution, and whose humble residence is guarded, when office hours are over, by the severest military precautions approved of by novel-writers. Such a pathetic survival of ancient manners is well illustrated by many little points about an ordinary Japanese dwelling.[81]

I went to school nearly 40 years later than Charlotte Brontë, and yet so closely
did her charity school and mine resemble each other that many of the features
with which my childhood made me familiar are reproduced in startling and
photographic exactness in the pages in which she describes Cowan Bridge.[82]

In terms of memory, unlike the gist passages that I read earlier, these passages
do not relay a general response to a novel: they are not aesthetic judgments.
Instead, novelistic characters or events have become touchstones in semantic
memory, easily retrieved points of comparison for events in everyday life.

When psychologists describe semantic memory, they do so in terms of
facts: who starred in a particular movie; where a capital is located; how government works. Usually, people do not remember how they first learned these
facts (in what is called "source amnesia"), probably because these facts are encountered often, from many sources, and because there's no good reason to
keep track of their origin.[83] Yet these nineteenth-century readers have not experienced source amnesia. Parts of these novels have entered semantic memory, still tagged with their source.

To understand why, I turn to a specialized area of memory research, concept formation. It engages the Platonic question of how we form abstract ideas.
Two dominant paradigms for how we create concepts are the prototype and the
exemplar. The prototype is what Gregory L. Murphy calls a "summary representation," in which "the entire category is represented by a unified representation
rather than separate representation for each member or for different classes."[84]
If a particular object/event shares a unified representation's most common features, then it falls squarely into that category; objects/events that share only a
few, or none, of those features will fall partially into it. Thus, participants identify "sparrow" as belonging to the category "bird" more quickly than they do
"ostrich." They know that ostriches are birds, but sparrows have more common
category features and therefore are identified more easily; sparrows are more
prototypical birds.

The competing paradigm for concept formation is the exemplar. In it, categories arise not from a summary representation but simply from having many
memories of the items in a particular concept: "A person's concept of dogs is the
set of dogs that the person remembers."[85] If one dog is especially easy for you to
retrieve, it becomes your category exemplar. If you recognize a specific bird as
more or less typical, it is not because you remember an abstract set of bird features but because you compare it to your remembered bird exemplar(s).

Psychological debate between prototypes and exemplars is rich, ongoing, and unresolved.[86] Yet among nineteenth-century readers, there is a clear winner: exemplars. Novels entered the long-term memory of nineteenth-century readers as containers from which could be extracted vivid pieces of shorthand: a bad marriage, unpleasant behaviors or sayings, embarrassment at a museum, being in suspense for a long time, attending an abusive school. Admittedly, the "container" metaphor is misleading: any act of retrieval involves active reconstruction, not the delivery of a preexisting trace. Yet nineteenth-century readers treat novels as just such containers, anyway. The writer who signed himself "Clericus" and compared his school to Cowan Bridge presumably had not read *Jane Eyre* when he was in school. Instead, Brontë's novel gives him an exemplar for his autobiographical experience and reinforces its retrievability.

Readers refer to their exemplars as confidently as earlier writers referred to the classics, sure that their addressees would recognize them. For example, in the testimony of an upholsterer, Thomas Broider, before a Select Committee of the House of Lords in 1888, Broider explains how poorly his boss paid him because of his youth: "It was customary then that he would not allow me to take what are called the best wages in the shop, 50 s. a week, owing to my youth. I was like David Copperfield."[87] Aside from revealing Dickens's reach among the working classes, Broider's quotation assumes that, when he compares himself to Dickens's character, his audience will know what he means. In ways that recall Wilde's claims about literature and life, nineteenth-century readers often use fiction as a better model for life than life. When Karl Pearson's Cambridge tutors informed his parents about his progress, they wrote, "He has fine abilities & is most industrious—he is no doubt a little peculiar. We think him somewhat like the character of Kenelm Chillingly in Bulwer's novel."[88] A fictional character is so well known that further description is unnecessary: invoking the exemplar tells an audience all it needs to know.

Although I have avoided focusing on a single author, of all nineteenth-century novelists, the translation of episodic into semantic memory took a particular form with Dickens that was less common for other authors. In general, semantic memory for exemplars exists at the level of the character or the event, often (at least so it seems from my evidence) unpleasant or odd ones. With Dickens there is the addition of memory for what characters say. In the classic Kintschian model surface code and textbase fade from long-term memory, leaving the situation model; as I have argued, even that situation model is less likely to be retrieved than an emotional gist. But in the case of Dickens readers remembered some of the textbase with great, if not always verbatim, detail, and they did so especially for the sayings of *The Pickwick Papers'* Sam Weller:

[From a military journal in 1837 on the evils of gambling]: In point of fact, a person might go into any of these houses with the certainty that he would be neither cheated or intimidated; he knew the odds were, as Sam Weller says, "rayther" against him, and that he could not lose more money than was in his pocket.[89]

[From the *Bengal Catholic Herald* in 1844, attacking an Australian anti-Catholic tract]: As for *Puseyism*, sending it amongst us to find a home, is coming on "rather strong" (as Sam Weller says).[90]

[From an American senator in 1854 on annexing Cuba]: Whenever we have had to deal with "manifest destiny" or "political necessity" in any treaty relating to our Northern boundary, it has been to cut off; and, if we could not sell out, we gave away, while we have been continually traveling south for acquisitions. This may be all accidental; probably it is; but, if you ever read Pickwick, sir, you remember that, as Sam Weller says, it was a most astonishing coincidence. [Laughter.][91] [actually "hex-traordinary and wonderful coincidence"]

[A soldier in Delhi in 1857]: You say that your letter was a very shabby and untidy one; but it didn't strike me to be so. I thought it just what it ought to be, except that I should have liked it to be a little longer; but, as Sam Weller says, "the perfection of letter writing is to leave off always so as to make the person to whom you write wish for more!"[92] [actually, "she'll vish there wos more, and that's the great art o' letter-writin."]

There are many, many more such quotations in the writings of Victorian readers, followed by a smaller but still substantial number of "As Micawber says"— though the Weller quotations come from all over *Pickwick* while the Micawber ones repeat just a few sayings. The force of novels as exemplars extended, in the case of Dickens, to actual quotations that could appear in the widest array of circumstances, produced in contexts as distant as possible from those of encoding. Quite apart from the plot of *The Pickwick Papers*, the quotations assert common ground with readers/hearers over a not-quite-respectable character whom they nevertheless all know. A gist memory of a character's language, fondly recalled, overtakes the novel's events.

In light of all these responses from nineteenth-century readers, while the psychological model of surface code, textbase, and situation model may describe memory for laboratory text, it needs to be complicated to account for actual readers' gist memories. These memories feature an "experiential envelope," which arises less from interacting with the text than from the reading experience itself; it consists of a loosely organized recollection of environmental context and emotional gist. If participants in a survey receive a series of questions about their situation model memories (such as, "How did the novel end?" or "What was a climactic event in the novel?") and their memories for environmental context and emotional reaction (such as, "Where were you when you read the novel?" or "How did you feel in reading the novel?"), subjects should be more confident in their answers to the second than the first.[93] My point is not that their memories of the experiential envelope are more true than their situation model memories, only that they are easier to access.

In addition, psychological theories of reading tend not to account for situations like the sayings of Sam Weller. In some cases reading can evidently become the subject of collective memory, of the kind studied by Henry Roediger and Magdalena Abel.[94] Characters become exemplar memories for entire social groups, especially vivid and easily accessible sources for world knowledge. Invoking them in conversation or in correspondence created for nineteenth-century readers an in-group status that marked common ground across differences.

Findings about easy reading, online and offline processes, gist memories, and category formation in this chapter may offer a starting point for other scholars to contest, revise, or correct. As digital databases add searchable evidence, larger, more accurate samples of readers may emerge that better represent the nineteenth-century population, as opposed to the literate sector on which I concentrate. In addition, search engines should also improve to allow better searches; for example, it would be valuable to have more information about the contexts in which readers remembered novels to determine how these might affect memory. In this chapter I make the best conclusions I can based on available evidence. It reveals that nineteenth-century readers enjoyed their easy reading despite all the attacks on it, that their enjoyment did not necessarily lead to long offline discussions, that their transportation coexisted with environmental encoding, and that novels became sources of exemplars detached from the original context. Easy reading in the nineteenth century was scorned as the shallowest of occupations and respected as the source of the deepest of memories.

# CHAPTER 6

# THAT'S ENTERTAINMENT?

**MY SURVEY** in the previous chapter noted that many nineteenth-century readers liked what they read: this chapter asks why. I wish that I could repeat a version of the previous chapter by collecting responses of nineteenth-century readers, but they did not write for later scholars. Although they were happy to note that they enjoyed a novel, they often did not provide much detail for what they liked beyond the fact that they found it "entertaining" or "diverting."

Given the enormous attention that the novel has received from literary scholarship, it might seem strange to someone outside of the field that so little time has been given to why readers enjoyed them. Scholars have much to say about the formal features of nineteenth-century novels, as well as their relation to economics, science, politics, imperialism, gender roles, class stratification, and much else. Nineteenth-century novels have become a master key to the century, as if everything significant about it could be filtered through them. Scholars have not ignored readers: they have examined such topics as readers' understandings of realism, their desires for happy endings, and the supposed evil effects of novel reading. Kate Flint's discussion in "The Victorian Novel and Its Readers" provides a concise overview of such issues.[1] But, perhaps because the topic seems so obvious, no one has ever bothered to analyze just why readers found novels entertaining.

This lack of attention is overdetermined by scholars' long struggle in the academy to make the novel into an object worth studying. In the early days of English departments, the novel looked like trash unsuited to serious research: since people could just read novels on their own, studying them seemed pointless.[2] To prove that they deserved study, scholars purged adjectives that nineteenth-century readers used to describe novels, like *entertaining* and *diverting*. Instead, the novel gained admission to serious literary study by becoming no fun, as I have argued in my account of the American reception of *Silas Marner*; a similar path has characterized the academic reception of films and, more recently, video games. More accurately, novels might be entertaining, even to scholars, as long as no one mentioned the fact; the more entertained scholars seemed to be, the less scholarly their work looked. For example, F. R. Leavis's characterization of Dickens as the "great entertainer" spurred decades of criticism to rescue him from the perceived putdown.[3]

Whatever we might want to say about nineteenth-century novels as indices of bourgeois subjectivity, imperialism, or the sex/gender system, we lose their historical significance if we take for granted their entertainment value. To judge from puffs routinely appended to novels, the best recommendation a novel could have was that it entertained:

> We cannot offer kinder advice to the reader than by recommending him to read this very entertaining novel.[4]

> One of the most entertaining novels of the season.[5]

> "Uncle Walter" is an exceedingly entertaining novel.[6]

As reviewers knew, entertainment mattered to readers, and it ought to matter to us because, without a good framework for discussing it, we cut off our ability to say much to nonacademic readers about why people bothered with novels.

Since demoting entertainment promoted scholarship, critical models of entertainment are sparse; William Warner's *Licensing Entertainment*, a major study of the rise of the eighteenth-century novel's respectability, for example, uses *entertainment* in the title but has little to say about it in the abstract, preferring to let novels speak for themselves as examples of changing attitudes.[7] More helpful is Deidre Lynch's *Loving Literature*, which describes how certain literary forms became invested with deep feeling by readers. Lynch's work foregrounds affect in exalting literary experience; she describes the mixed reactions stemming from "those particular conundrums that were generated for eighteenth-century readers by representations of readerly gratitude as authors' due and of books as, correspondingly, the gifts that should be repaid with that gratitude."[8] I share Lynch's investment in affect, but I am interested in a shallower, more transient form: the emotions arising from reading literature not profound enough to call for gratitude. Whereas Lynch cares about special works singled out for potentially deep emotion, I am interested in the more everyday affect evinced not by profoundly moving literature but by more ordinary reading.[9]

Within psychology, entertainment has also proven elusive; psychologists have investigated closely related topics but have kept entertainment just beyond what is worth studying. For example, cognitive psychologists have explored interest, and educational psychologists have examined motivation and its role in aiding or hindering learning.[10] Social psychologists, in turn, have explored identification, social interaction, and mood manipulation.[11] All are relevant to entertainment but not quite identical to it. The most extensive treatment comes from communication studies, although usually with visual media, especially film and television. While much of it is descriptive, some research tries to model the salient aspects of entertainment across the widest variety of situations.[12]

The first half of this chapter synthesizes insights from these disciplines to create a model for entertainment. As I argued in Chapter 4, nineteenth-century critics are at their most revealing when they discuss not easy literature but its opposite. With a work they find interesting, they fall into commonplaces. William Howitt, for example, maintains that interest depends on a work's "foundations being laid in human nature, and their superstructure raised in a true knowledge of that love of the marvellous, the beautiful, the new, the magnificent, and the tender, which for ever haunts the human soul."[13] Nineteenth-century critics are more savvy about entertainment not with a novel they like but with one they hate. In the second half of this chapter I test the strengths and weaknesses of my model of entertainment against specific examples: first, two novels widely considered among the worst ever, Gustave Strauss's *The Old Ledger* and "Rita's" *Like Dian's Kiss*; second, one novel that started as a failure and became a hit, Charles Dickens's *The Old Curiosity Shop*.

As Peter Vorderer and Francis F. Steen note, entertainment "includes various physiological, cognitive, affective, and behavioral components."[14] Although concentrating only on some simplifies a complex experience, some are easier to study historically than others. While it would be fascinating to know the physiology of nineteenth-century readers, we can do so only indirectly, as when they describe having experienced a breathless interest in what they read. Such comments tend to be fairly trite in nineteenth-century writing and are often most accessible in advertisements for new literature, where they indicate not reader experience but marketers' assumptions about readers' desire. Likewise, the physical behavior of entertained readers does not leave easy traces: when did readers move in their chairs? how quickly or slowly did they read? when did they take breaks? what distractions may have been around them? All these have potentially major effects, but we have no large-scale evidence of them.

Regarding the cognitive and emotional aspects of entertainment, in contrast, we do have evidence, although it tends to be offline, self-reported, and subject to retrospective bias. I base my discussion of nineteenth-century entertainment on them, even as I acknowledge that doing so oversimplifies. I also focus on reading as entertainment, as opposed to going to the theater, sports events, or concerts, because, again, the best evidence survives for reading. As I noted in my introduction, such investigations open themselves to an easy charge of anachronism: since most psychological findings derive from participants who postdate the nineteenth century, we cannot know if those findings apply to earlier periods. Yet literary scholars routinely apply approaches and insights honed in the twentieth- and twenty-first century academy to works written in earlier periods. Nervousness about the use of cognitive science is an arbitrary invocation of rigor that misrecognizes the field's enabling anachronisms. Also, there is no reason to decide a priori that contemporary psychological findings are irrelevant to the past. If it is wrong to assume that there is no difference between now and then, it is equally wrong to assume that there are no continuities either; assertions of historical difference do not guarantee truth any more than do ones of continuity.[15]

Spending hours to read a nine-hundred-page work of fiction, intricately plotted and packed with a vast group of characters, may not appear to many to be an obvious delight. That such an activity did indeed become widespread as entertainment is both remarkable and odd, and this chapter explores how it happened. Reading novels had to offer profound compensations for the sheer inconvenience of slogging through a long work. To explain what these were, I argue that reading for entertainment follows a time course, with a before, during, and after. The "before" is readers' cognitive and emotional mind-set when choosing what to read. In their influential theory of self-determination Deci and Ryan present evidence for three needs as core motivators: competence, autonomy, and relatedness. As always in psychology, these motivations are not meant to be exhaustive but are umbrella terms for especially salient needs.[16] Vorderer, Steen, and Chan have argued that these motivators pertain to entertainment generally, and, following in their path, I want to adapt them to the "before" of nineteenth-century entertainment.[17] By "competence," these authors describe the need to believe that the self is capable and effective: motivation fades if a task is too hard or too easy. In the case of reading, readers choose a novel because they believe that they will be equal to the challenges it poses. For readers content to spend most of their time in good-enough processing, their choices will be guided by their assumed level of competence; for others who perceive themselves as eager for more difficult material, they may find reading material that satisfied the first group beneath their competence.

In cognitive terms the emotional appeal of competence arises from the match between difficulty of material and desired effort. Feeling competent when reading means that you have adequate background knowledge and can access it without more effort than you want; likewise, it also means that you can easily transform the surface code of the novel into a situation model. Felt competence arises less from ease than from the match between expectation and perceived demands. In turn, this match provides a potential source for reader enjoyment when it is satisfied: people enjoy doing something that they feel they do well. Just as a novel can be unentertaining if it is too difficult for a reader's competence, it can also fail by falling below the reader's competence, either because it is too easy or because it does not meet reader expectations.

For nineteenth-century readers competence may have had a special edge because for most of the century literacy could not be assumed: many men and women were not competent to read any novel, no matter how easy or hard.[18] Reading a novel, even the silliest, put them in the charmed, though widening, circle of literacy. Admittedly, many readers experienced novels despite their illiteracy because other readers read them aloud; even those who could not read might listen. Here, questions of competence shift from pure literacy to comprehension: how comprehensible were these novels when heard? For example, many Victorian novels are thick with topical allusions. Much about Dickens might have been lost on those who did not have London under their feet, and Trollope's Barchester novels would mystify those without some grasp of ecclesiastical ranks. While many in Dickens's and Trollope's audience did indeed know these details, it's also worth considering that many did not. Their novels featured such topicality without, evidently, losing readers.[19] Other aspects of reading either compensated for the threat to reader competence or transformed it into a perceived realism that bolstered authenticity.

The second aspect of the "before" of entertainment is autonomy: nobody is forced to read a novel. As soon as coercion enters reading, its entertainment value shrinks (as literature professors know too well). Obvious as autonomy as a precondition of entertainment may be, it contrasts with other aspects of reading that occur without conscious agency or seem to do so. As I noted in Chapter 1, much reading is automatic, from recognizing words to using relevant knowledge; readers have little explicit awareness of these processes. At a conscious level, readers often use the metaphor of surrendering agency to the work, as if it cast a spell over them (see the quotation from Poulet in my introduction). Reading requires acts beyond conscious agency, either because it is automatic or because it seems to start outside the self. Nevertheless, this lack of agency is fun only if preceded by an all-important assertion of agency: choosing one novel rather than another or choosing to read rather than doing something else. Entertaining reading requires the autonomous choice to give up autonomy.

Cognitively, autonomy's attraction may arise from inhibition. When forced to do an activity, you become aware of other activities that you might have preferred, so that your attention is split between doing what you are forced to do and imagining what you could have done but cannot.[20] When you choose your own action, you may be aware of other potential choices, but they are less salient than when you have been forced because you know why you chose one action over others. In reading, inhibiting thoughts of all the other actions one might rather do would add a big cognitive load to the mind's already small capacity. It would make the potentially challenging experience of reading all the more difficult because it would wreck the desired match I have described between effort expected and effort required. More simply, thinking about what you would rather be doing makes reading harder and less fun.

For nineteenth-century readers, getting to choose may have been especially meaningful because no one could take leisure for granted. The sheer amount of labor required for an average day meant that leisure mattered because it was scarce. The autonomous choice of entertainment countered an omnipresent ethics of duty; for example, when Frances Power Cobbe recognized in 1881 that changes in laws gave women more power than they had ever had, she responded not by celebrating it but by writing *The Duties of Women*, a stern reminder of their responsibilities to themselves and others.[21] Valuing acting on one's own cut against the elevation of duty so harshly that in *Culture and Anarchy* Matthew Arnold uses the supposed popularity of "doing what one likes" as a symptom of cultural collapse. For nineteenth-century readers entertainment gave them choice. Duty may have led them to spend all day cooking and cleaning, administering the empire, watching children, copying legal briefs, or tending to the parish, but at least they could choose what novel to read.

The last category that Vorderer and Steen adapt from Ryan and Deci is relatedness: people seek out entertainment to form social bonds. This is at once obvious and complicated because the relatedness of fiction differs from that of life. While Ryan and Deci care about actual social relations, relations between people and fictive characters are parasocial. Literary critics interested in cognitive psychology have explored this parasociality by asking why people care about fictional characters, with books by Lisa Zunshine, Suzanne Keen, and Blakey Vermeule being especially helpful.[22] Although there are important differences among them, they converge on simulation; as Vermeule notes, "I have no doubt that the simulation theory captures crucial aspects of literary experience."[23] Critics agree that readers experience literature in part by treating it as a simulation of actual social experience.

Yet I find the idea of simulation less useful than others have. Keith Oatley, in support of it, has argued that "narrative stories are simulations that run not on computers but on minds."[24] While simulating experience has many uses, I am not sure why reading should be a source for it. The goals of imaginative simulation, such as exploring theory of mind, testing strategies for social relations, and developing the need for empathy, can be attained without reading a word, as when we imagine situations on our own, speculate about what other people are doing in real life, or listen to stories about events that happened to other people. Why should anybody read a novel for simulations when so many other, more predictable sources are easier to acquire and may better meet needs? If the goal is simulation, novels look like a bad source for them because they may not conform to the simulation desired by the reader. Some readers may want exciting simulations, others calming ones. With novels readers are not always certain what they will get: hence the name *novel*.

Unlike theorists who link reading fiction to social simulation, I emphasize that reading novels matters because it differs from "real life." Specifically, novels allow readers to feel linked to characters (and here I include narrators) whom they may or may not like but who cannot judge them back. Readers do not demand that everyone be likable, but they assume a likability threshold. If too many characters fall below it, motivation for reading fades. I write "like," not "love"; although some novel characters do indeed inspire love, for the average entertainment experience, liking characters suffices. The emotional energy required to love or hate a character may be more than most readers want to expend. A successfully likable novel balances characters who are just likable enough against characters who are just dislikable enough. The weak affective intensity of "liking" fuels novelistic entertainment and may be one of the salient inventions of the British novel: early modern drama, for example, strives for much higher emotional power, while other novelistic traditions, such as the French, care far less about likability.

Characters do not need to gain readers' goodwill: a reader, having chosen a novel, will give it a chance, though perhaps not for long. To succeed as entertainment, the key is for characters not to alienate the reader by being perceived as either incomprehensible or blatantly immoral. As such, likability is linked to interest and transportation. Characters lose both interest and likability if their actions make no sense: they deny readers the chance to find meaningful patterns of behavior. Immoral behavior is a more delicate matter because some characters who behave immorally can be likable if they have enough other traits to make them interesting.[25] Boring, generic immorality, in contrast, is unforgivable, and irritation forestalls the reader's desire for transportation.

Whatever we feel about characters, we do not worry about how they might respond to our reactions to them. Lucky for them, they will never know. As such, their ignorance reinforces our autonomy: we will not be held accountable. In life, however, potential vexations shadow our desire for social relations with others. We may not be competent to engage with them; we may deal with those we would rather not meet but must because of other obligations. In an entertainment situation we assume (not always correctly) that the simulations we encounter are ones that we can interpret successfully. Whatever our background knowledge, the author will provide what we need to know. If you dislike the characters in a novel, you have the option of not reading, unlike in life. Parasocial simulation provides the pluses of social relations without the minuses.

In terms of judging characters, the chief difference between us and nineteenth-century readers is that they were more easily alienated by perceived vulgarity. Entertainment value could be lost through immorality or dullness, but vulgarity had a particularly dreadful edge, and I will have more to say about it later in this chapter.[26] Otherwise, another partial difference between Victorian readers and contemporary ones is that practices such as reading aloud would have superimposed actual social relations on the parasocial simulations of fiction. It would be wrong to claim that twenty-first-century readers read only by themselves and Victorian readers read only in groups. Yet Victorian readers were more likely to experience novels in the company of others than contemporary readers are. I do not want to overstate this difference. While twenty-first-century readers may read by themselves, their reading may also fuel social relations: discussions in a book club, book recommendations to other people, reviews or impressions shared online. It may be, though, that for many nineteenth-century readers the novel was less a compensation for loneliness than it could appear to be later because so many novel-reading practices arose from creating and sustaining existing social relations.

Competence, autonomy, and relatedness all belong to the "before" of novel reading, the factors that bring readers to read novels. But once readers start reading, these factors change form to cope with the experience. In general, feeling competent is its own reward, but, with regard to reading fiction, competence has a payoff: being interested. A useful insight into how Victorian readers thought about interest comes from a classic study by Walter Kintsch, in which he distinguishes what makes a story cognitively (as opposed to emotionally) interesting. A cognitively interesting story needs low predictability but a high retrospective likelihood of seeing prior events as causally related: "We shouldn't be able to predict it, but it must be possible to postdict it."[27] A narrative with predictable events does not interest, while one whose events cannot be retrospectively shaped into coherence is boring, strange, or confusing (though different readers will have widely varying standards for creating such coherence). A good story has events unpredictable during the reading experience itself (online), but coherent in retrospect (offline).

Although Kintsch presents his formula as an abstraction, it's a useful measure because it describes lucidly how nineteenth-century authors separated their work from romance. In the rambling plots of early romance fiction, the relation of predictable to postdictable exists at the level of the episode rather than of the plot as a whole. The eighteenth-century novel slowly and reluctantly adapted the global plot structure that had been traditionally found in drama, and this adaptation needed ingenuity because of the difference in medium. Yet by the nineteenth-century period, cognitive interest had become an assumed criterion for judging success in fiction.

In terms of how reading affects the self, psychologists of entertainment look to pleasure: people go to the movies or listen to music to feel better, or, in psychological jargon, to gain "hedonic optimization."[28] Yet this concept does not explain why people eagerly undergo simulations of painful or horrific experiences. A better formulation for self-relevance is that entertainment steers between two goals: self-enhancement and self-improvement. Self-enhancement caters to narcissistic pleasure: entertainment makes readers feel good about themselves by catering to their moods, supporting their worldview, or glamorizing their social milieu.[29] If characters we like do well, we have the pleasure of feeling good about ourselves, as we do when characters we dislike meet justice.

Such desire exists in tension with self-improvement, the desire to become a better person.[30] At its core, self-improvement is another form of self-enhancement that reaches its goal by other means. Rather than supporting existing opinions, beliefs, and attitudes, self-improvement encourages readers to encounter upsetting, tragic, or at least face-threatening events and people. Much painful entertainment is perceived as more meaningful than entertainment that does not make comparable demands, so undergoing it supports an ultimate feeling of self-enhancement.[31] Yet the challenge to the self can only go so far: faced with too much distress, a reader may lose motivation.

In terms of wanting social relations literature offers a special satisfaction. Having lunch with friends, attending worship, or checking email can all support feeling connected to others. Yet only rarely are such interactions interesting: other peoples' problems, challenges, and aspirations, while not devoid of interest, are never quite as compelling as our own. Moreover, social relationships carry the burden of asking us at least to pretend to care about others. But literature, especially the nineteenth-century novel, offers events happening to other people that, at their best, are so interesting that we forget ourselves and imagine ourselves transported into another time and place. Even better, our interest carries no obligations because those other people do not exist.

Melanie Green is a leading researcher regarding transportation and its connection to a desire for relatedness. As she notes, "As individuals become increasingly enmeshed in a narrative world, it is likely that they will develop a strong sense of connection or familiarity with characters encountered repeatedly or continuously over time. . . . Individuals are able to use characters' situations and experiences to understand their own lives, and they tend to evaluate characters using criteria typically applied to individuals they meet in their daily lives."[32] For Green there is no gap between the social and the parasocial: readers treat characters as they do real people. Whether or not this is true for twenty-first-century literary critics, plenty of evidence reveals that nineteenth-century readers had such responses. For them, the movement from desire for relatedness to online transportation was smooth.

To bring together the different elements that I have described, a formula for online entertainment value might look like this: entertainment value = A (interest) + B (self-relevance) + C (transportation), where A, B, and C indicate different possible weights. Although, as written, the relation between the three factors looks additive, A, B, and C could take on negative as well as positive values. The most entertaining fiction would combine positive interest, self-relevance, and transportation weights. A different piece of fiction that, for a given reader, had high interest and high transportation but no self-relevance would be less entertaining. A more complex model might also include two- or three-way interactions among the variables, so that, for example, self-relevance and transportation might combine to produce an added entertainment value beyond what they contribute separately. I do not pursue such interactions because the available historical evidence does not (yet) provide enough detail to make them meaningful.

The last piece of the model continues a theme I discussed in Chapter 3: how one should feel after reading. A young Scottish student in 1846, paraphrasing Southey in *The Doctor*, claimed "that after reading a poem, or any other work, we should sit down and calmly consider whether its effect has been to make us wiser and better, to touch our feelings and warm our hearts. In proportion as it has had this, or a contrary effect, is the book to be applauded or condemned."[33] This virtuous advice was as widely ignored as one could have hoped. Instead, after reading a novel, readers register not whether it made them wiser and better but whether they liked it. As I noted in the previous chapter, Victorian readers were largely happy with their novels: it is not easy to find many complaining about what they read. As I also noted, this fact reveals less about nineteenth-century reactions than about conventions for writing about reading; readers may not have been motivated to write about novels they disliked, or such writing has not survived. In any case this last stage of reading as entertainment involves deciding if expectations have been met, exceeded, or disappointed.

I want to bring this model to bear on historical readers, yet, as I have noted, their actual words usually do not provide enough information to be able to determine much about their reactions. I therefore turn again to reviewers but only to reviewers put in the anomalous position of confronting truly bad novels. Usually, as Kenneth Graham argues in his survey of nineteenth-century criticism of the novel, "mid-Victorian critics of fiction anxious for their subject's prestige could hardly be expected to stress its undoubted ability to entertain. Rather, the need was to defend it from those who insisted it could do little more."[34] Yet certain novels were so bad that they jolted reviewers out of business as usual. Confronted with an aesthetic abyss, they were more revealing about just what assumptions they brought to entertainment, and the model that I have developed draws them out.

Many Victorian novels received bad reviews, but two stand out: Gustave Strauss's *The Old Ledger* (1865) and *Like Dian's Kiss* (1878) by Eliza Humphreys ("Rita"). While identifying them as aesthetic disasters has some antiquarian interest, the more compelling questions about them involve what reactions to them say about Victorian taste as a whole; my goal is not to close read these (truly dreadful) novels but to understand just why they inspired such disgust. In 1866 Robert Lush savaged Strauss's *The Old Ledger* in the *Athenaeum*:

> Our first impression, on opening this production, was, that, so many italics and inverted commas were never congregated into the same space before. Our last, on closing it, is, that it must be the very worst attempt at a novel that has ever been perpetrated. It cannot even claim the utility of an opiate. Its inanity, self-complacency, and vulgarity, its profanity, its indelicacy (to use no stronger word), its display of bad Latin, bad French, bad German, and bad English, the perpetual recurrence of abuse (or, as the author more euphemistically expresses it, "slightly digressive reflections") on great men living and dead, and wholly unconnected with the subject, all make the reader even more indignant than weary; and how much this means can only be conceived by an operation which few are likely to attempt, and fewer still to achieve—that of reading the book.[35]

Even for an age when reviewers rarely held back, this was scathing. Lush demolished every possible reason to read this novel: it was boring, irritating, and vulgar.

Furious, Strauss sued the *Athenaeum* for libel, and the case was heard on April 3, 1866. Strauss claimed that the review had stopped book sales and that he was entitled to £1,000 in damages. While this charge might have led to an interesting debate, the actual trial did not turn out as expected. The prosecuting attorney, Serjeant Ballantine, opened by claiming that the *Athenaeum* had published "not criticisms, but abuse, and coarse abuse." Yet, after this stirring start, his entire evidence failed because it consisted only of a certain "Dr. Gardiner" testifying that he had read *The Old Ledger* "and did not consider there was anything particularly objectionable in it."[36]

Hawkins, the counsel for the defense, gleefully responded:

> The learned counsel then gave a very humorous description of the principle [sic] incidents in the work, one of which was that a principle [sic] actor in it commits forgery to the amount of 7,000l., "being tempted" according to the novel to do so to enable him to carry on a little longer his connection with the gaming table, and also with a certain opera dancer. . . . The object of the writer was to insult and vilify every religious sect. (Laughter.)[37]

Whereas Lush singles out inanity and vulgarity, along with motiveless attacks, Hawkins focuses on immoral behavior: a novel that defended a man for forging £7000 to carry on an affair with a low woman had abandoned all civilized ethics. Even worse, according to Hawkins, the novel rewarded the forger because the queen eventually recognized his services.

Hawkins's speech left the prosecution in pieces. Ballantine confessed that he had not read Strauss's novel; after hearing Hawkins's description, he was so horrified that he wished to end the trial immediately. Hawkins, while still maintaining that the charge of libel was unjustified, did not object. Justice Erle had the last word, noting that "it appeared to him that Serjeant Ballantine had given very sound advice to his client when he recommended him not to proceed any further with the inquiry."[38]

All might have concluded there, but William Hepworth Dixon, the *Athenaeum*'s editor, perhaps angry that he had not received a real verdict, wrote an editorial, "The Rights of Criticism," which reprinted Lush's criticism and added more comments: "We found the book abominable, and we said so. Our readers, we may safely assume, were satisfied with our verdict, since it is alleged that the sale was instantly arrested, and was not resumed." He stressed that his motives in going to trial were not mercenary: "We . . . had every reason to fear that our only award from the Court would have been our costs *on paper*."[39]

A year later, in February of 1867, Strauss again took the *Athenaeum* to court for libel because, in his eyes, Hepworth Dixon's dig about being unlikely to be awarded costs attacked his perceived finances. At this second trial, after Strauss and Hepworth Dixon had testified, the jury erupted:

> A Juryman—Is it necessary for us to hear any more of this case, my lord?
> The Lord Chief Justice—You must, unless the learned counsel for the plaintiff consents to withdraw.

A Juryman—We think it might stop here.

Dr. Keneally [Strauss's lawyer]—You ought not to say that until you have heard the true character of the book.

A Juryman—We have heard enough of it. We don't want to hear anything more of it.

The Lord Chief Justice—I cannot stop the case without the consent of counsel. It is always possible that a jury's minds might be changed.

The jurymen shook their heads.[40]

Formal legal procedure, represented by the Lord Chief Justice and Dr. Keneally, squared off against pure exasperation, represented by the jury. The court officials wanted the trial to proceed as usual, but the jury responded to the thought of hearing more about *The Old Ledger* not as a legal procedure but as cruel punishment.

Despite this outburst, Dr. Keneally did his best, even dredging up the precedents of "Keates [*sic*] and Shelley" to argue that *The Old Ledger* had been maligned. Yet all his work mattered nothing in the face of the judge's blunt question: "Was the article as a whole reasonably fair and just?"[41] The jury returned for the defendant without even leaving the box. Although the newspaper article provides no specifics, the jury's speed suggests that it had decided long before and wanted to finish as soon as possible. The prospect of spending another second with *The Old Ledger* was so dreadful that customary legal niceties, like debating the case, could be dropped. Ending discussion as soon as possible was best for all.

*The Old Ledger*, like all novels reviewed in periodicals, started with heavy marks against it because the critic had no autonomy: he had to review it, whether or not he wanted to do so. My model would predict that in the absence of autonomy other components of entertainment—competence/interest and relatedness/transportation—would have to be especially strong to make the novel enjoyable; if they did not, the loss of autonomy would be galling. For the reviewer (Lush), the novel did not meet basic expectations: it would have some element of seriousness, at least of form if not of content, and its representations would follow norms of acceptable behavior. For Lush, this novel instead manifested "inanity" and "vulgarity," as seen in its "profanity," "indelicacy," and bad language.

"Profanity" and "indelicacy" are not intrinsically bad or uninteresting, but Lush specifies why they are so irritating in *The Old Ledger*: "the perpetual recurrence of abuse (or, as the author more euphemistically expresses it, 'slightly digressive reflections') on great men living and dead, and wholly unconnected with the subject" is inexcusable. Abuse might interest if linked to larger action, but when "wholly unconnected with the subject," it does not interest because, in Kintsch's terms, it has no postdictability. The lawyer for the *Athenaeum*, Mr. Hawkins, echoed Lush's claim: "In another portion of the work one of the learned judges was introduced, or rather dragged in the narrative, for no other purpose, as it appeared to him, than to make the utterly false and groundless representation concerning him."[42] For both, the novel's incoherence causes readers to lose interest.

If Lush's review focuses on interest, the defense's case spends time on relatedness. While a novel with bad characters might be tolerable if balanced by good ones, no one wanted to read about good things happening to bad people:

> It was astonishing that any one who wished a good literary character should have written such a book. . . . [The novel's] pith, he said, was the history of the career of a most immoral youth, whose life was plunged in vice, and who sought to retrieve his ruin by forgery. What were the comments on the author upon conduct and character such as this? The hero committed forgery in order to pay off gambling debts and support an opera-dancer. And what did the author think and say of this? Why, that, forsooth, the youth was "sorely tempted." Sorely tempted! No doubt, and so were many who were suffering penal servitude![43]

Nineteenth-century critics loved to attack immoral behavior in novels. Yet the lawyer Hawkins treated the immorality of Strauss's novel differently from the way novels had been attacked before, as in the savaging of Elizabeth Gaskell's *Ruth*. For earlier critics immorality was contagious: readers might believe that bad behavior was acceptable if they did not see it punished. Hawkins, in contrast, did not worry that *The Old Ledger* would wreck public morals. Instead, he could not imagine why readers would care about an obviously worthless protagonist. If the promise of entertainment was to be transported by parasocial relations into an alternative world, Strauss's book prevented such transportation with characters so repellent that no one liked them.

Useful as Strauss's *The Old Ledger* is as a test case, controversy arose from only one review. To get a broader perspective on entertainment, we need a novel that received more widespread condemnation. Happily, such a novel exists: *Like Dian's Kiss* (1878) by "Rita," the pen-name of Eliza Humphreys.

Whereas *The Old Ledger* received one bad review, *Like Dian's Kiss* earned waves of loathing:

> It would be a tempting of fate to say that this is the worst novel we could possibly be condemned to read, and so we will only say that it is the worst novel that, so far as our recollection carries us back, we have as yet read.[44]

> On the whole, we think "Like Dian's Kiss" worth notice as the worst novel we have ever read.[45]

> We have rarely read a novel in which the characters were less worthy of sympathy and their circumstances more incredible.[46]

> The whole story . . . leaves a very unhealthy and unsavoury impression behind it.[47]

*Like Dian's Kiss* went a step beyond being bad: it concentrated in itself everything that a Victorian critic might despise.

While reviews of *Like Dian's Kiss* did not lead to a court case, they did let reviewers explain just why novels failed, as when one noted that he had never read "any more preposterous story, worked out by means of more hateful individuals, or written in a style more widely removed from literary excellence."[48] Although *The Old Ledger* also had a preposterous story and hateful individuals, *Like Dian's Kiss* went even further. Its plot was even more nonsensical, its characters more irritating, and its prose more appalling.

In terms of my model, preposterousness is a failure of interest. If Kintsch's formula requires low predictability and high postdictability, *Like Dian's Kiss* did the opposite: its basic situations are predictable because so commonplace: "Now the ideas and situations in *Like Dian's Kiss* are far from being original when we first enter on the matter of the romance"; "The amount of unsuccessful love-making, where the 'reciprocity is all on one side,' involves much repetition and is scarcely amusing."[49] Yet characters nevertheless behave randomly, so they have no postdictability: "The heroine has . . . another suitor— her cousin, Bertie Fraser, whom she hates and accepts. Why, we cannot say. There is just as much reason for her accepting a man she hates while her heart is given to another as there is for anything else in this bewildering story."[50] Another reviewer comments, "It is almost incredible that a wealthy and noble family would accept an existence of the meanest poverty, and all to please a woman who married for the advantages and position that money can be-stow."[51] The combination of predictable situations and inexplicable behavior destroyed interest.

But the novel's failures were not only those of competence and interest: the reviewers also hated the characters. As I have noted, many novels contain loathsome characters, but *Like Dian's Kiss* exceeded its quota: "We cannot say that there is any pleasant company in this book." The heroine appears initially as "an intolerably precocious, pert, and ill-mannered child, named Maud Granville."[52] Another character is "one of the most obnoxious specimens of a vulgar *nouveau-riche* and incompetent amateur that ever cumbered the pages of fiction."[53] Although the hero at least has "well-nigh superhuman patience, forbearance, purity, and powers," he is set against "the vulgarity, ignorance, and brutality of the great amateur . . . and the inhuman coarseness of the mother."[54]

In *The Old Ledger* relatedness failed because readers had to like, or at least excuse, behavior that seemed blatantly immoral. *Like Dian's Kiss*, in contrast, made characters revoltingly vulgar: "That a young lady should 'take a flying leap into bed with her stockings on,' and that the son of a baron and baroness should decline to eat cabbage at the paternal table, because he 'has had too many experiences of cabbages on washing-days to risk it,' and 'always suspects the cook boils them in the copper,' are unusual incidents in either life or novels, but they are mild samples of the vulgarity of this novel."[55] The young lady leaping into bed and the young man brooding on cabbage and copper demonstrate behavior so crude that, for nineteenth-century reviewers, no one wanted to read about them.

Accusing a novel of vulgarity has an edge of snobbery to it: vulgar writing and behavior belong to supposedly common people. Yet the problem with *Like Dian's Kiss* was not that it represented common people but that it represented ladies and gentlemen behaving as if they were common. Such vulgarity had two equally bad possible origins: either the author really was ignorant of good manners, in which case she should not write novels, or she was trying to affront her audience, in which case her behavior was outrageous. Faced with such vulgarity, readers could pity the novelist for her ignorance or hate her for her bravado.

The novel's style was as bad as its characters:

Of the style, indeed, it may be unhesitatingly said that it could not be worse. Occasionally the author is wholly unintelligible.[56]

> We might adopt the Socratic method and respectfully put the matter to the author of *Like Dian's Kiss*, in the shape of a dialogue. You will admit, Madam, we might say, that the earlier pages of a work of fiction should not be overloaded with luscious epithets.[57]

The novel's prose exasperated reviewers because the author confused fine writing with inflated verbiage. The result was failure of likability: the work seemed to emanate from a defective sensibility. With *The Old Ledger* lawyers were shocked that Strauss could endorse immoral behavior; with *Like Dian's Kiss* reviewers were shocked that anyone could think such prose worth publishing. Nine-hundred pages of it wore down even the sturdiest reviewers.

In the larger history of the novel Humphreys's floridity responds to the same late century stylistic crisis that produced Meredith and James. They relocated within the novel the distinction between high and low styles that had traditionally been located between genres (poetry versus the novel). But for the reviewers, Humphreys's striving for literariness produced not distinction but nonsense. Life offered all too many opportunities for being trapped with disagreeable people and vulgar language; if fiction were to do the same, there was no reason to bother.

The critics' comments reveal deep assumptions behind what entertained Victorian readers. An interesting plot, likable characters, and a competent style create a positive feedback loop: cognitive curiosity stimulates readers to keep reading; a likability threshold for characters encourages readers to stick with them; and a competent writing style lets readers escape the distractions of bad writing. A common psychology underlies these traits: processing fluency. Autonomy aids fluency because, without it, readers struggle in working memory against all the other possible, preferred actions that they might do. Interest aids fluency by providing just enough challenges to keep up attention yet not enough to overwhelm the reader's background knowledge, reading strategies, or working-memory capacity. Relatedness aids fluency by allowing readers to draw on accessible autobiographical knowledge to supplement the text: they feel that they "know" the characters. As predicted by the model, enough fluency in one area may compensate for less in another: for a given reader an interesting novel may be entertaining even if characters are not likable and vice versa. The bigger point is that fluency provides a necessary, if not sufficient, ground for entertainment.

I stress fluency to counter a major objection to my model: everything that critics hated in *The Old Ledger* and *Like Dian's Kiss* can be found, at least partly, in the best Victorian novels, as well as the worst. Great nineteenth-century novels all have at least a few preposterous events; many contain vulgar and hateful characters; and some feature irritating or obtrusive writing styles. What makes them succeed while the novels I have discussed failed is that good novels, and even competent ones, placed preposterous events within a larger plot that combined low predictability and high postdictability, arranged characters across a spectrum of likability so as to reward readers' emotional investments, and used a writing style to further the story's interest rather than to detract from it. The result was overall cognitive and emotional reward rather than the disgust and irritation prominent in the reviews of *The Old Ledger* and *Like Dian's Kiss*.

Having looked at entertainment failures, I turn to a more familiar work, *The Old Curiosity Shop*, as a third and final example. Dickens's novel looks like a perfect work for thinking about the novel as entertainment because, as Paul Schlicke demonstrates, it is filled with people being entertained: at the Punch and Judy show, at Astley's, at the waxworks.[58] The usual path in literary criticism treats such representations as metafictional commentaries on novels, which define themselves by containing and criticizing them. I examine instead why Victorian readers perceived *The Old Curiosity Shop* as entertaining, so I focus on composition and reception.

Dickens had a hard time starting *The Old Curiosity Shop*. As scholars have often noted, it began as one sketch among others in the miscellany *Master Humphrey's Clock*, though after a few numbers Dickens almost entirely abandoned the Master Humphrey frame. Even after doing so, he still had trouble shaping his novel. It begins with the wrong plot, one not about Nell but about her brother, Fred Trent, and his scheme to steal her supposed fortune by marrying her off to the worthless Dick Swiveller. Yet Fred, who begins as the prime agent in the action, vanishes after a few chapters; in time Swiveller's morality improves; and Nell and her grandfather take over. For Dickens the third time was the charm: he failed with *Master Humphrey*, failed with Fred Trent, and succeeded with little Nell. His transformations of *The Old Curiosity Shop* offer a real-time model of the unentertaining becoming entertaining.[59]

Although in his later introduction to the novel, Dickens confessed that his pen "winces" at the memory of having had to abandon *Master Humphrey's Clock*, he seems to have missed it more than most critics, who treat it as an obviously bad idea; the same is true for the Fred Trent plot.[60] Indeed, critics sometimes seem irritated with Dickens for having tried the *Master Humphrey* framework at all; after the success of *Pickwick*, *Oliver Twist*, and *Nicholas Nickleby*, how could he think that his audience wanted short sketches? The Fred Trent plot has similarly appeared as a minor annoyance that he was bound to cut once he realized the true interest of Nell's story. Yet *The Old Curiosity Shop*'s development was not as inevitable as critics have often assumed. If one had to choose between (a) a series of short, easily digested stories with an intriguing tonal range from the macabre to the archly humorous; (b) a strong, melodramatic tale of a handsome young rake's schemes to squeeze money from his relations; or (c) a meandering narrative in which a vacuous old man and sickly sweet little girl wander around doing not much, it is not obvious that (c) would be the winner. Yet it was, and the question of why it was makes *The Old Curiosity Shop* a critical work for understanding the novel as entertainment.

Not only do (a) and (b) look more intrinsically interesting; they were especially attractive when *The Old Curiosity Shop* first appeared. In 1840–41 the novel seemed dead: Scott had died in 1832, and Edgeworth had stopped publishing; the silver-fork genre was drying up; and the new media of the day, such as popular magazines, annuals, anthologies, and gift books, wanted tales and sketches, not long novels.[61] Dickens himself published such short pieces in his *Sketches of Young Couples*, in honor of Victoria's engagement. The Fred Trent plot belongs to a situation of which nineteenth-century readers never tired, the criticism and punishment of regency-style rakes. This situation had been popular before Dickens, and it remained central to his fiction long after *The Old Curiosity Shop*. Nevertheless, puzzlingly, *Master Humphrey's Clock* and the Fred Trent plot lost out to what James Buzard aptly calls "the story-negating inertia of Nell."[62]

In terms of interest, self-relevance, and transportation the first incarnation of *The Old Curiosity Shop*, *Master Humphrey's Clock*, failed in terms of interest and relatedness. *Master Humphrey's Clock* had low predictability but also low postdictability. It includes the fantastic tales of the giants in the Guildhall, their own mini-Scott-like tale of sixteenth-century England, a letter from an obnoxious gentleman aspiring to Master Humphrey's club, the confession of a Jacobean child murderer (a piece much admired by Poe), a witchcraft story told by Mr. Pickwick, and comic sketches by Sam Weller and his father. While collections of sketches had succeeded before Dickens, they had a unifying setting and atmosphere, like the English countryside of Mary Russell Mitford's *Our Village*. Such unity linked the sketches to increase their postdictability: although each differed, they cohered retrospectively to map a region. *Master Humphrey's Clock* had no such coherence. Though individual tales may or may not have been interesting, the whole had no postdictability.

In terms of emotional connection the collection offers a good example of the trade-off between autonomy and relatedness. The short story maximizes the reader's sense of agency, since it invites not only skipping but "reading in" rather than "reading through": choosing whatever stories seemed most appealing. Yet such autonomy limits the relatedness that fosters transportation. The novel's strong suit is that committing to a long, complex narrative may persuade readers to become emotionally engaged with the characters and situations (and vice versa). Without such relatedness, readers may fail to care about them; Thomas Hood noted in the *Athenaeum* that there was no reason to like Master Humphrey and so readers did not: "We think no more of the gentle Hunchback [and his club] . . . than of as many printing-house readers and an Editor's Box."[63] The Dickens-hating *London Magazine* asked, "—Why is 'Master Humphrey's Clock' like the 'Auld Toun,' at Edinburgh?—Because he has a great many 'stories,' and all of them 'flats.' "[64]

Dickens's stories withheld conventional enhancement or improvement. Readers looking for in-group appeals on the basis of religion or politics or, more vaguely, on the basis of shared values would have found little, except for the return of the Pickwickians in *Master Humphrey's Clock*. In terms of improvement his stories offered no overt moral, so readers expecting didactic instruction would not have found any; the historical stories offer none of the detail that readers praised in Scott. Not all readers disliked *Master Humphrey's Clock*, but, against the background of previous collections, it offered few comparable satisfactions.[65] While individual stories may have been interesting, the overall structure blocked emotional connection and engagement.

Whereas the failure of *Master Humphrey's Clock* was plain in Dickens's plunging sales, the failure of the Fred Trent plot was more implicit to the novel itself.[66] Fred appears as a major character in the novel's second chapter, and he plots to marry Dick Swiveller to Nell in chapter 7. As is characteristic of Dickens, an event that has major causal consequences receives little textual space, so it is not surprising that we do not see more of Fred. After chapter 23, however, he largely disappears, but the scheme associated with him does not. In that chapter Fred turns it over to Quilp, as if to give himself permission to disappear from the book. After Fred's disappearance the plot associated with him fades as well. Swiveller, once he starts working for the Brasses, becomes a different character; Quilp abandons Nell for Kit Nubbles.

In terms of interest, if *Master Humphrey's Clock* had neither predictability nor postdictability, the Fred Trent plot was too predictable. Dickens's audience had seen similar plots, as recently as the attentions of Lord Frederick Verisopht and Sir Mulberry Hawk to Kate Nickleby (Fred even sounds like an abbreviated version of Lord Frederick). Readers could expect that Nell, after many trials and persecutions, would safely win out against Fred's nefarious schemes. This is exactly what happens in E. Stirling's dramatic adaptation of *The Old Curiosity Shop*, written before the novel was completed. Nell and her grandfather flee to Abel Cottage for refuge; just in time, Kit and Master Humphrey thwart the plans of Quilp, Fred, and Dick to abduct her.[67] Stirling's adaptation reveals what "should" have happened if Dickens had continued the Fred Trent plot, and it was old news.

By abandoning the Fred Trent plot, Dickens traded a predictable narrative for an unpredictable one. *The Old Curiosity Shop* takes character types who had appeared at the edges of previous novels (the very young, the very old, the very grotesque) and puts them front and center; it abandons the marriage plot that Jane Austen, Maria Edgeworth, Walter Scott, and even Dickens had used as the glue for long, complex narratives. To readers first coming to *The Old Curiosity Shop*, the loss of the Fred Trent plot took away their most familiar frame of reference, and they would have had little precedent for a long novel in which a very young girl either was the main character or died. Dickens liked to claim that he had received many letters from women begging him not to kill little Nell: true or not, it suggests both that readers worried that she might die and that they thought it plausible that she would live. However predictable Nell's death has seemed to academic critics, it did not seem so to Victorian readers; in retrospect, however, it is highly postdictable, given the many clues that Dickens provides to her incipient mortality.

I have noted that the scales in my model of entertainment rarely work independently, and the cognitive interest of *The Old Curiosity Shop*'s plot heightened its emotional pull. Readers willingly gave up their autonomy to follow Nell's story. She inspired emotional transportation not only because of her status as an innocent unjustly confronted with overwhelming odds but also because there was no guarantee that she would overcome them. Much fictional suspense is what Richard Gerrig terms "anomalous suspense": suspense that occurs despite readers' knowledge of the outcome.[68] The shocking difference in *The Old Curiosity Shop* was that the suspense was not anomalous. Dickens's abandonment of conventional masterplots meant that readers were in agony to discover what would happen because they had little in their previous experience to prepare them.

The online sign of their emotional transportation was anxiety: Dickens carried "the strain of the reader's anxiety to the highest pitch"; writers described the novel's readers as "all who have so anxiously followed that singularly captivating one through her brief life"; Margaret Oliphant remembered "how we defied augury, and clung to hope for her—how we refused to believe that Kit and the strange gentleman . . . could not do some miracle for her recovery."[69] If Dickens had kept the Fred Trent plot, readers would have felt much less anxiety: Fred would be punished, and Nell would be saved from a bad marriage. Moreover, Dickens preserves such a conventional plot in the imprisonment and rescue of Kit Nubbles and the punishment of Quilp and the Brasses. Yet what readers remembered was not the conventional rescue of Kit but the far less comforting story of Nell, which offered no comparably satisfying ending.

Some readers of *The Old Curiosity Shop* were furious with Dickens's Nellicide. Their anger points to the tension between autonomy and transportation at the heart of emotional relatedness. Readers provisionally give up their autonomy to read a work as long as *The Old Curiosity Shop*, and they want their transportation to be emotionally satisfying. That Dickens had not given them what they wanted seemed to upset a fundamental contract between writer and reader.

Their frustration reveals Dickens's greatest gamble: he hoped that readers would accept a new kind of self-relevance in exchange for not experiencing some of the conventional pleasures of the novel. Far from the gentle luxury of tears associated with nineteenth-century sentimentality, Victorian readers felt something far more racking in relation to Nell: her loss was not pleasurable, and many wished it had been otherwise. Nor did it offer conventional improvement. Children were supposed to die for good, morally legible reasons. Like Christ, fictional children died for the sins of others. Sarah Winter's important reading of the novel describes how thoroughly it upset the expectations of previous evangelical fiction: "The novel refuses to pursue the possibility of edification through the witnessing of [Nell's] death itself."[70] Dickens had plenty of material to make Nell's death into a social indictment, as he would later do with Jo in *Bleak House*: the Fred Trent plot sets up many possible people and motives to blame. But in abandoning Fred, Dickens also abandoned the convention whereby a child's death could immediately be coated in moral significance.

It has become a commonplace of criticism to see Nell's death as a sacrifice: as James Eli Adams notes, "The redemptive force of innocence . . . blurs into the ritual purgation offered by a scapegoat."[71] Yet this redemptive force was not evident to Victorian readers. Such a redemptive force would have tied Nell's death to a larger social or even religious message, as Winter argues. But it seemed to have none. In the most perceptive early response to *The Old Curiosity Shop*, the *Christian Remembrancer* objected to the lack of religious references because, without them, Nell's death was too barren: "To work up an elaborate picture of dying and death, without the only ingredient that can make the undisguised reality other than an 'uncouth hideous thing' . . . is not dealing fairly by us."[72] The reviewer pinpoints the originality of Dickens's treatment. With no Christian frame or sociopolitical justification, the death of little Nell was "undisguised reality," not a pile-up of clichés. This absence hit hard because Dickens omits her actual moment of death: no poignant last words absolving the guilty, no glimpse of heaven and eternal peace, no last-minute repentance from villains.

The result was almost unbearably painful, in a way that could have challenged many readers' sense of competence. For Edgar Allan Poe, while Nell's death is "of the highest order of literary excellence . . . there are few who will be willing to read the concluding passages a second time."[73] Where academic critics have seen an idealized, allegorical figure, nineteenth-century readers saw reality: "She has ceased to be a creature of the imagination, and we think of her as having really wandered about with the weary old man"; "The sad event [of her death] haunted us with the vividness of a real and present death."[74] Nell's death looked less like embarrassing sentimentality than chillingly harsh truth because of the absence of a comforting message, an impression so strong as to override the moral that Dickens does provide. Perhaps this absence drove so many readers to experience Nell's death in terms of a communal, collective response: knowing that others felt similarly filled out the eerie emptiness of the fictional experience.

What rescued *The Old Curiosity Shop* from the alienation that it might have inspired was, even beyond interest and transportation, a new kind of self-relevance: Nell's death resonated with readers as a profoundly meaningful event, a brutal confrontation with the reality of death. This confrontation had no "meaning" in a conventional sense, and the lack strengthened rather than weakened the novel's impact. A typical comment was that "her death is a tragedy of the true sort, that which softens, and yet strengthens and elevates."[75] For this writer, to pin down exactly why it both "softens" and "strengthens and elevates" would have detracted from what made Nell's death so compelling. As John Forster wrote to Dickens, "I had felt this death of dear little Nell as a kind of discipline of feeling and emotion which would do me lasting good, and which I would not thank you for as an ordinary enjoyment of literature."[76] The

Nell plot not only surpassed *Master Humphrey's Clock* and the Fred Trent plot in terms of entertainment; it also took them into new and startling directions for readers by redefining what they could expect from the "entertaining" genre of the novel.

As such, memories of little Nell combined into the gist representation of the novel. Even after the rest had fallen away, Nell's fate lingered in memories beyond what my model of entertainment might have predicted. This staying power arose from its unexpected harshness: the difficulty of assimilating its seeming unfairness gave it emotional and cognitive power that increased its memorability. In addition, once it became a cultural touchstone, readers would have had later opportunities to retrieve their memories of it, thus making it easier to access. The more that readers remembered Nell, the less they remembered much else, until one episode stood for the whole.

My purpose here, as throughout this book, has been to get beyond the "implied reader" to describe how readers interact with literature. I have used reader reactions and contemporary theories of entertainment to create a generalizable model for the most salient aspects of reading as entertainment. For psychologists, I hope that my discussion may encourage them to take more seriously entertainment as a condition of reading: the field is now so dominated by those who treat education as the goal of reading that entertainment has almost disappeared. For literary critics, I want to work against the embarrassment that has turned entertainment value into a black box, approachable only through hazy invocations of "pleasure" or "aesthetics." Rather than lists of themes, we need more discussions of why anyone would want to read a novel in the first place.

# CHAPTER 7

# ON INFLUENCE

**AS WITH ENTERTAINMENT** in the previous chapter, literary influence, understood as the way a later writer uses an earlier work or author as a model for imitation, rejection, or a range of possibilities in between, has no existing theory in psychology. I cannot point to well-established findings about it that could be adapted for literary analysis. Instead, as in my discussion of entertainment, I assemble findings from different psychological subfields that are most relevant. Whereas the previous chapter presented a model that has predictive value in assessing Victorian responses to entertainment, I avoid model building in this chapter. Instead, I focus on the specifics of a given work, Oscar Wilde's *The Picture of Dorian Gray*, and use it to unpack the different forms influence can take: I am more interested in that variety than in a single "right" model. Harold Bloom, in the most familiar model of literary influence, uses Freudian psychoanalysis to provide just enough of a framework to link specific evidence about verbal echoes to larger claims about artistic genius. Yet the success of this framework is also its weakness: it makes all influence look the same. Few attempts to criticize Bloom's theory have gotten much beyond it other than to maintain that influence can be positive as well as agonistic, a claim that inverts Bloom while bypassing the core problems raised by influence.[1]

For literary critics, empirical psychology offers not the truth about influence but a different way to describe conjectural origins.[2] A lingering belief in a myth of genius leads scholars to resist the usefulness of psychological description by insisting that the minds of great authors are unique; to describe them in terms of general processes elides the specialness that makes them worth studying in the first place. Yet as long ago as John Livingston Lowes's classic *The Road to Xanadu*, scholars have maintained that "the imagination works its wonders through the exercise, in the main, of normal and intelligible powers."[3] For Lowes the distinction between the creative mind and the "normal" one is false because it implies that there is no common ground, no overlap, between individual and general processes. Although Lowes wrote his work before most of the empirical findings I engage, his claims overlap with those that I am making because empirical results in psychology are probabilistic. They predict behavior based on group characteristics. A given author, like any individual, will share several, though not necessarily all, of these characteristics. At the same time, authors develop particular skills associated with writing and creativity, and they should use those skills better than the general population does. A description of authorial influence can begin with general processes and then lead to a conjectural history of how advanced skills of authorship and the literary-historical context modify them.

Since *influence* is an umbrella term that covers many things, it helps to make some basic distinctions regarding its scope.

1. Local to global: Local influence arises at the unit of the word or phrase: critics describe this influence when they produce verbal echoes to prove that a later writer echoes or alludes to another. Global influence arises when authors adapt entire plots or situations from earlier writers. The distinction between these two is not absolute, but local influence appears at a detailed linguistic level, global influence at the macrostructural level of event, character, or plot.

2. Specific to general: Authors may use words or phrases that have enough overlap with the language of previous writers and seem distinctive enough that the allusion appears specific. Such moments are ones that influence studies care about because they foreground the relation between artists. At other moments authors may employ conventional phrases that do not signal the influence of any particular work. Such high-frequency collocations indicate an author's general linguistic competence and genre familiarity. Similarly, authors may draw on masterplots or motifs characteristic of genre, without referring to any specific work. The distinction between specific and general does not have to be mutually exclusive: an author can be influenced by the conventions of a genre and also allude to a particular example of it.

3. Context dependent vs. context independent: When an author includes a quotation or near quotation from an earlier work, how much of the larger

context of the earlier work is relevant to the later one? Should an allusion be treated as the tip of an iceberg, a small sign of a large debt? Or should it be treated as language that has become uprooted from its original context, has lost its links in memory to the rest of the work, and is remembered by the later author chiefly as an isolated strip? No one can decide absolutely, but academic convention biases interpreters to treat a passing allusion as more than it seems. The scholarly convention has been to argue that an allusion must be a symptom of a deeper relationship. Such arguments, in striving to avoid superficiality, miss a key aspect of influence, which is that it can operate at different depths. By assuming that all relations are deep, scholars inadvertently oversimplify them. I maintain, instead, that moments of influence can vary in the depth of their relations to an earlier work.

Shared across these dimensions is the assumption that influence arises from long-term memory for written material, a topic I discussed in Chapter 3 and to which I now return. There, I explored gist representation, the generalized sense of a work that remains accessible in long-term memory after most of it has become hard to retrieve. Influence is interesting in this context because, in local influence, memory for text does not work the way it should. Readers usually do not remember for long the specific words that they have processed.[4] This lack of retention arises not from carelessness but from the limited capacity of working memory.[5] The mind is not an echo chamber for all the words in a text; instead, it is packed with gists, generalized representations based less on actual words than on the reader's transformation of them into a network of concepts.[6]

This transformation is usually a good thing. We typically do not need verbatim recall and do need a usable mental representation. Yet in the case of local, specific influence, something else happens. A later writer recalls the words (more or less) of an earlier writer and reshapes them by placing them in a new context and sometimes by revising them. Memory's power to dissolve language is suspended, and at least some version of the surface code survives.

No psychological model can predict what individual readers are most likely to remember, although a model can make some predictions about readers in general. Phrases are memorable for different reasons: they may have causal centrality; they may be surprising or unusual; or they may pack an emotional punch. Memory for phrases may also arise not from text characteristics but from a reader's: readers may attend carefully to a piece of language for reasons that they may or may not be able to describe but that make the language easier to remember later. For Victorian readers who often heard literature read out loud, for example, a particularly good performance might have made a literary phrase memorable. Especially with well-known works of literature, memorability could also arise from cultural dispersion: for Victorian readers the King James Bible would have been deep in memory not only from their own reading but also from hearing it everywhere.

But literary influence needs more than just memory; it also needs writing. Language from an earlier author appears in the work of a later author because memories, including pieces of language, are not stored in isolation but are linked with other items: the strength of the links varies constantly, as some are strengthened and others weakened. In writing, an allusion may occur when writers generate enough language strongly associated in memory with a remembered quotation that the quotation becomes accessible. If the writer chooses, it may then become part of writing, whether or not the writer is conscious of it as a quotation. According to spreading activation theory, facilitating memory for a stored trace happens automatically. The writer need not make a conscious effort to generate connections between language production and associated memory nodes.[7]

Yet activation does not guarantee that an author will use the quotation. During writing, countless quotations may be activated, but most decay rapidly in strength. A concept will enter conscious awareness only if activated repeatedly enough within a short frame of time that it surpasses a certain activation threshold and enters explicit awareness. Even then, it will not necessarily end up in writing. Writers may use remembered strips of language, modify them, or suppress them, depending on their writing goals. And even if they do use a quotation, there is no guarantee it will remain in a work, as they revise and polish.

Complicating this process is the challenge of source memory: the ability to remember where one has learned a chunk of information. Source memory varies dramatically. In some cases we can remember vividly the exact circumstances in which we learned something. Yet for much information in semantic memory, we have no reason to hold on to its source and so do not. Psychologists have explored cases in which source amnesia leads to unconscious plagiarism: participants genuinely believe that an idea is their own because their memory for its origin has vanished.[8] Literature may have a special status as a source of language because its language is understood to be special and unique. Although this status may mean that we generally have better memory for a literary source when we remember individual quotations, it is quite possible to remember quotations and have no recollection of their origin.

If we are not always certain of the source of our knowledge, how can we know how aware authors are of their influences? It would be easy to dismiss this question as misguided because it tries to determine what cannot be determined: authorial awareness. Yet such a dismissal avoids a core challenge of studying influence: it requires some positing of authorial consciousness, despite the many good reasons never to do so. Nineteenth-century authors, especially poets, were hyperaware of the possible charge of plagiarism, and their notes sometimes anticipate criticism by citing parallels between their language and that of previous authors. Yet it is often not possible to know a priori whether an allusion arises from unconscious plagiarism. In what follows, I offer some guidance in sorting out the depth of analysis appropriate to different kinds of literary influence.

To provide specifics, I turn to Oscar Wilde's *The Picture of Dorian Gray*, which, in addition to stealing heavily from earlier works, has the benefit of being all about influence. Before I address its plot, I want to focus on some moments of local influence to show their variety. For example, when Dorian goes to the theater where Sibyl Vane acts, he meets the Jewish manager, who is depicted with "greasy ringlets, and an enormous diamond blazed in the centre of a soiled shirt."[9] The phrase "greasy ringlets," sometimes followed by the mention of jewelry, was a Victorian formula for Jews: Rosina Bulwer-Lytton's *Memoirs of a Muscovite* (1844) portrayed "Mr. Solomons" as a man "with the long, black, greasy ringlets"; Bayard Taylor, writing of his travels in Russia, noted "Jews, with their greasy ringlets"; John Berwick Harwood's *Lord Ulswater* (1867) commented that a quasi-Jewish character had no "greasy ringlets" or "dubious jewellery"; James Picciotto, a reviewer of *Daniel Deronda* (1876), believed that Jews usually had "greasy ringlets" and wore "showy jewelry."[10]

The formula's prevalence in Victorian literature gives us several choices for interpreting Wilde's use of it. One could argue that it is unlikely to allude to a specific work. The more often a cue is found in different contexts, the harder it is to recover its initial context.[11] The phrase "greasy ringlets" in *Dorian Gray* looks like a formula unyoked from any particular origin to become part of a generalized set of associations around Jews, a cliché whose familiarity could be taken for granted; it could even be a case of unconscious plagiarism. Nevertheless, the fact that "greasy ringlets" is found in many Victorian works does not dispel the possibility that Wilde himself may have associated the phrase with a specific work. The phrase could be a general nod to Victorian cliché, or it could be a local one to some particular text. If so, however, nothing about that earlier work is distinctive enough to make it identifiable or to suggest that it matters more for Wilde's novel beyond its role as the phrase's source. In terms of my earlier distinctions this local allusion carries with it the larger context of Victorian literary anti-Semitism and not much more.

A more familiar mode of local allusion comes when Lord Henry muses on Dorian's life near the end of the novel: "Ah, Dorian, how happy you are! What an exquisite life you have had! You have drunk deeply of everything. You have crushed the grapes against your palate" (212). Lord Henry alludes to a specific text, the climax of Keats's "Ode on Melancholy," in which the vision of Melancholy's "Sovran shrine" comes only to "him whose strenuous tongue / Can burst Joy's grape against his palate fine."[12] At first glance this looks like a more straightforward allusion than "greasy ringlets" because, whereas "greasy ringlets" has several overlapping sources in Victorian writing, Keats's phrase is unique to his poem.

Yet this quotation, simple as it seems, raises two complex issues, one of language and one of context. Wilde substitutes *crushed* for Keats's *burst*. The switch may be part of the general phenomenon whereby readers remember not the exact words of the surface code but a gist representation. Readers mis-remember sentences in this way all the time. Since in English usage, *crushed* is associated with *grape* more frequently than Keats's *burst* is, the word substitution would be an easy one, an example of ordinary memory processes. As such, it would not be especially useful in interpreting the novel.

Yet the change could also be read as meaningful to the action at this moment. For example, the misremembering may characterize not Wilde's memory but Lord Henry's personality: Wilde may offer a slight criticism of Lord Henry by letting him substitute the commonplace *crushed* for the more piquantly explosive *burst*, as if he were too much a gentleman to quote exactly. Such an interpretation is more acceptable within the discipline of literary criticism. It makes what literary scholars are taught to value as a more interesting claim to see Wilde's misquotation as strategic than as an example of memory's usual vagaries. Yet this is a messy road: are all the novel's many slight misquotations equally strategic? If not, how do we decide which are and which are not without arbitrariness? While some scholars might object that there is nothing wrong with arbitrariness if one can produce a rhetorically convincing account, it would be hard to know in this case what would count as convincing. Wilde's seemingly obvious use of Keats resists interpretive closure.

Beyond the issue of language is that of context: how much of the larger context of Keats's poem is relevant at this moment in the novel? Just what is that context? Should we look in *Dorian Gray* for other possible signs of Keats's poem, such as references to melancholy moods, "Beauty that must die," or other Keatsian signs? Or does doing so permit a passing allusion to acquire more depth than it should? At what point does such a search become more a display of critical ingenuity than a reading of Wilde?

Beyond the text of Keats's ode, the "Keats" that Wilde recalls is not just a set of works or even the image of an author: Keats and his works had a Victorian publication history, critical response, and biographical tradition. When Wilde first read Keats, he presumably encoded some of this context, and as Wilde lived with Keats, his memory for the author and his works shifted and changed. As I have stressed, long-term memory for a literary work is not the text of the work. The lure of studying influence is that it seems to allow a direct, verifiable comparison between a source and a later text. Useful as that comparison may be, it depends on fantasies about the authorial mind as a perfect storage chamber of earlier works, a notion that has nothing to do with how works are remembered or come to have influence.

In the case of Wilde and Keats the relevant memory network for the Keats allusion may be less each word or phrase in the "Ode on Melancholy" than a generalized Victorian representation of the poem as a literary distillation of intense sensory pleasure. Whether or not Wilde memorized the whole ode, the Keats quotation may have entered his writing as a retrieval cue not for other words and phrases from the same poem but for a network of representations of decadent experience linked to Keats's poem by its late Victorian reception.[13] Lord Henry's allusion comes with a possible implied parenthesis: "You have crushed the grapes against your palate (just as all the other decadent young writers influenced by Keats say that they long to do—anyone who recognizes my almost correct quotation will know what I mean)." Allusions may be less to the earlier poem than to the way that lines from Keats have become decadent shorthand.

A different local allusion occurs in Sibyl's speech to Dorian after her disastrous performance: "My love! my love! Prince Charming! Prince of life! I have grown sick of shadows. You are more to me than all art can ever be" (87). As in the case of the Keats quotation, allusion is marked through the near repetition of a low-frequency, highly salient lexical sequence, here from Alfred Tennyson's "The Lady of Shalott."[14] Also like the Keats quotation, this allusion is a misquotation; Wilde substitutes "I have grown sick of shadows" for the Lady's "I am half-sick of shadows." Again, the interpretive questions are how to understand the misquotation and the relevance of the poem's context. Is the misquotation Wilde characterizing Sibyl, or is it memory being memory? Here, my preference is for the second, since, for the misquotation to belong to Sibyl, we would have to imagine that she knew the original. While it is plausible that Lord Henry would know Keats, it seems less likely that the impoverished and barely educated Sibyl would know Tennyson.

Yet even to make this distinction may assume a literal-minded character consistency not appropriate to the situation. One might counter that Sibyl at this moment "knows" Tennyson in spite of herself and rewrites him to produce a simplified, even trite, version of his poem, in line with her hackneyed romanticism in this scene. Or one might note that Tennyson's Victorian popularity makes Sybil's knowledge of him plausible, even though doing so assumes extra work by readers to invent a past for her. While the allusion is obvious, no appeal to psychology can make its interpretation simple.

As for the larger relevance of Tennyson's poem to the novel, the poem differs from Keats's lyric because it has a plot, like Wilde's novel, so it is possible to connect Tennyson's poem and Wilde's novel at the level of event as well as of language. In both, the moments captured by the quotation have high causal density for the narrative. The Lady, half-sick of shadows, turns from her loom to see Lancelot and subsequently dies. Sibyl, sick of shadows, has discovered true love and acts badly when Dorian visits with Lord Henry and Basil Hallward; her poor acting leads to Dorian's scorn and her suicide. Sibyl's identification with the Lady of Shalott flags later disaster for her in a way that Lord Henry's quotation of Keats does not about his or Dorian's future.

Yet Tennyson's poem, like Keats's, was also a Victorian icon. When Wilde uses the quotation, he may be referring less to the poem itself than to its Victorian status as shorthand for exquisitely doomed ladies.[15] For the knowing reader, Sibyl's quotation signals that she is not long for this novel. To academic scholars, since both works are easily accessible, it is tempting to assume that the right way to interpret the relation between them is to compare their words. Yet even as we know that works in memory bear little resemblance to works on the page, we also know that Wilde's memory is not recoverable except as critical fantasy. The Tennyson misquotation sits on the page, a loudly intertextual moment that does not easily disclose the extent of its intertextual reach—to the rest of Tennyson's poem, to the rest of Tennyson, or to the Victorian "Lady of Shalott" cult.

Although I have focused on Wilde's memory, interpreting influence requires readers' memories as well. Allusions imply readers who recognize and interpret the allusion. While I am comfortable with the "implied reader" as a literary critical construct, I have seen no psychological evidence that actual readers envision an implied reader as they read or use an implied reader to gauge their own performance. Literary scholars may at times strive to occupy a position as close as possible to their understanding of the implied reader, as Stanley Fish tries to do in the passage I discussed in Chapter 2. Yet understanding influence in terms of implied and actual readers may miss the point. Even if we envision the most perfectly informed readers, just how relevant their knowledge may be at any given moment is hardly clear. If we look to actual readers, their standards of coherence may be satisfied by recognizing an allusion as an allusion—and that is all. For others, even if they do recognize an allusion, associations that they may have formed with an earlier work may or may not be helpful in understanding. One reader's autobiographical experience with the "Ode on Melancholy," for example, may illuminate Lord Henry's remark, while another's may make his comment seem wrong or out of place; another may miss the allusion entirely.

Local allusions risk an explicit appeal to a reader's background knowledge because they assume a common ground. For an allusion to count, a reader has to recognize it, although readers may also detect quasi allusions, language that sounds like a possible allusion even if they cannot quite remember it. For readers who do recognize an allusion, the later work may become associated in memory with the earlier work. Those who recognize Sibyl's quotation from "The Lady of Shalott," for example, will have strengthened a memory association between Tennyson and Wilde so that whenever such readers return to Tennyson's poem, some aspect of Wilde's novel potentially becomes more accessible, whether or not it is actually retrieved. While an allusion's meaning remains uncertain in terms of influence, it shapes connections in long-term memory.

On the whole, local allusions disturb the forward progress of a work. As I have suggested, works often cue readers to retrieve relevant background knowledge, but readers often do so automatically and with little effort. Allusions, however, bring this automatic process to consciousness, at least for readers who recognize them. Because of the structure of memory, recollection is not pure: one passage potentially coactivates many other memories, at varying degrees of explicit awareness. What the reader does with these memories will vary radically, depending on goals, skills, and interest. Local allusions invite readers to infer connections between past and present, and readers may or may not accept.

I now turn to global allusion, in which large-scale gestures of plot, characterization, and theme in an earlier work shape a later one. At its most general, global influence marks the conventions of a genre rather than the effect of any particular work; such influence is the large-scale analogy of the formulaic "greasy ringlets" discussed earlier. My example here will instead be on the influence not of genre but of a particular work, Mary Ward's *Robert Elsmere* (1888), on Wilde's novel.

In terms of a memory, for a work to have global influence on a later author, it must leave behind a deep and integrated situation model for the reader-author that includes (accurately or not) crucial information about plot, characters, and overarching issues. Yet the earlier work cannot just be an inert memory: a later author reconstructs it as a model to achieve goals. Writers actively reconstruct the earlier work as they remember it. Once again, the conventional literary procedure of comparing two texts produces an illusion of rigor that masks what is most interesting about influence: the effect of works as they live in memory. A memory representation of a work stems not solely from words. It may also include an entire contextual apparatus: knowledge of a previous author's life and times, knowledge of other works by the same author, readers' autobiographical associations, and other background knowledge. Since all possible influences on a work end up being so multiple as to be unanalyzable, a useful account of global influence must choose the most salient ones.

What leads a later writer to be influenced by an earlier one? Harold Bloom's answer is straightforward: no writers are born knowing how to write, so all are formed by the influence of others. The greatest writers are influenced by their greatest precursors.[16] While that may be true, in a given writing situation writers have backgrounds, goals, and audiences that may make some works more attractive than others as possible models, either for imitation or for critical revision. About such choices, the psychology of memory has little to say. The psychology of writing, however, offers some insight.

In his work on psychology and writing, Ronald T. Kellogg usefully divides writing into stages: collecting, planning, translating, and revising. Collecting involves reading relevant background material; planning, generating and organizing ideas in relation to goals; translating, turning a set of private mental representations into a language bound by rules of semantics and syntax; and revising, creating local or global changes.[17] At each stage, successful writing involves constraint satisfaction. Of all the infinite options that a writer could take, skilled writers select those that, as they collect, plan, translate, and revise, best help them meet goals. Less-skilled writers are those who, given a goal, have more difficulty knowing what constraints that goal puts on them.

Constraints may serve as a memory probe for a writer to activate other pieces of writing, by themselves or others, that have been written successfully under similar constraints. More simply, a writer of comedy may remember other comedies while writing, a writer of thrillers other thrillers. The more accessible such traces are, the more likely they are to be retrieved. The interesting part involves what happens next, after writers have retrieved relevant earlier works. They can ignore, copy, or revise them. Ignoring them is unlikely because they are too salient as models for handling the situation, although writers may choose among several competing options. Pure imitation is also unlikely. Instead, as I have argued, long-term memory retains a gist representation that already reshapes an earlier work. In drawing on such a representation in planning, an author will further reshape it in accordance with his or her goals.

To return to the example of Wilde, although we cannot reconstruct his memory, we can reconstruct some of his goals in writing *Dorian Gray* and examine how those might have shaped his memory of an earlier novel. Mary Ward's *Robert Elsmere* had set the agenda for novels of the period. It was a late-Victorian phenomenon: its treatment of religious crisis and the hope for a humanistic spirituality created an intellectual furor. No other novel of the late 1880s matched its engagement of what were thought to be the most critical aspects of modern spirituality. As James Eli Adams notes, "For Elsmere, as for Carlyle, fervent belief becomes compatible with an entire absence of theology. The enormous popularity of the book suggests that many novel readers still hungered for such consolation."[18] Wilde was impressed enough by its success to sneer at it in "The Decay of Lying" (1889): Vivian calls it a "masterpiece of the *genre ennuyeux*, the one form of literature that the English people seems thoroughly to enjoy." Cyril, agreeing, cannot look on it as a "serious work" because its treatment of Christianity is ridiculous, yet he finds aspects of it to admire: "It contains several clever caricatures, and a heap of delightful quotations, and Green's philosophy very pleasantly sugars the somewhat bitter pill of the author's fiction."[19]

Wilde wrote these criticisms of Ward when he was editing *Woman's World* magazine and making a name for himself as a reviewer. By 1890, however, when he composed the first version of *Dorian Gray*, his situation had changed. Having abandoned *Woman's World* in October 1889 and needing new funds, he jumped when J. M. Stoddart, editor of the American magazine *Lippincott's*, offered him two hundred pounds for a short work to occupy an entire issue of the magazine.[20] Wilde suddenly found himself writing fiction for exactly the audience that Ward had conquered. When he wrote "The Decay of Lying," her work had little power for him: his comments were only a moment in a dismissive overview of contemporary writers. When he turned to *Dorian Gray*, however, his relation to *Robert Elsmere* changed because it was now a premier example of successful contemporary fiction. He wrote *Dorian Gray* for an audience primed by expectations Ward had created. Consequently, *Robert Elsmere* became a salient model for writing serious popular fiction of the kind requested by *Lippincott's*.

At the broad level of gist Ward's novel helped Wilde because he adapted her basic causal structure, as well as the roles of her main characters. Like *Robert Elsmere*, *Dorian Gray* addresses pressing spiritual and philosophical concerns through the plot vehicle of a younger man's seduction by an older one. Wilde also took over the schematic opposition of the two men: the younger is handsome, charismatic, naive, and open to experience; the older is cynical, manipulative, skeptical, and eager to dominate a younger man. Ward's Squire Wendover, a skeptical scholar, easily undermines the faith of Robert, a young clergyman, who gives up his living and marital happiness. In Wilde, Lord Henry's wit and cynicism open Dorian's eyes to the value of his youth and induce him to live the life of sensation that his portrait registers through its disintegration.

At the level of motif the key term in both novels is *influence*, one of Ward's favorite words. Robert notes of Wendover, "He found me in a susceptible state, and I recognize that his influence immensely accelerated a process already begun." Later, he tells his wife, "Being where I was before our intimacy began, his influence hastened everything."[21] When Wilde uses *influence* in *Dorian Gray*, he revises not particular moments in *Robert Elsmere* but a general image that Ward's book supplies for the evil of homosocial relationships. Basil admits Dorian's vitalizing influence on his art and warns Lord Henry against influencing Dorian; Lord Henry ignores him and tells Dorian, "There is no such thing as a good influence, Mr. Gray. All influence is immoral—immoral from the scientific point of view" (21). Although Lord Henry discusses influence in the abstract, the form of influence that he wields resembles that found in *Robert Elsmere*: the de-idealizing effect of a worldly-wise older man on a susceptible younger one.

Although Wilde sneered at Ward's treatment of Christianity by claiming that she had stolen it from the educator, political theorist, and idealist T. H. Green,

*Dorian Gray* emulates her novel as a vehicle for musings on modern spirituality. Wilde's disquisitions are often seen as indebted to Walter Pater, but their inclusion in his novel owes less to Pater than to Ward's precedent. Different as Dorian and Robert are, they have the same mission: to reimagine religion in a modern world. While it would oversimplify Wilde to treat the content of his philosophy as a revision of Ward's, that he includes Dorian's meditations at all stems largely from the appeal of the authority that Ward gained for the novel.

An added twist to Ward's influence was that *Robert Elsmere* earned its popularity in part by attacking Wilde. According to it, late Victorian novels should be long, serious, realistic works preoccupied with social, religious, and intellectual issues. As such, it reproached writers of sensation fiction, like Wilkie Collins and Mary Elizabeth Braddon, and of male adventure stories, including Robert Louis Stevenson and Rider Haggard. It also reproached Wilde, as Wilde himself noted. Cyril's remarks about *Robert Elsmere* in "The Decay of Lying" were originally more extensive than those quoted above: "It contains a few very clever sketches, one delightfully ill-natured caricature, and some admirable quotations. After all the pillory has always been a great source of amusement to the bystanders, and now that it has been removed from Cheapside into Paternoster Row, and that Jack Scribbler has taken the place of Jack Ketch as the showman, I see quite a future for the observant and industrious novelist."[22] The "delightfully ill-natured caricature" in *Robert Elsmere* is Ward's Mr. Wood, a pretentious poet encountered in the novel's descriptions of the London social scene. Edward Langham, an embittered Oxford don, views him at a salon:

> Close to him, he [Langham] found, was the poet of the party, got up in the most correct professional costume—long hair, velvet coat, eye-glass and all. His extravagance, however, was of the most conventional type. Only his vanity had a touch of the sublime. Langham, who possessed a sort of fine-ear gift for catching conversation, heard him saying to an open-eyed *ingenue* beside him,—"Oh, my literary baggage is small as yet. I have only done, perhaps, three things that will live." "Oh, Mr. Wood!" said the maiden, mildly protesting against so much modesty. He smiled, thrusting his hand into the breast of the velvet coat. "But then," he said in a tone of the purest candor, "at my age I don't think Shelley had done more!" (395–96)

Wilde is unflatteringly disguised by Wood, and the costume, the self-assurance, and the adoring female fan were all signals of a Wildean parody. The substitution of *wood* for *wild(e)* knocks Wilde down from rebel to poseur (though by "Wood," Ward also brings "Wilde" a little closer to "Ward"). Most cuttingly, Ward mocks Wilde's own genre in her comment that "only his vanity had a touch of the sublime," a pseudo-Wildean epigram. Wilde's cutting evaluation of *Robert Elsmere* retaliated against Ward for her own attacks, perhaps intermixed with some flattered recognition that she had acknowledged him at all.

In terms of memory, Wilde's challenge in using *Robert Elsmere* involved integrating two different, even antithetical, constructs: his understanding of the most successful aspects of Ward's novel with his own writing persona. While psychology might predict that such an integration would occur, actually describing it calls for more historical detail than psychology allows itself. A more complete understanding of the constraints on influence requires locating the author in a sociology of literary production of the kind created by Pierre Bourdieu:

> The social microcosm that I call the literary field is a space of objective rela-
> tionships among positions—that of the consecrated artist and that of the *artiste
> maudit*, for example—and one can only understand what happens there if one
> locates each agent or each institution in its relationships with all the others. It is
> this peculiar universe, this "Republic of Letters," with its relations of power and
> its struggles for the preservation or the transformation of the established order,
> that is the basis for the strategies of producers, for the form of art they defend,
> for the alliances they form, for the schools they found, in short, for their specific
> interests.[23]

In the case of *Dorian Gray* Bourdieu's model highlights the fact that Wilde's venue, the American *Lippincott's*, had less prestige than Ward's, the London publishing house of Smith, Elder. Although later criticism might contrast Wilde as elite male aesthete and Ward as a hack, Wilde makes his bid for prestige from a site of comparative disadvantage. Bourdieu helps establish Wilde's process in writing as situated cognition, in which mental activities occur not in a vacuum but in a network of power relations.

The most immediate effect of the difference between Ward and Wilde's publication settings was that Wilde had much less space for his novel than Ward. She wrote a triple-decker; he was commissioned for just one issue of a magazine. He substitutes a peculiarly foreshortened time frame for her leisurely plot, provides only a few characters instead of her vast cast, and uses rapid transformations in place of her gradual metamorphoses of character. This formal shrinkage becomes a thematic aspect of the novel in its flexible treatment of time. Events that take place over the course of many years are collapsed into the notorious chapter 11, while other events take place in a few months, separated by an eighteen-year gap. Even at the level of individual characters, long events are experienced as having lasted only a few seconds, while short events take an eternity, as in Dorian's experience of Sibyl's bad acting.

At a broader level Wilde responds to Ward's precedent by integrating two other elements from his memory into what he takes from her: (1) a version of his own aesthetic philosophy and (2) generic plot elements from contemporary sensation fiction. He reaches both above and below Ward in constructing *Dorian Gray*. He reaches above by foregrounding a far more sophisticated contemporary philosophy than her "religion of humanity"; his philosophy arises from a deeper education in aesthetic, philosophical, and political history and represents a more comprehensive knowledge of major intellectual trends. It is also easily accessible to him as a writer because he has already formulated it in his earlier writing, so the writing situation itself produces cues to memory.

At the same time, Wilde reaches below Ward in deriving elements of his plot not from the serious realistic novel but from the sensation literature that her novel rejected. Next to the staid *Robert Elsmere*, Wilde's novel teems with sordid incidents: Sibyl's suicide, scandals surrounding Dorian, and Basil's murder. Such elements are the macrostructural parallels to the "greasy ringlets" that I described earlier: motifs from earlier literature that influence later literature but that are too generic to be narrowed down to a single source. Kerry Powell's essay "Tom, Dick, and Dorian Gray: Magic Picture Mania in Late-Victorian Fiction" catalogues the obscure Victorian works before *Dorian Gray* using the motif of the magic picture.[24] Such stories, along with the general motifs of sensation fiction, form a collective category of popular fiction that Wilde accesses in planning his novel: he borrows motifs from it without being indebted to any single work.

Yet the strength of a Bourdieuian analysis is also a weakness because it locates Wilde's every artistic decision in the all-encompassing need to situate himself in a field of cultural production. Each choice looks predetermined in ways that leave little room for unpredictability: moments in which Wilde may have mistaken his audience, taken unexpected risks, been uncertain of his relations in the cultural field, written largely for himself, or written against what Bourdieu calls "specific interests." Neither the psychology of memory and writing nor the sociology of culture quite explains the most striking aspect of Wilde's revision of *Robert Elsmere*. Put flatly, *Dorian Gray* reads as an outing of *Robert Elsmere*. It eroticizes the obsessive homosocial influence in Ward's novel by jettisoning the novel's heteroerotic components and foregrounds expressions of desire between men. Wilde plays up the eros of pedagogy at which Ward only hints, and he transforms passages in Ward's novel about the hero's tormented secrecy into a metaphor for the homosexual double life. In Ward this secrecy is Robert's hesitation to confess his newfound unbelief to his wife; eventually, he does confess it, and their marriage changes irrevocably. Wilde adapts the motif of the secret but not the confession: Dorian's portrait, a far more dangerous secret than Robert's, leads him, when he does reveal it, to murder Basil.

Critics have usually assumed that because Wilde was gay, his novel must be as well. Yet the more one knows about the novel's origins, the stranger Wilde's choices appear. He could have met all the constraints of his writing situation, in ways consistent with his earlier career, without such homoerotic foregrounding. He could have stayed with envisioning different relations between religion and belief, exchanging Ward's exhaustive realism for his bejeweled epigrams, and moving from her laborious time frame to his flexible one. J.-K. Huysmans's *À rebours* even provided Wilde with a model for such a work. He might have balanced both indebtedness to and reaction against Ward in a less homoerotic revision of *Robert Elsmere*, which could have played well with his late Victorian audience.

The most useful findings from psychology for understanding this aspect of Wilde's work arise from what social psychologists call "reactance": "Whenever free choice is limited or threatened, the need to retain our freedoms makes us want them . . . significantly more than before."[25] It has been a major concern in social psychology because it hampers programs intended to encourage healthy or socially beneficial behavior. It arises if individuals believe that they should control an outcome and if their threatened freedom is important or attractive. Reactance grows in proportion to the number of threatened freedoms, and implied threats of limitation may be as important as real limitations in creating it.[26]

Research on reactance has explored situations in which persuasive messages backfire; for example, smokers exposed to graphic antismoking messages end up more likely to resist such messages than those exposed just to textual messages.[27] What in ordinary language might be called stubbornness and, in an older vocabulary, pride, arises for psychologists in relation to a concern I discussed in the previous chapter: the desirability of perceived autonomy.

The desire to preserve it in the face of perceived threat overrides rational cost-benefit analysis.

To integrate the category of reactance into influence study, I argue that influence can generate a strange kind of reactance. In psychology "reactance" belongs within the study of persuasion: a persuasive argument may or may not generate reactance in participants, and psychologists study how and why it occurs. To extend reactance to influence, we have to imagine persuasion operating not at the level of a particular argument but at the level of a literary work. For influence to occur, later authors persuade themselves that an earlier work offers the best model for meeting their writing goals. The earlier work is not in itself the source of persuasion, in the sense of putting forth discrete arguments; its persuasive power exists only through the later author's response.

In this extended understanding of reactance a work that a later author uses as a model might also give rise to a backfire effect, so that the earlier work's helpfulness becomes a source of perceived restriction, even more frustrating to an author for being self-imposed. The more developed an author's relationship to an earlier work, the greater an investment he or she may have in reacting against it. Literary critics have had trouble imagining why authors would critically revise earlier works outside of Bloom's oedipal scenario of the struggle for originality. The desires to assert originality and to react against previous writers may co-occur, but the second does not need the first. Whereas Bloom sees an agonistic relation to earlier works as arising from the impossible obligations of originality, even an author not especially striving for originality may feel that using another work as a model, necessary though it may be, confines creative autonomy.

An author may react less against the earlier work itself than against the literary system that led it to succeed. In the case of Wilde and Ward, Wilde's reactance against Ward is inseparable from his reaction against the market that privileged her work over his. Since her novel insulted him as loudly as it could without mentioning him by name, it is not surprising that *Dorian Gray* adapts *Robert Elsmere* as it takes revenge on it. For example, these two passages both describe influence in terms of the pleasure that an older man takes in enlightening a younger man, an enlightenment that comes near to a corruption:

> Elsmere had his will with all the rest of the world, Mr. Wendover knew perfectly well who it was that at the present moment had his will with Elsmere. He had found a great piquancy in this shaping of a mind more intellectually eager and pliant than any he had yet come across among younger men; perpetual food too,

for his sense of irony, in the intellectual contradictions, wherein Elsmere's developing ideas and information were now, according to the squire, involving him at every turn. "His religious foundations are gone already, if he did but know it," Mr. Wendover grimly remarked to himself one day about this time, "but he will take so long finding it out that the results are not worth speculating on." (310)

To a large extent the lad was his [Lord Henry's] own creation. He had made him premature. That was something. Ordinary people waited till life disclosed to them its secrets, but to the few, to the elect, the mysteries of life were revealed before the veil was drawn away. . . . The pulse and passion of youth were in him, but he was becoming self-conscious. It was delightful to watch him. With his beautiful face, and his beautiful soul, he was a thing to wonder at. It was no matter how it all ended, or was destined to end. He was like one of those gracious figures in a pageant or a play, whose joys seem to be remote from one, but whose sorrows stir one's sense of beauty, and whose wounds are like red roses. (61)

In both passages older men revel in the pedagogical pleasure of demolishing the moral foundations of their students; even better, they get to enjoy from afar their pupils' consequent spiritual wrecks. Wendover gloats about the victory of his intellectual skepticism over Elsmere's naive faith; Lord Henry licks his lips as he watches Dorian become self-conscious. In both cases they luxuriate in knowing other men better than they know themselves, as they stand serenely on dry land while their pupils battle the flood.

When literary scholars juxtapose such passages, they point out verbal parallels, so that one work looks like a distinct source for the other. As I have been arguing, such a method is wrong for the influence I describe. The passage from Ward has a misleading aura of specificity as a source. To use Kintsch's terms, I am arguing that Ward influences Wilde at the level not of the surface code but of the situation model. The quotation from *Robert Elsmere* is an inadequate substitute for what cannot be represented: Wilde's long-term memory for Ward's novel. The *Robert Elsmere* that mattered for Wilde as he wrote *Dorian Gray* was a gist representation, not recoverable except indirectly through his own comments about it and through his use of it in *Dorian Gray*. The most prominent result of this reactance is that Wilde dramatically heats up the homoeroticism implicit but unstated in Ward's text. Wendover's condescending knowingness about Elsmere's naiveté becomes Lord Henry's aesthetic detachment: "It was delightful to watch him."

Until now, when I have described influence, I have assumed that it occurs between two different writers. This misses the fact that, in memory, writers' most easily accessed memories are not of other writers' works but of their own. Writers are more likely to be influenced by their own earlier work than by that of any other writer. Educational psychologists have described the "generation effect," in which learners remember material that they have generated on their own better than material that has been handed to them.[28] The influence of writers' earlier work on their later work is a particularly pointed case of it, since such material should be primary in writers' background knowledge.

The interesting question involves just how writers use their earlier work's accessibility. Some may choose largely to repeat: what worked before may work again. They may echo old gestures even if the circumstances of writing have changed to make them outdated. Other writers, in contrast, may experience a version of reactance against their earlier writing: what was once a product of inspiration can be felt, in retrospect, as constraint. Such reactance, I argue, occurs in *The Picture of Dorian Gray* as Wilde reacts against an earlier version of his authorial persona, whom I will call "Wilde." Wilde rewrites *Robert Elsmere* to make it more consistent with his earlier persona, but he simultaneously writes against that persona because he is taking up a new genre, the short novel, that asks for different conventions. "Wilde," who initially seems the most effective means of countering Ward's influence, is ultimately another influence to be countered. Even as Wilde rewrites *Robert Elsmere* to make it look like a novel by "Wilde," *Dorian Gray* departs from that earlier persona, as if it had become a more serious threat even than Ward.

Evidence for the reaction of Wilde against "Wilde" appears in Lord Henry's collapse. Lord Henry begins as the mouthpiece of Wildean wit but loses authority until he looks like an afterthought. In making Dorian premature, he makes himself superannuated:

> "I have sorrows, Dorian, of my own, that even you know nothing of. . . . Ah, Dorian, how happy you are! What an exquisite life you have had! . . . Nothing has been hidden from you. And it has all been to you no more than the sound of music. It has not marred you. You are still the same."
>
> "I am not the same, Harry." (212–13)

Lord Henry transforms Dorian into Pater's La Gioconda, to whom all history has been "but as the sound of lyres and flutes."[29] Dorian's curt "I am not the same" undermines Lord Henry's fantasy, though Dorian is characteristically too self-obsessed to care. The reader knows what Lord Henry does not, that Dorian conceals a secret life that would appear extreme even to Lord Henry. By this late point, Lord Henry's wit competes with the novel's plot, with the result that he appears less all-knowing than he did earlier.

Wilde surpasses Ward in everything, including self-criticism. The result is the novel's most pointed rejection of both Ward and "Wilde": its well-calibrated undecidability. Ward and "Wilde" were both easy reads: Ward, the didactic late Victorian author investigating faith and doubt; "Wilde," the witty aesthete. The Wilde of *The Picture of Dorian Gray* is anything but an easy read. The magic picture that registers Dorian's decay is at once a severe moral condemnation and one point of view among others: its magic does not make it right. Dorian's death might be proof of the wages of sin, but the novel avoids making any such condemnation explicit. Lord Henry is both a witty stand-in for Wilde and a bit of a fool, ignorant of the Dorian he professes to admire. When contemporary critics attacked the novel for its supposed celebration of homoeroticism and perverse morality, they took a part for the whole, catching Wilde's rebelliousness and missing his irony.

While *Dorian Gray* owes much to Wilde's generalized gist representation of both *Robert Elsmere* and his own earlier work, neither is a singular source in the way that Keats and Tennyson are. There are almost too many sources for *Dorian Gray*, as I noted earlier. The likelihood of any single work being easily detectible by a reader at the level of global influence is less than for the local influence I discussed earlier. In those cases a near-quotation signaled the presence of earlier work, inviting the reader to retrieve relevant background knowledge, whether or not the reader actually did so. Wilde, in contrast, does not cue *Robert Elsmere*'s relevance as he does for Keats and Tennyson. While he may have assumed familiarity with *Robert Elsmere* as part of the common ground he shares with his audience, he does not insist on it for the reader to comprehend his novel. The novel may project an ideal reader who knows Ward's work, but it also allows for a merely very good reader who, with no knowledge of Ward, can understand it anyway. In contrast, it does seem to assume a reader with some knowledge of Wilde's earlier career, presumably because *Lippincott's* was counting on such familiarity.

Influence becomes for me a particularly valuable test case for the interdisciplinarity that I have attempted in this book, in which neither psychology nor literary studies has to emerge as winner. For literary scholars there may always be the temptation to believe that, in the long run, important insights will come from literary studies, no matter how much one invokes psychology; psychologists may find the opposite. But my goal has been to argue that such decisions cannot be made in advance: one cannot set out to use psychology to save literary studies or vice versa. One can, however, take seriously a shared interest in reading in both disciplines as a little-acknowledged starting point for a shared project of trying to understand just why literature matters.

# ON METHODOLOGY

**LITERARY SCHOLARS** have always known that reading is complex, but they have located that complexity at the level of interpretation, not at the level of reading, both in the moment and as it lives in memory. Although a firm line between interpretation and reading does not exist, this book provides a framework for understanding aspects of reading that usually have been invisible. In so doing, I want to encourage scholars to think more deeply about their own reading processes, as well as those of their colleagues, students, and historical readers. Rather than providing more close readings of literary works, I have explored reading as a process.

An implicit thread in this book has been the challenge of working between disciplines—in my case, between literary criticism and cognitive psychology. Cognitive psychology has been interesting to me both in itself and as a tool for professional defamiliarization. Most of all, it has helped me recognize methodological assumptions that I did not know I had. To clarify some of these, I turn to a moment in a classic essay, Roman Jakobson's "Linguistics and Poetics." Jakobson argues for the mutual relevance of linguistics and poetics, an argument that I continued in my previous book, *Romanticism and the Rise of English*. Here, I am interested in Jakobson's model of the communication chain:

CONTEXT

ADDRESSER         MESSAGE         ADDRESSEE

CONTACT

CODE[1]

The six nodes in this diagram correspond to basic sites of literary production and reception. For a literary work the addresser is the author; the message, the work; the addressee, the audience; the context, the situations in which the work is written and received; the contact, the medium of communication; and the code, the language of the work. Others have developed more complete versions of this chain, but I prefer the simplicity of Jakobson's.

Within literary scholarship each node in this image has received exhaustive attention. For authors, we have magisterial biographies; for message, edited editions; for context, historicist work about setting; for contact, scholarship in book history and media studies; for code, histories of language; and for the addressee, accounts of audiences, literacy, and education. Yet if the nodes have been well researched, the links among them have not. In Jakobson the diagram displays a network of potential relationships among two or more nodes: it is a small web, not a set of distinct items. Each potential link brings with it a host of questions about how the two nodes need to be defined to allow a connection between them.

When scholars address relations between nodes, they often do so at the level of theory or in broad overviews of critical trends rather than in practical criticism or close reading. Practical criticism, in contrast, typically combines outstanding scholarship about individual nodes with ad hoc fuzziness about relations between them. For example, numerous author biographies are impressive monuments to archival effort. Yet deep discussions of the relation between biography and text remain surprisingly thin. New Critics argued influentially against the relevance of biography for analysis, and Foucault and Barthes both wrote major essays contesting the traditional status of the author.[2] These essays are widely assigned in theory courses and widely ignored in practical criticism. Instead, biographical facts in practical criticism surface almost at random, as if they are relevant at some times and not at others. The logic by which some facts count as evidence and others do not never materializes. Even more, basic questions about agency, the literary conventions for what counts as "life," and the assumptions behind positing individual life as the source for literary writing remain unanswered.

Similarly, the advent of historicism over the past thirty years has encouraged contextual readings of literary works, yet many are plagued by an underdeveloped analysis of just what the interrelation between context and literariness should be. Mary Poovey describes this impoverishment in terms of the need for a theory of mediation, with reference to a conference that she attended:

Mediation appears as an *issue* in cultural analysis when a scholar wants to place literary or visual texts in relation to other factors, forces, or influences that somehow exist as history—that is, outside of the texts in question. It appears as a *problem* when it goes unnoticed and unremarked. Thus, too many of the papers I heard at the conference began with a narrative that reconstructed some historical events, debates, or developments . . . [and] then moved on to an interpretation . . . that was informed . . . by what the scholar had learned about the historical matter. The problem with this model is that such easy segues from context to text leave too many important questions unanswered.[3]

Poovey identifies with historicism the same challenges that I have described in biography. Despite the aptness of her analysis, few scholars have risen to her challenge; her essay, published in 2006, has barely been acknowledged, much less answered. The right response is not to abandon contextual readings as a dead end. Rather, the point is about methodology. If one wants to do contextual readings, basic questions about mediation should matter more than they now do.

As I noted, *Romanticism and the Rise of English* addressed one of the links in Jakobson's chart, that of code to message, to argue that the disciplinary practice of close reading took for granted not only the agency of the author but also the history of the language at a given moment. *The Gist of Reading*, in contrast, looks at a different link, that of message to addressee, to move beyond either reader response (the critic fantasizes about the reader's reactions) or archival evidence (the critic uncovers the historical responses of an individual reader). Psychology has been my tool for decoupling reading and interpretation, a linkage so common in literary criticism that the claim "there is no reading without interpretation" has become a truism, though it rests on a host of unexamined assumptions about both.

I am suspicious of the category of "cognitive literary studies" because cognitive psychology remains agnostic about hermeneutics: it describes what readers do in general but makes no claims about meaning. At the same time, I do believe that many psychological findings other than the ones discussed in this book can be helpful or at least provocative to literary critics. For example, media studies has stressed the physical medium in which readers encounter works: such scholarship has countered the earlier treatment of works as if they existed in a vacuum. Yet are readers necessarily as sensitive to medium as scholars want them to be? At least in the lab, comprehension processes of readers when faced with written, oral, and visual versions of a story are quite similar: participants demonstrate general comprehension skills apart from the particularities of medium and even of language.[4] Reading a novel in a codex versus reading it on a digital device may be different but not as distinct as scholars in media studies claim.

Yet I care less that literary scholars turn to psychology than that they turn back to literary criticism, to pervasive, unasked questions about method. In their desire to keep abreast of changing events and prove their relevance, scholars face strong pressure to engage current issues, such as the environment, diversity, the effects of war and globalization, or the dominance of virtual reality. These topics are indeed interesting and important. Yet I worry that the increasing preoccupation with them among literary scholars indicates as much embarrassment with the status of the literary as it does engagement with nonliterary issues.

For literary scholarship to make innovative contributions, it must first take seriously its own methodological provocations. The web of links outlined by Jakobson offers a rich source for investigation, which will not occur in disciplines other than those devoted to literary study. Rather than deserting our object of study in the name of relevance, the most serious contribution we can make to debates about the future of the humanities will arise from making the literary event even more central than it has been. What we bring to the table in interdisciplinary conversations is disciplinary expertise: if we desert it, we lose the reason anyone would want to hear what we have to say in the first place.

Literary scholars have avoided questions like the ones that Poovey raises because, as I noted in my introduction, criticism focuses on the particular rather than the general. If an analysis of the individual work is interesting enough, then the analysis of its relationship to other nodes in Jakobson's chart can, evidently, be taken for granted. Focusing too much on such relations may seem to threaten the primacy of the message, the literary work. Yet disciplinary practice has become so ingrained that many assumptions about those relations are not even perceptible as such.

*Critical thinking* has become widespread as a term for what literary study is supposed to teach. But as John Guillory has noted, using it to defend humanistic study runs into trouble because doing so implies, wrongly, that other modes of inquiry like the sciences do not also promote critical thinking.[5] It has nevertheless become a general term for "humanities speak," an all-purpose discourse that enables scholars to talk across disciplinary borders at the cost of the insights most specific to their discipline. Yet critical thinking by literary scholars will be most valuable if it arises first from attention to literature; such thinking will, in the long run, provide the most trenchant contributions to interdisciplinary debates. I am arguing for attention to methodology as an alternative either to endless close readings or to abandoning literary analysis. Long-held disciplinary habits work hard against such attention, but that means only that it is time to develop new ones.

# NOTES

## Introduction: Interdisciplinarity

1. Ellen Messer-Davidow, *Disciplining Feminism: From Social Activism to Academic Discourse* (Durham, NC: Duke University Press, 2002), 20.

2. Keith E. Stanovich, *How to Think Straight About Psychology*, 8th ed. (Boston: Allyn and Bacon, 2007), 152–53; Stanovich's entire discussion of probabilistic claims (152–63) is valuable.

3. Danielle S. McNamara and Joseph P. Magliano, "Toward a Comprehensive Model of Comprehension," in *The Psychology of Learning and Motivation*, vol. 51, ed. Brian Ross (San Diego: Academic Press, 2009), 297–384, 305.

4. Richard J. Gerrig, "Suspense in the Absence of Uncertainty," *Journal of Memory and Language* 28, no. 6 (1989): 633–48.

5. My thinking on this topic has been helped by Elaine Auyoung, "What We Mean by Reading," work in progress.

6. See David W. Martin, *Doing Psychology Experiments*, 6th ed. (Belmont, CA: Thomson/Wadsworth, 2004), 26–42.

7. Jerome L. Myers, Edward J. O'Brien, Jason E. Albrecht, and Robert A. Mason, "Maintaining Global Coherence During Reading," *Journal of Experimental Psychology: Learning, Memory, and Cognition* 20, no. 4 (1994): 876–86; Jerome L. Myers and Edward J. O'Brien, "Accessing the Discourse Representation During Reading," *Discourse Processes* 26, no. 2–3 (1998): 131–47; Edward J. O'Brien, Anne E. Cook, and Kelly A. Peracchi, "Updating Situation Models: Reply to Zwaan and Madden (2004)," *Journal of Experimental Psychology: Learning, Memory, and Cognition* 30, no. 1 (2004): 289–91; Edward J. O'Brien, Anne E. Cook, and Sabine Guéraud, "Accessibility of Outdated Information," *Journal of Experimental Psychology: Learning, Memory, and Cognition* 36, no. 4 (2010): 979–91; Panayiota Kendeou, Emily R. Smith, and Edward J. O'Brien, "Updating

During Reading Comprehension: Why Causality Matters," *Journal of Experimental Psychology: Learning, Memory, and Cognition* 39, no. 3 (2013): 854–65.

8. See William F. Battig, "Parsimony in Psychology," *Psychological Reports* 11, no. 2 (1962): 555–72.

9. Zac Rowlinson, "Conference Report: Science and Literary Criticism," *Excursions* 4, no. 1 (2013): www.excursions-journal.org.uk/index.php?journal=excursions&page=article&op=view&path%5B%5D=94&path%5B%5D=133.

10. See Martin, *Doing Psychology Experiments*, 506.

11. For an overview see Steven J. Heine and Matthew B. Ruby, "Cultural Psychology," in *Wiley Interdisciplinary Reviews* 1, no. 2 (2010): 254–66. See also the vigorous debate in psychology about nature and nurture in language development (e.g., W. Tecumseh Fitch, Marc D. Hauser, and Noam Chomsky, "The Evolution of the Language Faculty: Clarifications and Implications," *Cognition* 97, no. 2 [2005]: 179–210; and the response by Ray Jackendorff and Steven Pinker, "The Nature of the Language Faculty and Its Implications for Evolution of Language," *Cognition* 97, no. 2 [2005]: 211–25).

12. I use *model* here in the sense of a formal or mathematical description, derived from empirical work on cognition, that is meant to explain a basic psychological process (see Jerome R. Busemeyer and Adele Diederich, *Cognitive Modeling* [Los Angeles: Sage, 2010], 2–3).

13. For the problems see Ed Yong, "Replication Studies: Bad Copy," *Nature*, May 16, 2012, 298–300; John P. A. Ioannidis, "Why Most Published Research Findings Are False," *PLOS Medicine* 2, no. 8 (2005): e124; Joseph P. Simmons, Leif D. Nelson, and Uri Simonsohn, "False-Positive Psychology: Undisclosed Flexibility in Data Collection and Analysis Allows Presenting Anything as Significant," *Psychological Science* 22, no. 11 (2011): 1359–66; John P. A. Ioannidis, "Why Science Is Not Necessarily Self-Correcting," *Perspectives on Psychological Science* 7, no. 6 (2012): 645–54; Gregory Francis, "Too Good to Be True: Publication Bias in Two Prominent Studies from Experimental Psychology," *Psychonomic Bulletin and Review* 19, no. 2 (2012): 151–56; for responses see Geoff Cumming, "The New Statistics: Why and How," *Psychological Science* 25, no. 1 (2014): 7–29; Open Science Collaboration, "Estimating the Reproducibility of Psychological Science," *Science* 349, no. 6251 (2015): 943–50.

14. Alan Liu, "Local Transcendence: Cultural Criticism, Postmodernism, and the Romanticism of Detail," *Representations* 32, no. 1 (1990): 75–113, 82; see also Thomas Pfau's acute commentary on the secularization of divine infinity into the "*proceduralism of modern knowledge production*" (italics in the original), in "'The Philosophy of Shipwreck: Gnosticism, Skepticism, and Coleridge's Catastrophic Modernity," *Modern Language Notes (MLN)* 122, no. 5 (2007): 949–1004, 957.

15. See, e.g., Michel Foucault, "The Subject and Power," *Critical Inquiry* 8, no. 4 (1982): 777–95; see also my "Romantic Loves: A Response to *Historicizing Romantic Sexuality*," in *Historicizing Romantic Sexuality*, ed. Richard C. Sha, *Romantic Circles Praxis Series* (2006), www.rc.umd.edu/praxis/sexuality/elfenbein/elfenbein.html.

16. Roland Barthes, "On Reading," in *The Rustle of Language*, trans. Richard Howard (New York: Hill and Wang, 1986), 33–43, 42.

17. George Mandler, "Emotion," in *The Oxford Companion to the Mind*, ed. Richard L. Gregory (Oxford: Oxford University Press, 1987), 219–20, 220.

18. Gregory quoted in Sedgwick and Frank, "Shame in the Cybernetic Fold," chapter 3 of Sedgwick, *Touching Feeling: Affect, Pedagogy, Performativity* (Durham, NC: Duke University Press, 2003), 93–122, 112; Sedgwick and Frank quoted on 113; for a criticism of this passage from a social psychological perspective see Margaret Wetherell, "Trends in the Turn to Affect: A Social Psychological Critique," *Body and Society* 21, no. 2 (2015): 139–66.

19. John D. Bransford, Ann L. Brown, and Rodney R. Cocking, *How People Learn: Brain, Mind, Experience, and School* (Washington: National Academy Press, 1999), 10–12.

20. See, e.g., Arthur C. Graesser, Keith K. Millis, and Rolf A. Zwaan, "Discourse Comprehension," *Annual Review of Psychology* 48 (Feb. 1997): 163–89; Peter Dixon and Marissa Bortolussi, "The Scientific Study of Literature: What Can, Has, and Should Be Done," *Scientific Study of Literature* 1, no. 1 (2011): 59–71.

21. Jeffrey Walker, review of Norman Holland, *The Brain of Robert Frost: A Cognitive Approach to Literature*, in *The Yearbook of English Studies* 21 (1991): 312–13, 313; Sabine Gross, "Cognitive Readings; or, The Disappearance of Literature in the Mind," review of Mark Turner, *Reading Minds: The Study of English in the Age of Cognitive Science*, in *Poetics Today* 18, no. 2 (1997): 271–97, 282; Michael Fisher, "Literary Change and Cognitive Science," review of Ellen Spolsky, *Gaps in Nature: Literary Interpretation and the Modular Mind*, in *Poetics Today* 17, no. 2 (1996): 262–65, 265.

22. For a useful, skeptical overview of interdisciplinarity see Jerry A. Jacobs and Scott Frickel, "Interdisciplinarity: A Critical Assessment," *Annual Review of Sociology* 35 (August 2009): 43–65.

23. Sidonie Smith, contribution to "Enumerating the Obstacles," part of a four-part *PMLA* forum on interdisciplinarity, *PMLA* 111, no. 2 (1996): 293–94, 294.

24. Peter J. Rabinowitz, *Before Reading: Narrative Conventions and the Politics of Interpretation* (1987; repr. Columbus: Ohio State University Press, 1998); Norman N. Holland, *Literature and the Brain* (Gainesville, FL: PsyArt Foundation, 2009); Wolfgang Iser, *The Act of Reading: A Theory of Aesthetic Response* (Baltimore: Johns Hopkins University Press, 1978); Stanley E. Fish, *Is There a Text in This Class? The Authority of Interpretive Communities* (Cambridge, MA: Harvard University Press, 1980); Nicholas Dames, *The Physiology of the Novel: Reading, Neural Science, and the Form of Victorian Fiction* (Oxford: Oxford University Press, 2007). See also John Maynard, *Literary Intention, Literary Interpretation, and Readers* (Peterborough, ON: Broadview, 2009), 299–360; and Paul B. Armstrong, *How Literature Plays with the Brain: The Neuroscience of Reading and Art* (Baltimore: Johns Hopkins University Press, 2013).

25. Quoted in David Frisby, "The Popper-Adorno Controversy: The Methodological Dispute in German Sociology," *Philosophy of the Social Sciences* 2, no. 1 (1972): 105–19, 113.

26. For foundational work on cognitive approaches to metaphor see George Lakoff and Mark Turner, *More Than Cool Reason: A Field Guide to Poetic Metaphor* (Chicago: University of Chicago Press, 1989); for examples of work following their lead see Margaret H. Freeman, "Poetry and the Scope of Metaphor: Toward a Cognitive Theory of

Literature," in *Metaphor and Metonymy at the Crossroads: A Cognitive Perspective*, ed. Antonia Barcelona (Berlin: Mouton de Gruyter, 2000), 253–81; Roberta Trites, *Literary Conceptualizations of Growth: Metaphors and Cognition in Adolescent Literature* (Amsterdam: John Benjamins, 2014); on theory of mind see Lisa Zunshine, *Why We Read Fiction: Theory of Mind and the Novel* (Columbus: Ohio State University Press, 2006); and Lisa Zunshine, "Lying Bodies of the Enlightenment: Theory of Mind and Cultural Historicism," in *Introduction to Cognitive Cultural Studies*, ed. Lisa Zunshine (Baltimore: Johns Hopkins University Press, 2010), 115–33; and Paula Leverage et al., eds., *Theory of Mind and Literature* (West Lafayette, IN: Purdue University Press, 2011); on evolutionary psychology see Brian Boyd, Joseph Carroll, and Jonathan Gottschall, eds., *Evolution, Literature, and Film: A Reader* (New York: Columbia University Press, 2010); and Nancy Easterlin, *A Biocultural Approach to Literary Theory and Interpretation* (Baltimore: Johns Hopkins University Press, 2012); on neuroscience see Frederick Luis Aldama, "What the Brain Sciences Might Tell Us About Our Making of and Engaging with Strange Fiction," *Style* 47, no. 3 (2013): 283–95; Arthur M. Jacobs, "Neurocognitive Poetics: Methods and Models for Investigating the Neuronal and Cognitive-Affective Bases of Literature Reception," *Frontiers in Human Neuroscience* 9 (2015): 1–22; G. Gabrielle Starr, *Feeling Beauty: The Neuroscience of Aesthetic Experience* (Cambridge, MA: MIT Press, 2013); and Anthony J. Sanford and Catherine Emmott, *Mind, Brain, and Narrative* (Cambridge: Cambridge University Press, 2012); on narratology see David Herman, "Narrative Theory After the Second Cognitive Revolution," in Zunshine, *Introduction to Cognitive Cultural Studies*, 155–75; and David Herman, *Storytelling and the Sciences of the Mind* (Cambridge, MA: MIT Press, 2013).

## Chapter 1: Doing What Comes Automatically

1. Stanislas Dehaene et al., "How Learning to Read Changes the Cortical Networks for Vision and Language," *Science* 330, no. 6009 (2010): 1359–64, 1359.

2. For an overview of these processes see Robert A. Mason and Marcel Adam Just, "Identifying Component Discourse Processes from the fMRI Time Course Signatures," in *Reading—From Words to Multiple Texts*, ed. M. Anne Britt, Susan R. Goldman, and Jean-François Rouet (New York: Routledge, 2013), 147–59.

3. Judith Butler, from her "Commencement Address at McGill University, 2013," excerpts online at Brainpickings, www.brainpickings.org/2013/06/07/judith-butler-mcgill -2013-commencement-address.

4. For examples of how psychologists examine such effects, see Colin M. MacLeod, "Half a Century of Research on the Stroop Effect: An Integrative Review," *Psychological Bulletin* 109, no. 2 (1991): 163–203.

5. On automaticity and preattentive processing see Anne Treisman, Alfred Viera, and Amy Hayes, "Automaticity and Preattentive Processing," *American Journal of Psychology* 105, no. 2 (1992): 341–62; on the importance of automaticity in learning to read see S. Jay Samuels and Richard F. Flor, "The Importance of Automaticity for Developing Expertise in Reading," *Reading and Writing Quarterly* 13, no. 2 (1997): 107–21; and Stephanie A. Lai, Rebekah George Benjamin, Paula J. Schwanenflugel, and Melanie R. Kuhn,

"The Longitudinal Relationship Between Reading Fluency and Reading Comprehension in Second-Grade Children," *Reading and Writing Quarterly* 30, no. 2 (2014): 116–38; for a traditional view of reading and automaticity see Gordon D. Logan, "Automaticity and Reading: Perspectives from the Instance Theory of Automatization," *Reading and Writing Quarterly* 13, no. 2 (1997): 123–46; and Charles Perfetti, "Reading Ability: Lexical Quality to Comprehension," *Scientific Studies of Reading* 11, no. 4 (2007): 357–83; and for more recent important work see Katherine A. Rawson and Erica L. Middleton, "Memory-Based Processing as a Mechanism of Automaticity in Text Comprehension," *Journal of Experimental Psychology: Learning, Memory, and Cognition* 35, no. 2 (2009): 353–70.

6. Agnes Moors, "Automaticity," in *The Oxford Handbook of Cognitive Psychology*, ed. Daniel Reisberg (Oxford: Oxford University Press, 2013), 163–75, 169; I draw on Moors's discussion extensively in this paragraph.

7. On semantic priming see Eva Van Den Bussche, Wim Van Den Noortgate, and Bert Reynvoet, "Mechanisms of Masked Priming: A Meta-analysis," *Psychological Bulletin* 135, no. 3 (2009): 452–77; and Simon van Gaal et al., "Can the Meaning of Multiple Words Be Integrated Unconsciously?" *Philosophical Transactions of the Royal Society B (Biological Sciences)* 369 (2014): http://rstb.royalsocietypublishing.org/content/369/1641/20130212; on morphological priming see Joanna Morris and Linnaea Stockall, "Early, Equivalent ERP Masked Priming Effects for Regular and Irregular Morphology," *Brain and Language* 123, no. 2 (2012): 81–92; on orthographic and phonological priming see Johannes C. Ziegler, Daisy Bertrand, Bernard Lété, and Jonathan Grainger, "Orthographic and Phonological Contributions to Reading Development: Tracking Developmental Trajectories Using Masked Priming," *Developmental Psychology* 50, no. 4 (2014): 1026–36. For a helpful online demonstration see www.u.arizona.edu/kforster/priming/masked_priming_demo.htm.

8. Matthew J. Traxler, *Introduction to Psycholinguistics: Understanding Language Science* (Chichester, West Sussex: John Wiley and Sons, 2012), 104.

9. Charles Dickens, *Bleak House* (1852–53), ed. Stephen Gill (Oxford: Oxford University Press, 2008), 39.

10. For the classic discussion see Victor Shklovsky, "Art as Technique," in *Russian Formalist Criticism: Four Essays*, trans. Lee T. Lemon and Marion J. Reis (Lincoln: University of Nebraska Press, 1965), 3–24.

11. Lai et al., "The Longitudinal Relationship," 119.

12. Moors, "Automaticity," 165–67.

13. Fernanda Ferreira, Karl G. D. Bailey, and Vittoria Ferraro, "Good-Enough Representations in Language Comprehension," *Current Directions in Psychological Science* 11, no. 1 (2002): 11–15; and Hossein Karimi and Fernanda Ferreira, "Good-Enough Linguistic Representations and Online Cognitive Equilibrium in Language Processing," *Quarterly Journal of Experimental Psychology* 69, no. 5 (2016): 1013–40.

14. Sanford B. Barton and Anthony J. Sanford, "A Case Study of Anomaly Detection: Shallow Semantic Processing and Cohesion Establishment," *Memory and Cognition* 21, no. 4 (1993): 477–87, 479; see also the discussion of shallow processing in Sanford and Emmott, *Mind, Brain, and Narrative*, 103–9.

15. Myrtle Whitlock Martin, review of *Handbook on Tuberculosis for Public Health Nurses*, by Violet H. Hodgson, *American Journal of Nursing* 40, no. 4 (1940): 488; B. W. Hodder, review of *Industrialization in West Africa*, by J. O. C. Onyemelukwe, *Geographical Journal* 152, no. 2 (1986): 264; Regina M. Benjamin, "Oral Health Care for People Living with HIV/AIDS," *Public Health Reports* 127, suppl. 2 (2012): 1–2, 1.

16. Karimi and Ferreira, "Good-Enough Linguistic Representations," 1014. The description has close parallels with the account of decision making described by Daniel Kahneman in *Thinking, Fast and Slow* (New York: Farrar, Straus and Giroux, 2011), 59–70.

17. David A. Swinney, "Lexical Access During Sentence Comprehension: (Re)consideration of Context Effects," *Journal of Verbal Learning and Verbal Behavior* 18, no. 6 (1979): 645–59.

18. For examples of similar effects obtained with visual presentation, see Walter Kintsch and Ernest F. Mross, "Context Effects in Word Identification," *Journal of Memory and Language* 24, no. 3 (1985): 336–49; Robert E. Till, Ernest F. Mross, and Walter Kintsch, "Time Course of Priming for Associate and Inference Words in a Discourse Context," *Memory and Cognition* 16, no. 4 (1988): 283–98; and Kerrie E. Elston-Güttler and Angela D. Friederici, "Native and L2 Processing of Homonyms in Sentential Context," *Journal of Memory and Language* 52, no. 2 (2005): 256–83.

19. Mark S. Seidenberg, Michael K. Tanenhaus, James M. Leiman, and Marie Bienkowski, "Automatic Access of the Meanings of Ambiguous Words in Context: Some Limitations of Knowledge-Based Processing," *Cognitive Psychology* 14, no. 4 (1982): 489–537.

20. On inhibitory control of attention and its importance for reading see Penny Chiappe, Lynn Hasher, and Linda S. Siegel, "Working Memory, Inhibitory Control, and Reading Disability," *Memory and Cognition* 28, no. 1 (2000): 8–17.

21. A classic statement of this model is Allan M. Collins and Elizabeth F. Loftus, "A Spreading-Activation Theory of Semantic Processing," *Psychological Review* 82, no. 6 (1975): 407–28.

22. "Through the strait pass of suffering" (792), in *Final Harvest: Emily Dickinson's Poems*, ed. Thomas H. Johnson (Boston: Little, Brown, 1961), 197.

23. Edward J. O'Brien, Michelle Rizzella, Jason E. Albrecht, and Jennifer G. Halleran, "Updating a Situation Model: A Memory-Based Text Processing View," *Journal of Experimental Psychology: Learning, Memory, and Cognition* 24, no. 5 (1998): 1200–1210, 1210. O'Brien has generously made all the passages in his 1998 experiment available on his web page at http://pubpages.unh.edu/eob/.

24. Alan Baddeley, *Working Memory, Thought, and Action* (Oxford: Oxford University Press, 2007), 1.

25. Marcel Adam Just and Patricia A. Carpenter, "A Capacity Theory of Comprehension: Individual Differences in Working Memory," *Psychological Review* 99, no. 1 (1992): 122–49.

26. O'Brien et al., "Updating a Situation Model." Important antecedents include Jason E. Albrecht and Jerome L. Myers, "Role of Context in Accessing Distant Information During Reading," *Journal of Experimental Psychology: Learning, Memory, and Cognition* 21, no. 6 (1995): 1459–68; and Jason E. Albrecht and Edward J. O'Brien, "Updating

a Mental Model: Maintaining Both Local and Global Coherence," *Journal of Experimental Psychology: Learning, Memory, and Cognition* 19, no. 5 (1993): 1061–70.

27. Anne E. Cook and Edward J. O'Brien, "Knowledge Activation, Integration, and Validation During Narrative Text Comprehension," *Discourse Processes* 51, no. 1–2 (2014): 26–49, 27.

28. Here Cook and O'Brien draw on Walter Kintsch's *Comprehension: A Paradigm for Cognition* (Cambridge: Cambridge University Press, 1998), 96–101.

29. Panayiota Kendeou, Emily R. Smith, and Edward J. O'Brien, "Updating During Reading Comprehension: Why Causality Matters," *Journal of Experimental Psychology: Learning, Memory, and Cognition* 39, no. 3 (2013): 854–65.

30. For a classic discussion of how psychologists understand their treatment of linguistic memory as differing from a purely mechanistic one, see James J. Jenkins, "Remember That Old Theory of Memory? Well, Forget It," *American Psychologist* 29, no. 11 (1974): 785–95.

31. Albrecht and Myers, "Role of Context," 1468.

32. Roman Jakobson, "Two Aspects of Language," in *Language in Literature*, ed. Krystyna Pomorska and Stephen Rudy (Cambridge, MA: Harvard University Press, 1987), 95–114, 111.

33. R. Brooke Lea, David Rapp, Andrew Elfenbein, Aaron D. Mitchel, and Russell Swinburne Romine, "Sweet Silent Thought: Alliteration and Resonance in Poetry Comprehension," *Psychological Science* 19, no. 7 (2008): 709–16.

34. R. Brooke Lea, Chelsea Voskuilen, and Andrew Elfenbein, "Rhyme as Memory Cue: Do Poets Resonate?" poster at the 2010 Society for Text and Discourse, Chicago, Illinois. For more on rhyme's psychological effects see Matthew S. McGlone and Jessica Tofighbakhsh, "Birds of a Feather Flock Conjointly (?): Rhyme as Reason in Aphorisms," *Psychological Science* 11, no. 5 (2000): 424–28.

35. Arthur Henry Hallam, "On Some of the Characteristics of Modern Poetry, and on the Lyrical Poems of Alfred Tennyson," *Englishman's Magazine* 1 (1831): 616–28, 618.

36. For the pioneering article in this field see Elizabeth J. Marsh and Lisa K. Fazio, "Learning Errors from Fiction: Difficulties in Reducing Reliance on Fictional Stories," *Memory and Cognition* 34, no. 5 (2006): 1140–49.

37. Lisa K. Fazio, Sarah J. Barber, Suparna Rajaram, Peter A. Ornstein, and Elizabeth J. Marsh, "Creating Illusions of Knowledge: Learning Errors That Contradict Prior Knowledge," *Journal of Experimental Psychology: General* 142, no. 1 (2013): 1–5, 3.

38. For a thorough investigation see David N. Rapp and Jason L. G. Braasch, eds., *Processing Inaccurate Information: Theoretical and Applied Perspectives from Cognitive Science and the Educational Sciences* (Cambridge, MA: MIT Press, 2014).

39. See also Deborah A. Prentice, Richard J. Gerrig, and Daniel S. Bailis, "What Readers Bring to the Processing of Fictional Texts," *Psychonomic Bulletin and Review* 4, no. 3 (1997): 416–20, for evidence of the power of reading to influence reader belief; in this case participants were more likely to accept false facts in a fictional text set at a different university than they were when the same facts appeared in a text set at their own university.

40. David N. Rapp, "The Consequences of Reading Inaccurate Information," *Current Directions in Psychological Science* 25, no. 4 (2016): 281–85, 282.

41. Dickens, *Bleak House*, 5–6.

42. See Shklovsky, "Art as Technique."

43. For a cognitive perspective see Adam L. Alter, "The Benefits of Cognitive Disfluency," *Current Directions in Psychological Science* 22, no. 6 (2013): 437–42.

## Chapter 2: Three Readers Reading

1. David H. Richter, *Falling into Theory: Conflicting Views on Reading Literature* (Boston: St. Martin's, 1994), 205.

2. Umberto Eco, "*Intentio lectoris*: The State of the Art," in *The Limits of Interpretation* (Bloomington: Indiana University Press, 1990), 44–63, 57.

3. For two interesting exceptions see Greta Golick, " 'One Quart Milk, Five Eggs I Should Say': Marginalia in Anglo-Canadian Cookbooks," in "Reading Notes," ed. Dirk Van Hulle and Wim Van Mierlo, special issue, *Variants* 2/3 (2004): 95–114; and Mike Esbester, "Nineteenth-Century Timetables and the History of Reading," *Book History* 12 (2009): 156–85. Esbester, in particular, emphasizes the value of exploring nonliterary reading in the history of reading.

4. Georges Poulet, "The Phenomenology of Reading," *New Literary History* 1, no. 1 (1969): 53–68, 57.

5. Quoted in A. Norman Jeffares, *W. B. Yeats: Man and Poet*, 2nd ed. (London: Routledge and Kegan Paul, 1962), 267.

6. Arthur C. Graesser, Murray Singer, and Tom Trabasso, "Constructing Inferences During Narrative Text Comprehension," *Psychological Review* 101, no. 3 (1994): 371–95, 371–72.

7. Ibid., 371.

8. John D. Bransford and Marcia K. Johnson, "Contextual Prerequisites for Understanding: Some Investigations of Comprehension and Recall," *Journal of Verbal Learning and Verbal Behavior* 11, no. 6 (1972): 717–26, 722.

9. Colleen M. Zeitz, "Expert-Novice Differences in Memory, Abstraction, and Reasoning in the Domain of Literature," *Cognition and Instruction* 12, no. 4 (1994): 277–312; Barbara Graves, "The Study of Literary Expertise as a Research Strategy," *Poetics* 23, no. 6 (1996): 385–403.

10. Danielle S. McNamara, Eileen Kintsch, Nancy Butler Songer, and Walter Kintsch, "Are Good Texts Always Better? Interactions of Text Coherence, Background Knowledge, and Levels of Understanding in Learning from Text," *Cognition and Instruction* 14, no. 1 (1996): 1–43.

11. An excellent overview of the kinds of conscious activities that readers perform appears in Michael Pressley and Peter Afflerbach, *Verbal Protocols of Reading: The Nature of Constructively Responsive Reading* (Hillsdale, NJ: Erlbaum, 1995).

12. Jane Austen, *Emma* (1816), ed. Stephen M. Parrish, 3rd ed. (New York: Norton, 2000), 429.

13. Joseph Litvak, "Reading Characters: Self, Society, and Text in *Emma*," *PMLA* 100, no. 5 (1985): 763–73, 765.

14. See Ruth Garner, *Metacognition and Reading Comprehension: Cognition and Literacy* (Norwood, NJ: Ablex, 1987).

15. See, e.g., Helen Rogers, " 'Oh, What Beautiful Books!' Captivated Reading in an Early Victorian Prison," *Victorian Studies* 55, no. 1 (2012): 57–84; Joan Swann and Daniel Allington, "Reading Groups and the Language of Literary Texts: A Case Study in Social Reading," *Language and Literature* 18, no. 3 (2009): 247–64.

16. Stanley Fish, *Is There a Text in This Class? The Authority of Interpretive Communities* (Cambridge, MA: Harvard University Press, 1980), 28.

17. Ibid., 33–34

18. Ibid., 28.

19. Pressley and Afflerbach, *Verbal Protocols*, 2–3.

20. Ibid., 9.

21. Ibid., 9–11.

22. Many students in this experiment had difficulty providing much interpretive material at all: H was exceptional in attempting to provide a global structure for what she had read.

23. Roland Barthes, *S/Z: An Essay*, trans. Richard Miller (New York: Hill and Wang, 1974), 11.

24. Water Kintsch, *Comprehension: A Paradigm for Cognition* (Cambridge: Cambridge University Press, 1998).

25. Austen, *Emma*, 286–91.

26. Ibid., 292–94.

27. Leane Zugsmith, "The Three Veterans," in *Seventy-Five Short Masterpieces*, ed. Roger B. Goodman (New York: Bantam, 1961), 275–78; originally published in the *New Yorker* (1935) and reprinted by permission of Condé Nast.

## Chapter 3: Reading On- and Offline

1. Elizabeth Freund, *The Return of the Reader: Reader-Response Criticism* (London: Methuen, 1987), 152.

2. For a good overview of research into both kinds of processing see Marta Minguela, Isabel Solé, and Stephanie Pieschl, "Flexible Self-Regulated Reading as a Cue for Deep Comprehension: Evidence from Online and Offline Measures," *Reading and Writing* 28, no. 5 (2015): 721–44.

3. Paul van den Broek and Kathleen E. Kremer, "The Mind in Action: What It Means to Comprehend During Reading," in *Reading for Meaning: Fostering Comprehension in the Middle Grades*, ed. Barbara M. Taylor, Michael F. Graves, and Paul van den Broek (New York: Teachers College, 1999), 1–31, 2.

4. See David Caplan and Gloria S. Waters, "Verbal Working Memory and Sentence Comprehension," *Behavioral and Brain Sciences* 22, no. 1 (1999): 77–94; Morton Ann Gernsbacher and Michael P. Kaschak, "Neuroimaging Studies of Language Production

and Comprehension," *Annual Review of Psychology* 54 (Feb. 2003): 91–114; Charles A. Perfetti and Donald J. Bolger, "The Brain Might Read That Way," *Scientific Studies of Reading* 8, no. 3 (2004): 293–304; Jason D. Yeatman, Robert F. Dougherty, Elena Rykhlevskaia, Anthony J. Sherbondy, Gayle K. Deutsch, Brian A. Wandell, and Michal Ben-Shachar, "Anatomical Properties of the Arcuate Fasciculus Predict Phonological and Reading Skills in Children," *Journal of Cognitive Neuroscience* 23, no. 11 (2011): 3304–17.

5. George E. P. Box, "Robustness in the Strategy of Scientific Model Building," in *Robustness in Statistics*, ed. Robert L. Launer and Graham N. Wilkinson (New York: Academic Press, 1979), 201–36, 202.

6. On architectures in psychology see Sashank Varma, "Criteria for the Design and Evaluation of Cognitive Architectures," *Cognitive Science* 35, no. 7 (2011): 1329–51.

7. Paul van den Broek, Michael Young, Yuhtsuen Tzeng, and Tracy Linderholm, "The Landscape Model of Reading: Inferences and the Online Construction of a Memory Representation," in *The Construction of Mental Representations During Reading*, ed. Susan R. Goldman and Herre van Oostendorp (Mahwah, NJ: Erlbaum, 1999), 71–98; and Paul van den Broek, Robert F. Lorch Jr., Tracy Linderholm, and Mary Gustafson, "The Effects of Readers' Goals on Inference Generation and Memory for Texts," *Memory and Cognition* 29, no. 8 (2001): 1081–87.

8. Arthur C. Graesser, Keith K. Millis, and Rolf A. Zwaan, "Discourse Comprehension," *Annual Review of Psychology* 48 (Feb. 1997): 163–89, 174.

9. See, e.g., Arthur C. Graesser, Murray Singer, and Tom Trabasso, "Constructing Inferences During Narrative Text Comprehension," *Psychological Review* 101, no. 3 (1994): 371–95; David C. Rubin, *Memory in Oral Traditions: The Cognitive Psychology of Epic, Ballads, and Counting-Out Rhymes* (New York: Oxford University Press, 1995); Walter Kintsch, *Comprehension: A Paradigm for Cognition* (Cambridge: Cambridge University Press, 1998); Howard Eichenbaum and Neal J. Cohen, *From Conditioning to Conscious Recollection: Memory Systems of the Brain* (Oxford: Oxford University Press, 2001), 471.

10. Graesser, Millis, and Zwaan, "Discourse Comprehension," 175.

11. Rubin, *Memory in Oral Traditions*, 155–61; Kintsch, *Comprehension*, 217–21.

12. Meredyth Daneman and Patricia A. Carpenter, "Individual Differences in Working Memory and Reading," *Journal of Verbal Learning and Verbal Behavior* 19, no. 4 (1980): 450–66; Marcel Adam Just and Patricia A. Carpenter, "A Capacity Theory of Comprehension: Individual Differences in Working Memory," *Psychological Review* 99, no. 1 (1992): 122–49; Murray Singer and Kathryn F. M. Ritchot, "The Role of Working Memory Capacity and Knowledge Access in Text Inference Processing," *Memory and Cognition* 24, no. 6 (1996): 733–43.

13. Randall W. Engle, "Working Memory Capacity as Executive Attention," *Current Directions in Psychological Science* 11, no. 1 (2002): 19–23, 20.

14. Desiree Budd, Paul Whitney, and Kandi Jo Turley, "Individual Differences in Working Memory Strategies for Reading Expository Texts," *Memory and Cognition* 23, no. 6 (1995): 735–48; Kintsch, *Comprehension*, 217–21.

15. Paul van den Broek and Mary Gustafson, "Comprehension and Memory for Texts: Three Generations of Reading Research," in *Narrative Comprehension, Causality, and*

*Coherence: Essays in Honor of Tom Trabasso*, ed. Susan R. Goldman, Arthur C. Graesser, and Paul van den Broek (Mahwah, NJ: Erlbaum, 1999), 15–34, 22.

16. Arthur C. Graesser and Rolf A. Zwaan, "Inference Generation and the Construction of Situation Models," in *Discourse Comprehension: Essays in Honor of Walter Kintsch*, ed. Charles A. Weaver III, Suzanne Manner, and Charles R. Fletcher (1995; New York: Routledge, 2009), 117–40, 124.

17. George Eliot, *Middlemarch* (1871–72) (Harmondsworth: Penguin, 1982), 29.

18. Paul van den Broek, David N. Rapp, and Panayiota Kendeou, "Integrating Memory-Based and Constructionist Processes in Accounts of Reading Comprehension," *Discourse Processes* 39, no. 2–3 (2005): 299–316, 306.

19. Mikhail M. Bakhtin, *The Dialogic Imagination: Four Essays*, ed. Michael Holquist, trans. Caryl Emerson and Michael Holquist (Austin: University of Texas Press, 1981), 262–63.

20. Tracy Linderholm, Sandra Virtue, Yuhtsuen Tzeng, and Paul van den Broek, "Fluctuations in the Availability of Information During Reading: Capturing Cognitive Processes Using the Landscape Model," *Discourse Processes* 37, no. 2 (2004): 165–86, 168.

21. Susan R. Goldman and Elizabeth U. Saul, "Flexibility in Text Processing: A Strategy Competition Model," *Learning and Individual Differences* 2, no. 2 (1990): 181–219; Ellen Spolsky, *Gaps in Nature: Literary Interpretation and the Modular Mind* (Albany: State University of New York Press, 1993).

22. Tom Trabasso and Paul van den Broek, "Causal Thinking and the Representation of Narrative Events," *Journal of Memory and Language* 24, no. 5 (1985): 612–30; Charles R. Fletcher, John E. Hummel, and Chad J. Marsolek, "Causality and the Allocation of Attention During Comprehension," *Journal of Experimental Psychology: Learning, Memory, and Cognition* 16, no. 2 (1990): 233–40; Paul van den Broek, "The Causal Inference Maker: Towards a Process Model of Inference Generation," in *Comprehension Processes in Reading*, ed. D. A. Balota, G. B. Flores d'Arcais, and K. Rayner (New York: Erlbaum, 1990), 423–45.

23. Eliot, *Middlemarch*, 30.

24. Gerald C. Cupchik, Garry Leonard, Elise Axelrad, and Judith D. Kalin, "The Landscape of Emotion in Literary Encounters," *Cognition and Emotion* 12, no. 6 (1998): 825–47.

25. Linderholm et al., "Fluctuations"; Van den Broek et al., "The Effects of Readers' Goals."

26. Linderholm et al., "Fluctuations," 168.

27. Pierre Bourdieu, *Distinction: A Social Critique of the Judgement of Taste*, trans. Richard Nice (Cambridge, MA: Harvard University Press, 1984), 440–51; Deborah Brandt, *Literacy in American Lives* (Cambridge: Cambridge University Press, 2001); Peter Smagorinsky, "If Meaning Is Constructed, What Is It Made From? Toward a Cultural Theory of Reading," *Review of Educational Research* 71, no. 1 (2001): 133–69.

28. Ruth Garner, *Metacognition and Reading Comprehension* (Norwood, NJ: Ablex, 1987).

29. John Woolford, "Periodicals and the Practice of Literary Criticism, 1855–64," in

*The Victorian Periodical Press: Samplings and Soundings*, ed. Joanne Shattock and Michael Wolff (Toronto: University of Toronto Press, 1982), 109–42; Laurel Brake, "Literary Criticism and the Victorian Periodicals," *Yearbook of English Studies* 16 (1986): 92–116.

30. Isobel Armstrong, *Victorian Poetry: Poetry, Poetics, and Politics* (London: Routledge, 1993), 284–317; E. Warwick Slinn, *Victorian Poetry as Cultural Critique: The Politics of Performative Language* (Charlottesville: University of Virginia Press, 2003), 32–55.

31. See William George Clark, "Preface," *Essays by George Brimley*, 3rd ed. (London: Routledge, 1882), vi–x; Maurice B. Cramer, "Browning's Literary Reputation at Oxford, 1855–1859," *PMLA* 57, no. 1 (1942): 232–40.

32. Margaret Oliphant, "Modern Light Literature: Poetry," *Blackwood's Edinburgh Magazine* 79 (1856): 125–38, 129. Subsequent citations of this source are referenced parenthetically in the text.

33. To describe states like the ones described by Oliphant, psychologists sometimes appeal to Mihály Csíkszentmihályi's theory of "optimal experience" or "flow": see his *Flow: The Psychology of Optimal Experience* (New York: Harper and Row, 1990); Melanie C. Green and Timothy C. Brock, "In the Mind's Eye: Transportation-Imagery Model of Narrative Persuasion," in *Narrative Impact: Social and Cognitive Foundations*, ed. Melanie C. Green, Jeffrey J. Strange, and Timothy C. Brock (Mahwah, NJ: Erlbaum, 2002), 315–41, esp. 325–26; and Jeff Mcquillan and Gisela Conde, "The Conditions of Flow in Reading: Two Studies of Optimal Experience," *Reading Psychology* 17, no. 2 (1996): 109–35.

34. Margaret Oliphant, *The Autobiography of Mrs. Oliphant* (1899), ed. Elisabeth Jay (Peterborough: Broadview, 2002), 50.

35. Thomas McNicoll, "New Poems," *London Quarterly Review* 6 (1856): 493–507. Subsequent citations of this source are referenced parenthetically in the text.

36. Clark, "Preface," viii.

37. See Angela Leighton, "Touching Forms: Tennyson and Aestheticism," *Essays in Criticism* 52, no. 1 (2002): 56–75, 58–60.

38. George Brimley, "Tennyson's Poems" (1855), in *Essays by George Brimley*, 3rd ed. (London: Routledge, 1882), 1–91, 8; Robert O. Preyer, "The Romantic Tide Reaches Trinity: Notes on the Transmission and Diffusion of New Approaches to Traditional Studies at Cambridge, 1820–1840," in *Victorian Science and Victorian Values: Literary Perspectives*, ed. James Paradis and Thomas Postlewait (New Brunswick, NJ: Rutgers University Press, 1985), 39–68.

39. George Brimley, review of *Men and Women*, *Fraser's* 53 (1856): 105–16, 110. Subsequent citations of this source are referenced parenthetically in the text.

40. Jason E. Albrecht and Edward J. O'Brien, "Updating a Mental Model: Maintaining Both Local and Global Coherence," *Journal of Experimental Psychology: Learning, Memory, and Cognition* 19, no. 5 (1993): 1061–70.

41. William Morris, "*Men and Women* by Robert Browning" (1856), in *The Hollow Land and Other Contributions to the Oxford and Cambridge Magazine*, ed. Eugene D. LeMire, William Morris Library (Bristol: Thoemmes, 1996), 259–88, 259. Subsequent citations of this source are referenced parenthetically in the text.

42. Thomas Cleghorn, "Writings of Charles Dickens," *North British Review* 3 (May 1845): 65–87, 85.

43. Patrick Brantlinger, *The Reading Lesson: The Threat of Mass Literacy in Nineteenth-Century British Fiction* (Bloomington: Indiana University Press, 1998), 1–24; see also Kelly J. Mays, "The Disease of Reading and Victorian Periodicals," in *Literature in the Marketplace: Nineteenth-Century British Publishing and Reading Practices*, ed. John O. Jordan and Robert L. Patten (Cambridge: Cambridge University Press, 1995), 165–94; Pamela K. Gilbert, "Ingestion, Contagion, Seduction: Victorian Metaphors of Reading," *LIT: Literature Interpretation Theory* 8 (1997): 83–104; and Kenneth Brewer, "Lost in a Book: Aesthetic Absorption, 1820–1880" (PhD diss., Stanford University, 1998).

44. Melanie C. Green and Timothy C. Brock, "The Role of Transportation in the Persuasiveness of Public Narratives," *Journal of Personality and Social Psychology* 79, no. 5 (2000): 701–21; Richard J. Gerrig, *Experiencing Narrative Worlds: On the Psychological Activities of Reading* (New Haven, CT: Yale University Press, 1993); Richard J. Gerrig and David N. Rapp, "Psychological Processes Underlying Literary Impact," *Poetics Today* 25, no. 2 (2004): 265–81.

45. I. A. Richards, *Principles of Literary Criticism* (1924; London: Routledge, 1967), 192–93.

46. See K. Anders Ericsson and Walter Kintsch, "Long-Term Working Memory," *Psychological Review* 102, no. 2 (1995): 211–45.

47. Isaac d'Israeli, *The Literary Character, Illustrated by the History of Men of Genius* (London: John Murray, 1818), 191.

48. John Brewer, *The Pleasures of the Imagination: English Culture in the Eighteenth Century* (New York: Farrar, Straus and Giroux, 1997), 187.

49. Bernard Barton, "To Walter Scott Esq., on Reading His *Lady of the Lake*," in *Metrical Effusions, or Verses on Various Occasions* (Woodbridge: S. Loder, 1812), 206–8, 207.

50. Teun van Dijk and Walter Kintsch, *Strategies of Discourse Comprehension* (New York: Academic Press, 1983); see also Charles R. Fletcher and Susan T. Chrysler, "Surface Forms, Textbases, and Situation Models: Recognition Memory for Three Types of Textual Information," *Discourse Processes* 13, no. 2 (1990): 175–90.

51. Aaron Hill, "After Reading an Unknown Author's Book," *The Works of the Late Aaron Hill*, 4 vols. (London, 1753), 3:104.

52. J. Paul Hunter, *Before Novels: The Cultural Contexts of Eighteenth-Century English Fiction* (New York: Norton, 1990), 156–61.

53. Henry Ellison, "After Reading Wordsworth's 'Laodamia,'" from *Madmoments* (1839); Josiah D. Canning, "On Reading Beattie's 'Minstrel,'" from *Poems* (1838); Caroline Oliphant, "On Reading Lord Byron's *Childe Harold*," from *Life and Songs* (1869); Henry Kirke White, "Lines on Reading the Poems of Warton, Age 14," from *The Poetical Works* (1830); Edward Moxon, "Lines, Written After Reading Burns's *Poems and Life*, June 12, 1825," in *The Prospect and Other Poems* (1826); Thomas Park, "To the Poet Laureate, After Reading His Epic Entitled 'Madoc,'" in *Morning Thoughts* (1818); all poems accessed from the ProQuest Literature Online Database (subscription only). Note that these poems

were written early in the century, even though the database takes them from editions published later.

54. Eefje Claassen, *Author Representations in Literary Reading* (Amsterdam: John Benjamins, 2012), 219–20.

55. On repetition see Michael C. W. English and Troy A. W. Visser, "Exploring the Repetition Paradox: The Effects of Learning Context and Massed Repetition on Memory," *Psychonomic Bulletin and Review* 21, no. 4 (2014): 1026–32; on schema effects see Vanessa E. Ghosh and Asaf Gilboa, "What Is a Memory Schema? A Historical Perspective on Current Neuroscience Literature," *Neuropsychologia* 53 (Jan. 2014): 104–14.

56. See Michael Benton, *Literary Biography: An Introduction* (Chichester, West Sussex: Wiley and Sons, 2009).

57. Algernon Charles Swinburne, "Emily Brontë," in *Miscellanies* (London: Chatto and Windus, 1886), 260–70, 269–70.

58. I thank Cannon Schmitt for clarifying my ideas on this issue.

59. Raymond W. Gibbs Jr., "Authorial Intentions in Text Understanding," *Discourse Processes* 32, no. 1 (2001): 73–80. Gibbs's point is not that readers understand the intentions of actual authors but that they assume a communicative stance; see also Claassen, *Author Representations*.

60. Michael Saler, *As If: Modern Enchantment and the Literary Prehistory of Virtual Reality* (Oxford: Oxford University Press, 2012), 36–37.

## Chapter 4: Hard Reading

1. For a useful account of college student beliefs about reading see Robert F. Lorch, Elizabeth P. Lorch, and Madeline A. Klusewitz, "College Students' Conditional Knowledge About Reading," *Journal of Educational Psychology* 85, no. 2 (1993): 239–52.

2. See Barbara A. Marinak and Linda B. Gambrell, "Reading Motivation: Exploring the Elementary Gender Gap," *Literacy Research and Instruction* 49, no. 2 (2010): 129–41.

3. Wendy Griswold, Terry McDonnell, and Nathan Wright, "Reading and the Reading Class in the Twenty-First Century," *Annual Review of Sociology* 31 (2005): 127–41, 127; see also Wendy Griswold, Elizabeth Lenaghan, and Michelle Naffziger, "Readers as Audiences," in *The Handbook of Media Audiences*, ed. Virginia Nightingale (Oxford: Wiley-Blackwell, 2011), 19–40.

4. Johannes Fabian, "Keep Listening: Ethnography and Reading," in *The Ethnography of Reading*, ed. Jonathan Boyarin (Berkeley: University of California Press, 1993), 80–97, 92.

5. See, e.g., C. Clayton Childress and Noah E. Friedkin, "Cultural Reception and Production: The Social Construction of Meaning in Book Clubs," *American Sociological Review* 77, no. 1 (2012): 45–68.

6. John Wesley, "Thoughts Upon Taste" (1780), in *The Works of the Late Reverend John Wesley, A. M.*, 7 vols. (New York: B. Waugh and T. Mason, 1835), 7:452–55, 455.

7. William Cowper to the Rev. Mr. Hurdis, March 23, 1792, quoted in *The Life and Posthumous Writings of William Cowper*, ed. William Hayley, 2 vols. (New York: T. and J. Swords, 1803), 2:15–16, 15.

8. Charles Darwin, *Charles Darwin: His Life Told in an Autobiographical Chapter and in a Selected Series of His Published Letters*, ed. Francis Darwin (London: John Murray, 1908), 23.

9. Percival Stockdale, *Memoirs of the Life and Writings of Percival Stockdale*, 2 vols. (London: Longman, Hurst, Rees, and Orme, 1809), 2:293.

10. Sir William Rowan Hamilton, quoted in Robert Percival Graves, *Life of Sir William Rowan Hamilton*, 2 vols. (London: Longman, Green, 1882), 1:199 (my emphasis).

11. Francis Bacon, "Of Studies," in *Francis Bacon: A Critical Edition of the Major Works*, ed. Brian Vickers (Oxford: Oxford University Press, 1996), 439–40, 439.

12. John Locke, "Some Thoughts Concerning Reading and Study for a Gentleman" (1703), in *The Works of John Locke*, 10 vols., 11th ed. (London: W. Otridge and Son, 1812), 3:269–76, 270.

13. For work especially on the Bible and reading see, in particular, David S. Katz, *God's Last Words: Reading the English Bible from the Reformation to Fundamentalism* (New Haven, CT: Yale University Press, 2004); Jonathan Sheehan, *The Enlightenment Bible: Translation, Scholarship, Culture* (Princeton, NJ: Princeton University Press, 2005); Gordon Campbell, *Bible: The Story of the King James Version, 1611–2011* (Oxford: Oxford University Press, 2010); Timothy Larsen, *A People of One Book: The Bible and the Victorians* (Oxford: Oxford University Press, 2011); Stephen Prickett, "From Novel to Bible: The Aestheticizing of Scripture," in *Biblical Religion and the Novel, 1700–2000*, ed. Mark Knight and Thomas Woodman (Farnham, Surrey: Ashgate, 2006), 13–24.

14. Anton Wilhelm Böhm, *Plain Directions for Reading the Holy Scriptures* (London: Joseph Downing, 1721), 33.

15. Dykes Alexander Fox, *Thoughts upon the Private and Social Reading of the Holy Scriptures* (London: A. W. Bennett, 1859), 5; attributed to Fox in William Cushing, *Anonyms: A Dictionary of Revealed Authorship* (Cambridge: William Cushing, 1889), 670.

16. W. Miles Myres, ed., *The Book of Common Prayer, A.D. 1886* (London: Griffith, Farran, Okeden, and Welsh, 1887), 96.

17. Anon., *Hints on Bible Reading and Study* (London: Hodder and Stoughton, 1868), 9.

18. Böhm, *Plain Directions*, 6.

19. Edward Bickersteth, *A Scripture Help, Designed to Assist in Reading the Bible Profitably* (1820), 12th ed. (London: L. B. Seely, 1825), 286.

20. Ibid., 278.

21. William Carpenter, *An Introduction to the Reading and Study of the English Bible* (London: S. W. Partridge, 1868), 61.

22. *Hints on Bible Reading*, 12–14.

23. Edward Bickersteth, *A Scripture Help, Designed to Assist in Reading the Bible Profitably*, 18th rev. ed. (London: R. B. Seeley and W. Burnside, 1840), 60. For this edition Bickersteth expanded his discussion of Bible study; see also John Leifchild, *A Help to the Private and Domestic Reading of the Holy Scriptures* (London: J. Nisbet, 1828), 4.

24. Bickersteth, *A Scripture Help* (1825 ed.), 283; Leifchild, *A Help*, 4–5.

25. Leifchild, *A Help*, 4.

26. Böhm, *Plain Directions*, 28–29.

27. Bickersteth, *A Scripture Help* (1840 ed.), 60.

28. See Robert West, "The Temporal Dynamics of Prospective Memory: A Review of the ERP and Prospective Memory Literature," *Neuropsychologia* 49, no. 8 (2011): 2233–45.

29. On cognitive ethics and reading see Nicholas Dames, *The Physiology of the Novel: Reading, Neural Science, and the Form of Victorian Fiction* (Oxford: Oxford University Press, 2007), 81–82.

30. Anon., *Extracts from the Reports of Her Majesty's Inspectors of Schools* (London: Longman, Brown, Green and Longmans, 1852), 59, 63.

31. Thomas R. Malthus, *An Essay on the Principle of Population*, 2 vols. in 1 (London: J. M. Dent, 1973); this is the revised edition of 1826. On moral restraint see 2:151–67; the second quotation is on 2:214.

32. For a thorough discussion see Atsuko Betchaku, "Thomas Chalmers, David Stow, and the St. John's Experiment: A Study in Educational Influence in Scotland and Beyond, 1819–c.1850," *Journal of Scottish Historical Studies* 27, no. 2 (2007): 170–90. On Stow see Sir Henry P. Wood, *David Stow and the Glasgow Normal Seminary* (Glasgow: Jordanhill College of Education, 1987); and William Fraser, *Memoir of the Life of David Stow* (London: James Nisbet, 1868).

33. David Stow, *Bible Emblems for the Use of Parents and Teachers* (London: Griffith and Farran, 1857), viii.

34. David Stow, *The Training System Adopted in the Model Schools of the Glasgow Educational Society* (Glasgow: W. R. M'Phun, 1836), 161–62.

35. Ibid., 103–4 (an earlier version appeared in 1832).

36. Walter Kintsch and Teun A. van Dijk, "Toward a Model of Text Comprehension and Production," *Psychological Review* 85, no. 5 (1978): 363–94.

37. Quoted in Mary Sturt, *The Education of the People: A History of Primary Education in England and Wales in the Nineteenth Century* (London: Routledge and Kegan Paul, 1967), 120.

38. Horace Mann, "Seventh Annual Report of the Secretary of the Board of Education," *Common School Journal* 6, no. 5–12 (1844): 65–196, 99 (emphasis in the original).

39. See Richard Johnson, "Educational Policy and Social Control in Early Victorian England," *Past and Present* 49 (Nov. 1970): 96–119.

40. The UK Reading Experience Database provides hundreds of examples; see UK RED, www.open.ac.uk/Arts/reading/UK/index.php.

41. John Ruskin, "Of Kings' Treasuries," in *Sesame and Lilies* (1865), ed. Deborah Epstein Nord (New Haven, CT: Yale University Press, 2002), 27–28. Subsequent citations of this source are referenced parenthetically in the text.

42. See George Levine, *Dying to Know: Scientific Epistemology and Narrative in Victorian England* (Chicago: University of Chicago Press, 2002).

43. Mary Poovey, *Genres of the Credit Economy: Mediating Value in Eighteenth- and Nineteenth-Century Britain* (Chicago: University of Chicago Press, 2008), 313, 405–9; see also Stephen Arata, "Literature and Information," *PMLA* 130, no. 3 (2015): 673–78.

44. See Elizabeth Helsinger, "Authority, Desire, and the Pleasures of Reading," in

*Sesame and Lilies*, ed. Deborah Epstein Nord (New Haven, CT: Yale University Press, 2002), 113–41, esp. 114–21.

45. Stephen Arata, "On Not Paying Attention," *Victorian Studies* 46, no. 2 (2004): 193–205, 201.

46. Poovey, *Genres of the Credit Economy*, chap. 5, "Delimiting Literature, Defining *Literary Value*"; see also Jesse Cordes Selbin, "'Read with Attention': John Cassell, John Ruskin, and the History of Close Reading," *Victorian Studies* 58, no. 3 (2016): 493–521.

47. Blanche Wilder Bellamy and Maud Wilder Goodwin, *Open Sesame: Poetry and Prose for School-Days*, vol. 3 (Boston: Ginn, 1890), vi.

48. Angeline Parmenter Carey, *A Guide to the Study of Literary Criticism* (Indianapolis, IN: William Burford, 1895), 22–23.

49. P. W. Horn, "The Cultural Value of Education," *Journal of Education* 81, no. 6 (1915): 143–45, 145; L. A. Williams, "On Literary Taste," *High School Journal* 4, no. 8 (1921): 173–75, 175.

50. Rowena Keith Keyes, *Recommended English Reading for High Schools* (New York: Noble and Noble, 1922), 62; see also the Ruskin chapter epigraph in Jessie Anderson Chase's *Three Freshmen: Ruth, Fran, and Natalie* (Chicago: A. C. McClurg, 1898), 42.

51. Herbert M. Kliebard, *The Struggle for the American Curriculum, 1893–1958*, 3rd ed. (New York: Routledge, 2004), 1–25; Michael P. Riccards, *The College Board and American Higher Education* (Madison, NJ: Fairleigh Dickinson University Press, 2010), 21.

52. Claude M. Fuess, *The College Board: Its First Fifty Years* (New York: Columbia University Press, 1950), 10; Riccards, *The College Board*, 24.

53. Commission on English, *Examining the Examination in English: A Report to the College Entrance Examination Board* (Cambridge, MA: Harvard University Press, 1931).

54. Ibid., 16–28.

55. John A. Valentine, *The College Board and the School Curriculum: A History of the College Board's Influence on the Substance and Standards of American Education, 1900–1980* (New York: College Entrance Examination Board, 1987), 14.

56. J. Rose Colby, ed., *"Silas Marner" by George Eliot* (New York: Appleton, 1900), 298.

57. J. N. Hook, "A Century of Change in English Teaching," *English Education* 14, no. 2 (1982): 113–24, 113.

58. Winifred Quincy Norton, *Entrance English Questions Set by the College Entrance Examination Board, 1901–1928*, 2nd ed. (Boston: Ginn, 1929), 125.

59. Ibid., 101.

60. Ibid., 84–85.

61. George Armstrong Wauchope, ed., *George Eliot's "Silas Marner"* (Boston: Heath, 1902), ix.

62. Colby, *"Silas Marner" by George Eliot*, 11.

63. May McKitrick, ed., *George Eliot's "Silas Marner"* (New York: American Book Company, 1911), 209.

64. Emma Miller Bolenius, *Teaching Literature in the Grammar Grades and High School* (Boston: Houghton Mifflin, 1915), 245.

65. As Gerald Graff argues, while "civic uplift" helped shape the canon, it was not

prominent in textbooks (*Professing Literature: An Institutional History*, 20th anniversary ed. [Chicago: University of Chicago Press, 2007], 131).

66. Colby, *"Silas Marner" by George Eliot*, 8.

67. Gilbert Sykes Blakely, *Teachers' Outlines for Studies in English* (New York: American Book Company, 1908), 25.

68. Colby, *"Silas Marner" by George Eliot*, 280, 285.

69. Mary Harriot Norris, ed., *George Eliot's "Silas Marner"* (Boston: Leach, Shewell, and Sanborn, 1890), 287.

70. Ellen Garrigues, ed., *George Eliot's "Silas Marner"* (New York: Holt, 1911), 251.

71. John Guillory, *Cultural Capital: The Problem of Literary Canon Formation* (Chicago: University of Chicago Press, 1993), 168–75.

72. Riccards, *The College Board*, 39–53.

73. Jay E. Greene, ed., *"Silas Marner" by George Eliot and "The Pearl" by John Steinbeck* (New York: Noble and Noble, 1953), v.

74. McKitrick, *George Eliot's "Silas Marner,"* 213.

75. Greene, *"Silas Marner" by George Eliot and "The Pearl" by John Steinbeck*, 419.

76. M. Atkinson Williams, quoted in H. B. Lathrop, "Recent Literature in the High-School Classroom," *English Journal* 13, no. 7 (1924): 463–77, 463.

77. Anon., "Reading Lists of Colleges Held Too Old," *Chicago Daily Tribune*, Oct. 20, 1935, D3.

78. J. H., "The Schoolteacher's Novel," *Saturday Review of Literature*, March 20, 1937, 13.

79. William Leonard, "A Wide Disparity Between Old and New in Latest Release," *Chicago Tribune*, July 21, 1968, E12.

80. J. H., "The Schoolteacher's Novel," 13.

81. C. Edward Jones, *Sources of Interest in High School English* (New York: American Book Company, 1912), 36–44.

82. Charles Maxwell McConn, "High-School Students' Rankings of English Classics," *English Journal* 1, no. 5 (1912): 257–72, 263; Sarah T. Muir, "Pupil Reactions to the Classics," *English Journal* 11, no. 3 (1922): 167–73, 168; Frances Mary Hughes, "What Do High-School Teachers Say About the Classics at Present Used?" *English Journal* 13, no. 5 (1924): 331–35, 334; Vera Elder and Helen S. Carpenter, "Reading Interests of High-School Children," *Journal of Educational Research* 19, no. 4 (1929): 276–82, 278; William G. Brink, "Reading Interests of High-School Pupils," *School Review* 47, no. 8 (1939): 613–21, 620.

83. Margaret A. Edwards, "A Little Learnin': Satin Gowns in Childress, Texas," *ALA Bulletin* 50, no. 6 (1956): 379–87, 385.

84. On the concept of "desirable difficulties" in education see Mark A. McDaniel and Andrew C. Butler, "A Contextual Framework for Understanding When Difficulties Are Desirable," in *Successful Remembering and Successful Forgetting*, ed. Aaron S. Benjamin (New York: Psychology Press, 2011), 175–98.

85. I am again drawing here on the well-known arguments of John Guillory in *Cultural Capital*, 168–75.

86. Mary Poovey, "Recovering Ellen Pickering," *Yale Journal of Criticism* 13, no. 2 (2000): 437–52, 451.

## Chapter 5: Easy Reading

1. Anon., "Editor's Outlook: Information versus Fiction," *Chatauquan* 6 (1886): 358.

2. For an ambitious attempt to collect such experiences, see the *Reading Experience Database*, www.open.ac.uk/Arts/RED/; for a thoughtful account of databases' limitations see the review by Ed Potten in *Library* 13, no. 3 (2012): 351–55.

3. François Fénelon, *Dialogues on Eloquence in General, Particularly That Kind Which Is Fit for the Pulpit*, trans. W. Stevenson, rev. James Creighton (London: W. Baynes, 1808), 257.

4. See D. E. Berlyne, "Novelty, Complexity, and Interestingness," in *Studies in the New Experimental Aesthetics: Steps Toward an Objective Psychology of Aesthetic Appreciation*, ed. D. E. Berlyne (New York: John Wiley and Sons, 1974), 175–80.

5. Edward Young, "Epistle 2: From Oxford," in *Two Epistles to Mr. Pope* (London, 1730), 22.

6. Samuel Johnson, "[On Easy Writing]," *Idler* (1759), in *Samuel Johnson: Selected Poetry and Prose*, ed. Frank Brady and W. K. Wimsatt (Berkeley: University of California Press, 1977), 265–68, 265.

7. See Andrew Elfenbein, *Romanticism and the Rise of English* (Stanford, CA: Stanford University Press, 2009), 108–44.

8. For one of the best treatments of how a romantic poet transformed the easy style see William Keach's "Shelley's Speed," chap. 5 of his *Shelley's Style* (New York: Methuen, 1984).

9. Edward Young, *Conjectures on Original Composition*, ed. Edith J. Morley (Manchester: Manchester University Press, 1918), 8.

10. See, e.g.: "Just such another wanton Ganymede / Set [Jove] afire with, and enforc'd the god / Snatch up the goodly boy" (*The Two Noble Kinsmen*, 4.2.15–17, *The Riverside Shakespeare*, ed. G. Blakemore Evans [Boston: Houghton Mifflin, 1974], 1667).

11. For a partial bibliography see Erdmann Waniek, "*Werther* lesen und Werther als Leser," *Goethe Yearbook* 1 (1982): 51–92; Richard D. Altick, "The Reading Public in England and America in 1900," in *Writers, Readers, and Occasions: Selected Essays on Victorian Literature and Life* (Columbus: Ohio State University Press, 1989), 209–30; Tom Keymer, *Richardson's "Clarissa" and the Eighteenth-Century Reader* (Cambridge: Cambridge University Press, 1992); Kate Flint, *The Woman Reader, 1837–1914* (Oxford: Clarendon, 1993); Kathryn Sutherland, "'Events . . . Have Made Us a World of Readers': Reader Relations, 1780–1830," in *The Romantic Period*, ed. David B. Pirie, vol. 5 of the *Penguin History of Literature* (Harmondsworth, Middlesex: Penguin, 1994), 1–48; Reinhard Wittmann, "Was There a Reading Revolution at the End of the Eighteenth Century?" in *A History of Reading in the West*, ed. Guglielmo Cavallo and Roger Chartier, trans. Lydia G. Cochrane (Amherst: University of Massachusetts Press, 1999), 284–312; Stephen Colclough, *Consuming Texts: Readers and Reading Communities, 1695–1870* (Houndmills, Basingstoke: Palgrave, 2007); and Nicholas Paige, "Rousseau's Readers Revisited: The Aesthetics of *La Nouvelle Heloise*," *Eighteenth-Century Studies* 42, no. 1 (2008): 131–54.

12. William St. Clair, *The Reading Nation in the Romantic Period* (Cambridge: Cambridge University Press, 2004), 5–6.

13. Gertrude Savile, *Secret Comment: The Diaries of Gertrude Savile, 1721–1757*, ed. Alan Saville (Devon: Kingsbridge History Society, 1997), 144.

14. See also Colclough's comments on Savile in *Consuming Texts*, 60–63.

15. Mary Granville, *The Autobiography and Correspondence of Mary Granville, Mrs. Delany*, ed. Lady Llanover, 3 vols. (London: Richard Bentley, 1861), 3:162, writing in 1752.

16. Lady Eleanor Butler, *A Year with the Ladies of Llangollen*, ed. Elizabeth Mavor (Harmondsworth, Middlesex: Penguin, 1986), 128–29, writing in 1788.

17. Thomas Green, *Extracts from the Diary of a Lover of Literature* (Ipswich: J. Raw, 1810), 23, writing in 1797.

18. Joseph Hunter, *Journal*, 1798, excerpted online in the UK Reading Experience Database, British Library, Add 24, 879, p. 17, www.open.ac.uk/Arts/reading/UK/record_details.php?id=10812.

19. Ellen Weeton, *Miss Weeton: Journal of a Governess*, ed. Edward Hall, 2 vols. (London: Oxford University Press, 1936–39), 2:72, writing in 1813.

20. Beattie, quoted in William Forbes, *An Account of the Life and Writings of James Beattie* (New York: Brisban and Brannan, 1807), 28–29, writing in 1759.

21. Leah Price, *The Anthology and the Rise of the Novel: From Richardson to George Eliot* (Cambridge: Cambridge University Press, 2000), 17–20.

22. Lady Mary Wortley Montagu, *The Letters and Works of Lady Mary Wortley Montagu*, ed. Lord Wharncliffe, 2 vols. (Paris: Galignani, 1837), 2:373.

23. Henrietta Knight, Lady Luxborough. *Letters Written by the Late Honourable Lady Luxborough, to William Shenstone, Esq.* (London: J. Dodsley, 1775), 369.

24. Quoted in William Beatty Warner, *Licensing Entertainment: The Elevation of Novel Reading in Britain, 1684–1750* (Berkeley: University of California Press, 1998), 178.

25. Elizabeth Carter, *A Series of Letters Between Mrs. Elizabeth Carter and Miss Catherine Talbot, from the Year 1741 to 1770*, ed. Montague Pennington, 4 vols. (London: F. C. and J. Rivington, 1809), 2:71.

26. Thomas Gray, *The Correspondence of Gray, Walpole, West and Ashton (1734–1771)*, ed. Paget Jackson Toynbee, 2 vols. (Oxford: Clarendon, 1915), 2:25–26.

27. David Garrick, *The Private Correspondence of David Garrick*, 2 vols. (London: Henry Colburn and Richard Bentley, 1831), 1:116.

28. Anna Seward, *Letters of Anna Seward Written Between the Years 1784 and 1807*, 6 vols. (Edinburgh: Archibald Constable, 1811), 1:127.

29. John Davis, *Travels of Four Years and a Half in the United States of America* (London: T. Ostell, 1803), 396.

30. Quoted in Anon., *Minutes of Evidence Taken Before the Select Committee on the Copyright Acts of 8 Anne, C. 19; 15 Geo. III, C. 53; 41 Geo. III, C. 107; and 54 Geo. III., C. 116* (London: Printed for the House of Commons, 1818), 125.

31. Quoted in Anon., *Second Report from Selection Committee on Illicit Distillation in Ireland* (London: Printed for the House of Commons, 1816), 99.

32. Claudia L. Johnson, "'Let Me Make the Novels of a Country': Barbauld's *The*

*British Novelists* (1810/1820)," in "The Romantic-Era Novel," ed. Amanda Gilroy and Wil Verhoeven, special issue, *NOVEL: A Forum on Fiction* 34, no. 2 (2001): 163–79.

33. Dino Franco Felluga, *The Perversity of Poetry: Romantic Ideology and the Popular Male Poet of Genius* (Albany: State University of New York Press, 2005), 40–42.

34. Quoted in Anon., *Report from the Select Committee on Public Libraries* (London: Printed for the House of Commons, 1849), 134.

35. Richard H. Hutton, *Scott* (London: Macmillan, 1895), 43.

36. Charles Dickens, *The Christmas Books*, ed. Michael Slater, 2 vols. (Harmondsworth, Middlesex: Penguin, 1971), 1:72.

37. Ibid., 1:73.

38. Audrey Jaffe, "Spectacular Sympathy: Visuality and Ideology in Dickens's *A Christmas Carol*," *PMLA* 109, no. 2 (1994): 254–65, 259; see also Joss Marsh, "Dickensian 'Dissolving Views': The Magic Lantern, Visual Story-Telling, and the Victorian Technological Imagination," *Comparative Critical Studies* 6, no. 3 (2009): 333–46, on the place of the episode in the history of media.

39. In statistics the standard measure of interrater reliability is Cohen's kappa; for this research Cohen's kappa = 0.75, which indicates moderate to good reliability (see Jacob Cohen, "A Coefficient of Agreement for Nominal Scales," *Educational and Psychological Measurement* 20, no. 1 [1960]: 37–46).

40. My broader approach to sampling is influenced by Don A. Dillman, Jolene D. Smyth, and Leah Melani Christian, *Internet, Mail, and Mixed Mode Surveys: The Tailored Design Method*, 3rd ed. (Hoboken, NJ: John Wiley and Sons, 2009), esp. chap. 3, "Coverage and Sampling"; for a more technical discussion see Sharon L. Lohr, *Sampling: Design and Analysis*, 2nd ed. (Boston: Brooke/Cole Cengage Learning, 2010).

41. For classic work on these terms see Endel Tulving, "How Many Memory Systems Are There?" *American Psychologist* 40, no. 4 (1985): 385–98; Endel Tulving and Donald M. Thomson, "Encoding Specificity and Retrieval Processes in Episodic Memory," *Psychological Review* 80, no. 5 (1973): 352–73; J. R. Barclay, John D. Bransford, Jeffrey J. Franks, Nancy S. McCarrell, and Kathy Nitsch, "Comprehension and Semantic Flexibility," *Journal of Verbal Learning and Verbal Behavior* 13, no. 4 (1974): 471–81; on storage see Robert A. Bjork and Elizabeth L. Bjork, "A New Theory of Disuse and an Old Theory of Stimulus Fluctuation," in *From Learning Processes to Cognitive Processes: Essays in Honor of William K. Estes*, ed. Alice F. Healy, Stephen M. Kosslyn, and Richard M. Shiffrin, 2 vols. (Hillsdale, NJ: Erlbaum, 1992), 2:35–67.

42. See Daniel L. Schacter, ed., *Memory Distortions: How Minds, Brains, and Societies Reconstruct the Past* (Cambridge, MA: Harvard University Press, 1995).

43. Fergus I. M. Craik and Robert S. Lockhart, "Levels of Processing: A Framework for Memory Research," *Journal of Verbal Learning and Verbal Behavior* 11, no. 6 (1972): 671–84; for an important criticism of Craik and Lockhart see Michael Eysenk, "Levels of Processing: A Critique," *British Journal of Psychology* 69, no. 2 (1978): 157–69.

44. Dr. J. W. Hudson, quoted in Anon., *Report from the Select Committee on Parliamentary Papers* (London: House of Commons, July 7, 1853), 57; interlocutor is Mr. Drummond.

45. Emily B. Todd, "Walter Scott and the Nineteenth-Century American Literary Marketplace: Antebellum Richmond Readers and the Collected Editions of the Waverley Novels," *Papers of the Bibliographical Society of America* 93, no. 4 (1999): 495–517.

46. See Tulving, "How Many Memory Systems?"

47. For what readers remember in the lab, see Gabriel A. Radvansky, David E. Copeland, and Rolf Zwaan, "A Novel Study: Investigating the Structure of Narrative and Autobiographical Memories," *Memory* 13, no. 8 (2005): 796–814; and David E. Copeland, Gabriel A. Radvansky, and Kerri A. Goodwin, "A Novel Study: Forgetting Curves and the Reminiscence Bump," *Memory* 17, no. 3 (2009): 323–36.

48. See David C. Howell, "Correlation and Regression," in *Statistical Methods for Psychology*, 7th ed. (Belmont, CA: Wadsworth, Cengage Learning, 2010), 245–92.

49. Frances Andrews Tenney, *War Diary of Luman Harris Tenney, 1861–1865* (Cleveland, OH: Evangelical Publishing House, 1914), 144, writing in 1865.

50. Richard Owen, *The Life of Richard Owen*, 2 vols. (London: John Murray, 1894), 1:347–48, writing in 1849.

51. Mary Matthews Bray, *A Sea Trip in Clipper Ship Days* (Boston: Richard G. Badger, 1920), 107, writing in the 1860s.

52. William Powell Frith, *John Leech: His Life and Work*, 2 vols. (London: R. Bentley, 1891), 2:123–24, date unspecified.

53. John Buckley Castieau, "Manuscript Diaries," National Library of Australia, *Reading Experience Database: Australia*, Record 24028, www.open.ac.uk/Arts/reading/recorddetails2.php?id=24028, writing in 1884.

54. Leslie Stephen, *The Selected Letters of Leslie Stephen*, ed. John Bicknell, 2 vols. (Columbus: Ohio State University Press, 1996), 1:80, *Reading Experience Database: UK*, Record 3944, www.open.ac.uk/Arts/reading/recorddetails2.php?id=3944, writing in 1870.

55. Samuel Butler, *The Life and Letters of Dr. Samuel Butler*, 2 vols. (London: John Murray, 1896), 2:22, writing in 1832.

56. Letter of Martha Swan, quoted in Susan Inches Lesley, *Recollections of My Mother* (Boston: George H. Ellis, 1886), 395, writing in 1847.

57. "R. L. C.," "Judge Story" [review of *Life and Letters of Joseph Story*], in *The Christian Reformer; or the Unitarian Magazine and Review* 8 (1852): 412–28, 413.

58. James Macdonell, quoted in W. Robertson Nicoll, *James Macdonell, Journalist* (New York: Dodd, Mead, 1897), 184, writing in 1870.

59. Alphonso David Rockwell, *Rambling Recollections: An Autobiography* (New York: P. B. Hoeber, 1920), 279.

60. Mary Russell Mitford, *Letters of Mary Russell Mitford*, 2nd series, ed. Henry Fothergill Chorley, 2 vols. (London: Richard Bentley, 1872), 2:101, writing in 1849.

61. Frederick William Robertson, *Life and Letters of Frederick W. Robertson*, ed. Stopford Augustus Brooke, 2 vols. (London: Smith and Elder, 1866), 2:124.

62. Alice M. Diehl, *The True Story of My Life* (London: John Lane, 1908), 329.

63. Edward Martin Taber, *Stowe Notes, Letters, and Verses* (Boston: Houghton Mifflin, 1913), 270–71, writing in 1893.

64. Edward Dowden, *Fragments from Old Letters, E. D. to E. D. W., 1869–1892* (London: J. M. Dent, 1914), 102, writing in 1874.

65. Connop Thirlwall, *Letters Literary and Theological of Connop Thirlwall*, ed. John James Stewart Perowne and Louis Stokes (London: Richard Bentley, 1881), 202–3, writing in 1852.

66. Gertrude Bell, *The Letters of Gertrude Bell*, ed. Lady Bell, 2 vols. (New York: Boni and Liveright, 1927), 2:687, writing in 1924.

67. Jane Welsh Carlyle, "Journal for October 1855–July 1856," writing in 1855 (*The Carlyle Letters Online: A Victorian Cultural Reference*, http://carlyleletters.dukeupress.edu/content/vol30/#ed-30-jane-welsh-carlyle-journal [italics in original]).

68. Andrew K. H. Boyd, *Twenty-Five Years of St. Andrews*, 2 vols. (London: Longmans, Green, 1892), 2:246.

69. Benjamin Coulson Robinson, *Bench and Bar: Reminiscences of One of the Last of an Ancient Race*, 3rd ed. (London: Hurst and Blackett, 1894), 103.

70. Anon., *Boiler Explosions: Report to the Secretary of the Board of Trade upon the Working of the Boiler Explosions Acts, 1882 and 1890. Parliamentary Paper C.7081* (London: Eyre and Spottiswode, 1894), 15.

71. Joseph Phipps Townsend, *Rambles and Observations in New South Wales* (London: Chapman and Hall, 1849), 261.

72. R. E. H. Greyson, *Selections from the Correspondence of R. E. H. Greyson*, 2 vols. (London: Longman, Brown, Green, Longmans, and Roberts, 1857), 1:211, date unspecified.

73. Marianne North, *Recollections of a Happy Life, Being the Autobiography of Marianne North*, ed. Janet Catherine North Symonds, 2 vols. (London: Macmillan, 1892), 2:176.

74. "N." [Letter to *The Academy*], August 27, 1898, 199–200, 199.

75. Robert Collyer, quoted in John Haynes Holmes, *The Life and Letters of Robert Collyer, 1823–1912* (New York: Dodd, Mead, 1918), 1:71, date unspecified.

76. Charles Henry Jones, *The Life and Public Services of J. Glancy Jones*, 2 vols. (Philadelphia: J. B. Lippincott, 1910), 2:119, writing in 1861.

77. Steven M. Smith and Edward Vela, citing Arthur Glenberg in "Environmental Context-Dependent Memory: A Review and Meta-analysis," *Psychonomic Bulletin and Review* 8, no. 2 (2001): 203–20, 204.

78. John W. Diggle, *The Lancashire Life of Bishop Fraser*, 4th ed. (London: Sampson Low, Marston, Searle, and Rivington, 1890), 462; Marsh's *Emilia Wyndham* appeared in 1846.

79. Frederic Kenyon Brown (writing as "Al Priddy"), *Through the Mill: The Life of a Mill Boy* (Boston: Pilgrim Press, 1911), 14.

80. Halliday Macartney, quoted in Demetrius Charles de Kavanagh Boulger, *The Life of Sir Halliday Macartney, K. C. M. G.* (London: John Lane, 1908), 263, writing in the 1870s.

81. Henry Faulds, *Nine Years in Nipon: Sketches of Japanese Life and Manners* (Boston: Cupples and Hurd, 1888), 257–58.

82. "Clericus," "Life in an Orphan School," *University Magazine and Free Review* 11 (1899): 239–52, 241.

83. See Arthur P. Shimamura and Larry R. Squire, "A Neuropsychological Study of Fact Memory and Source Amnesia," *Journal of Experimental Psychology: Learning, Memory, and Cognition* 13, no. 3 (1987): 464–73; for more about source amnesia see Chapter 7.

84. Gregory L. Murphy, *The Big Book of Concepts* (Cambridge, MA: MIT Press, 2002), 42.

85. Ibid., 49.

86. For important moments in this debate see Eleanor Rosch, "Cognitive Representations of Semantic Categories," *Journal of Experimental Psychology: General* 104, no. 3 (1975): 192–233; Douglas L. Medin and Marguerite M. Schaffer, "Context Theory of Classification Learning," *Psychological Review* 85, no. 3 (1978): 207–38; Lawrence W. Barsalou, "Ideals, Central Tendency, and Frequency of Instantiation as Determinants of Graded Structure in Categories," *Journal of Experimental Psychology: Learning, Memory, and Cognition* 11, no. 4 (1985): 629–54; Gail McKoon and Roger Ratcliff, "Contextually Relevant Aspects of Meaning," *Journal of Experimental Psychology: Learning, Memory, and* Cognition 14, no. 2 (1988): 331–43; and Edward J. Wisniewski and Douglas L. Medin, "On the Interaction of Theory and Data in Concept Learning," *Cognitive Science* 18, no. 2 (1994): 221–81.

87. Broider, quoted in Anon., *First Report from the Select Committee of the House of Lords on the Sweating System* (London: Henry Hansard and Son, 1888), 440.

88. Quoted in Theodore. M. Porter, *Karl Pearson: The Scientific Life in a Statistical Age* (Princeton, NJ: Princeton University Press, 2004), 24.

89. Anon., "A Sermon on Gambling," *United Service Journal* 3 (Oct. 1837): 211–18, 216.

90. Anon., "Australian Tract Society," *Bengal Catholic Herald*, April 13, 1844, 203.

91. Senator Hale, 1854 senate debate on annexation of Cuba, quoted in *Great Debates in American History*, ed. Marion Mills Miller, 14 vols. (New York: Current Literature Publishing, 1913), 3:96.

92. Keith Young, *Delhi—1857: The Siege, Assault, and Capture*, ed. General Sir Henry Wylie Norman and Mrs. Keith Young (London: W. and R. Chambers, 1902), 249, writing in the 1850s.

93. I have carried out such surveys among my students; confidence is uniformly higher for memories of the autobiographical setting of reading even than for the content of what was read.

94. Henry L. Roediger III and Magdalena Abel, "Collective Memory: A New Arena of Cognitive Study," *Trends in Cognitive Sciences* 19, no. 7 (2015): 359–61.

## Chapter 6: That's Entertainment?

1. Kate Flint, "The Victorian Novel and Its Readers," in *The Cambridge Companion to the Victorian Novel*, ed. Deirdre David (Cambridge: Cambridge University Press, 2001), 17–36.

2. See Claudia L. Johnson, "F. R. Leavis: The 'Great Tradition' of the English Novel and the Jewish Part," *Nineteenth-Century Literature* 56, no. 2 (2001): 198–227.

3. F. R. Leavis, *The Great Tradition* (London: Chatto and Windus, 1948), 29.

4. Anon., advertisement for *Nightmare Abbey* from the *Monthly Review*, repr. in Thomas Love Peacock's *Maid Marian* (London: T. Hookham and Longman, Hurst, Rees, Orme, and Brown, 1822), 263.

5. Anon., advertisement for *Walter Colyton, Fraser's* 3 (Feb. 1831): 99.

6. Anon., from the *Morning Post*, repr. in Ewa Felińska, *Revelations of Siberia: By a Banished Lady*, 2 vols. (London: Colburn, 1852), p. 15 of advertising supplement at the back of vol. 2.

7. William Beatty Warner, *Licensing Entertainment: The Elevation of Novel Reading in Britain, 1684–1750* (Berkeley: University of California Press, 1998).

8. Deidre Lynch, *Loving Literature: A Cultural History* (Chicago: University of Chicago Press, 2015), 35.

9. My interest in shallow or weak affect owes a debt to Sianne Ngai's discussion of interest in *Our Aesthetic Categories: Zany, Cute, Interesting* (Cambridge, MA: Harvard University Press, 2012), 136–47.

10. On interest see Laura K. M. Graf and Jan R. Landwehr, "A Dual-Process Perspective on Fluency-Based Aesthetics: The Pleasure-Interest Model of Aesthetic Liking," *Personality and Social Psychology Review* 19, no. 4 (2015): 395–410; Paul J. Silvia, "Interest: The Curious Emotion," *Current Directions in Psychological Science* 17, no. 1 (2008): 57–60; "What Is Interesting? Exploring the Appraisal Structure of Interest," *Emotion* 5, no. 1 (2005): 89–102; on learning and motivation see the annual *Psychology of Learning and Motivation*.

11. On identification see Anneke de Graaf, Hans Hoeken, José Sanders, and Johannes W. J. Beentjes, "Identification as Mechanism of Narrative Persuasion," *Communication Research* 39, no. 6 (2012): 802–23; on social interaction see Li-Shiue Gau, Daniel L. Wann, and Jeffrey D. James, "Examining Relations of Entertainment with Social Interaction Motives and Team Identification," *Perceptual and Motor Skills* 111, no. 2 (2010): 576–89; on mood manipulation see Dolf Zillman, "Mood Management Through Communication Choices," *American Behavioral Scientist* 31, no. 3 (1988): 327–41.

12. For helpful work in this area see Mary Beth Oliver and Arthur A. Raney, "Entertainment as Pleasurable and Meaningful: Identifying Hedonic and Eudaimonic Motivations for Entertainment Consumption," *Journal of Communication* 61, no. 5 (2011): 984–1004; Mary Beth Oliver and Anne Bartsch, "Appreciation as Audience Response: Exploring Entertainment Gratifications Beyond Hedonism," *Human Communication Research* 36, no. 1 (2010): 53–81; and K. Maja Krakowíak and Mary Beth Oliver, "When Good Characters Do Bad Things: Examining the Effect of Moral Ambiguity on Enjoyment," *Journal of Communication* 62, no. 1 (2012): 117–35.

13. William Howitt, *Pantika: Or, Traditions of the Most Ancient Times*, 2 vols. (London: Manning and Smithson 1834), 1:vi.

14. Peter Vorderer, Francis F. Steen, and Elaine Chan, "Motivation," in *Psychology of*

*Entertainment*, ed. Jennings Bryant and Peter Vorderer (2006; Mahwah, NJ: Erlbaum, 2008), 3–18, 4.

15. See Richard C. Sha, "The Uses and Abuses of Otherness: Halperin and Shelley on the Otherness of Ancient Greek Sexuality," in *Historicizing Romantic Sexuality*, ed. Richard C. Sha, at Romantic Circles, www.rc.umd.edu/praxis/sexuality/sha/sha.html.

16. Edward L. Deci and Richard M. Ryan, "The 'What' and 'Why' of Goal Pursuits: Human Needs and the Self-Determination of Behavior," *Psychological Inquiry* 11, no. 4 (2000): 227–68.

17. Vorderer, Steen, and Chan, "Motivation," 6–7.

18. See David Vincent, *Literacy and Popular Culture: England, 1750–1914* (Cambridge: Cambridge University Press, 1989).

19. For an illuminating discussion of Victorian topicality in relation to Victorian farce see Richard Schoch, *Not Shakespeare: Bardolatry and Burlesque in the Nineteenth Century* (Cambridge: Cambridge University Press, 2002), 37–41; what Schoch notes about nineteenth-century burlesque can be applied to novels as well: "We can recognize that ignorance—both ours and the original audience's—is the constitutive condition of burlesque spectating" (39).

20. On inhibition see Michael C. Andersen and Benjamin J. Levy, "Theoretical Issues in Inhibition: Insights from Research on Human Memory," in *Inhibition in Cognition*, ed. David S. Gorfein and Colin M. MacLeod (Washington: American Psychological Association, 2007), 81–102; I am grateful to Sashank Varma for his help with this point.

21. Frances Power Cobbe, *The Duties of Women* (1881), 7th American ed. (Boston: George H. Ellis, 1882).

22. See Lisa Zunshine, *Why We Read Fiction: Theory of Mind and the Novel* (Columbus: Ohio State University Press, 2006); Suzanne Keen, *Empathy and the Novel* (Oxford: Oxford University Press, 2007); and Blakey Vermeule, *Why Do We Care About Literary Characters?* (Baltimore: Johns Hopkins University Press, 2010).

23. Vermeule, *Why Do We Care*, 41.

24. Keith Oatley, *Such Stuff as Dreams: The Psychology of Fiction* (Chichester, West Sussex: John Wiley and Sons, 2011), 17.

25. Richard J. Gerrig, "Moral Judgments in Narrative Contexts" (commentary on Cass R. Sunstein, "Moral Heuristics"), *Behavioral and Brain Sciences* 28, no. 4 (2009): 550.

26. On varieties of attitudes toward vulgarity in the nineteenth century see Susan David Bernstein and Elsie B. Michie, eds., *Victorian Vulgarity: Taste in Verbal and Visual Culture* (Farnham, Surrey: Ashgate, 2009).

27. Walter Kintsch, "Learning from Text, Levels of Comprehension, or: Why Anyone Would Read a Story Anyway," *Poetics* 9, no. 1 (1980): 87–98, 93.

28. See Dorina Miron, "Cognition and Emotion in Entertainment," in *Psychology of Entertainment*, ed. Jennings Bryant and Peter Vorderer (2006; Mahwah, NJ: Erlbaum, 2008), 343–64, 360–61.

29. For contrasting views see Margaret A. Marshall and Jonathon D. Brown, "On the Psychological Benefits of Self-Enhancement," in *Self-Criticism and Self-Enhancement: Theory, Research, and Clinical Implications*, ed. Edward C. Chang (Washington: Ameri-

can Psychological Association, 2008), 19–35; and, in the same volume, C. Randall Colvin and Robert Griffo, "On the Psychological Costs of Self-Enhancement," 123–40.

30.  See Constantine Sedikides and Erica G. D. Hepper, "Self-Improvement," *Social and Personality Psychology Compass* 3, no. 6 (2009): 899–917.

31.  Anne Bartsch, Anja Kalch, and Mary Beth Oliver, "Moved to Think: The Role of Emotional Media in Stimulating Reflective Thoughts," *Journal of Media Psychology* 26, no. 3 (2014): 124–40; and Mary Beth Oliver, Erin Ash, Julia K. Woolley, Drew D. Shade, and Keunyeong Kim, "Entertainment We Watch and Entertainment We Appreciate: Patterns of Motion Picture Consumption and Acclaim over Three Decades," *Mass Communication and Society* 17, no. 6 (2014): 853–73.

32.  Melanie C. Green, Timothy C. Brock, and Geoff F. Kaufman, "Understanding Media Enjoyment: The Role of Transportation into Narrative Worlds," *Communication Theory* 14, no. 4 (2004): 311–27, 319; see also Melanie C. Green and Timothy C. Brock, "In the Mind's Eye: Transportation-Imagery Model of Narrative Persuasion," in *Narrative Impact: Social and Cognitive Foundations*, ed. Melanie C. Green, Jeffrey J. Strange, and Timothy C. Brock (Mahwah, NJ: Erlbaum, 2002), 315–42.

33.  "On the Poetry of the Age," in *Grange Magazine*, vol. 1 (Edinburgh: R. Grant, 1846), 195–202, 198; the title page notes that this is "a series of papers in prose and verse by the pupils of the Grange school."

34.  Kenneth Graham, *English Criticism of the Novel, 1865–1900* (Oxford: Clarendon, 1965), 6–7.

35.  Robert Lush, review of *The Old Ledger*, *Athenaeum*, Jan. 13, 1866, 48.

36.  "Assize Intelligence," *London Daily News*, April 4, 1866, 6.

37.  Ibid.

38.  Ibid.

39.  William Hepworth Dixon, "The Rights of Criticism," *Athenaeum*, April 7, 1866, 463.

40.  *London Daily News*, Feb. 8, 1867, 6.

41.  Ibid.

42.  *London Daily News*, April 4, 1866, 6.

43.  Anon., "Spring Assizes: Strauss v. Francis," *Times* (London), April 4, 1866, 11.

44.  Anon., review of *Like Dian's Kiss*, *Spectator*, April 27, 1878, 543.

45.  Anon., review of *Like Dian's Kiss*, *Pall Mall Budget*, June 14, 1878, 24–25, 25.

46.  Anon., review of *Like Dian's Kiss*, *Saturday Review*, April 13, 1878, 470–71, 471.

47.  Anon., "Contemporary Literature," *British Quarterly Review* 68 (July 1878): 146.

48.  Anon., review of *Like Dian's Kiss*, *Spectator*, April 27, 1878, 543.

49.  Anon., review of *Like Dian's Kiss*, *Saturday Review*, April 13, 1878, 471; Anon., "Contemporary Literature," *British Quarterly Review* 68 (July 1878): 146.

50.  Anon., review of *Like Dian's Kiss*, *Pall Mall Budget*, June 14, 1878, 25.

51.  Anon., review of *Like Dian's Kiss*, *Saturday Review*, April 13, 1878, 471.

52.  Ibid.

53.  Anon., review of *Like Dian's Kiss*, *Academy* 13 (May 25 1878): 457–58, 457.

54.  Anon., "Contemporary Literature," *British Quarterly Review* 68 (July 1878): 146.

55. Ibid., 145–46.

56. Anon., review of *Like Dian's Kiss, Spectator*, April 27 1878, 543.

57. Anon., review of *Like Dian's Kiss, Saturday Review*, April 13, 1878, 470.

58. Paul Schlicke, *Dickens and Popular Entertainment* (London: Allen and Unwin, 1985), 87–136.

59. For a definitive account of the biographical and publication context see Robert L. Patten, *Charles Dickens and "Boz": The Birth of the Industrial-Age Author* (Cambridge: Cambridge University Press, 2012), esp. chap. 6.

60. From Dickens's "Preface to the Cheap Edition of His Novels" (1848), in *The Old Curiosity Shop*, ed. Elizabeth M. Brennan (Oxford: Oxford University Press, 1999), 5.

61. In addition, as John M. L. Drew notes, "By the standards of 1840 . . . Dickens was decidedly moving up in the world of literary journalism by ceasing to be a mere writer of parts, and becoming the editor of his own magazine" (*Dickens the Journalist* [Houndmills, Basingstoke: Palgrave, 2003], 49).

62. James Buzard, "Enumeration and Exhaustion: Taking Inventory in *The Old Curiosity Shop*," in *Contemporary Dickens*, ed. Eileen Gillooly and Deirdre David (Columbus: Ohio State University Press, 2009), 189–206, 194. Nell's inertia also forms a large part of Steven Marcus's analysis of the novel in *Dickens from Pickwick to Dombey* (New York: Norton, 1965), 140–51.

63. Thomas Hood, review of *Master Humphrey's Clock, Athenaeum*, Nov. 7, 1840, 887–88, 887.

64. Anon., "Charivari," *London Magazine*, May 1840, 331.

65. For a review that takes an unusual favorable stance on *Master Humphrey*, see the article in which the reviewer is pleased that Dickens seems to be forsaking his dangerous tendency to draw compelling villains: "Fools[,] knaves, and villains are drawn with a richness of gusto, and a force of individuality which cannot fail to leave a strong and lasting impression" (*Era* 84 [Sunday, May 3, 1840], 386).

66. For specifics about declining sales see Robert L. Patten, *Dickens and His Publishers* (1978; repr. Santa Cruz: Dickens Project, 1991), 110.

67. Edward Stirling, *The Old Curiosity Shop: A Drama in Two Acts* (London: Thomas Hailes Lacy, [1840]); available from HathiTrust.

68. Richard J. Gerrig, "Suspense in the Absence of Uncertainty," *Journal of Memory and Language* 28, no. 6 (1989): 633–48.

69. Anon., "Little Nell in Dickens's *Old Curiosity Shop*," *National Repository* 3 (Sept. 1878): 233–37, 235; Rev. John O. Adams, "Sculpture," in *The Universalist and Ladies' Repository* 11 (1843): 17–20, 19; Margaret Oliphant, "Charles Dickens," *Blackwood's Edinburgh Magazine* 77 (April 1855): 451–66, 458.

70. Sarah Winter, *The Pleasures of Memory: Learning to Read with Charles Dickens* (New York: Fordham University Press, 2011), 162.

71. James Eli Adams, *A History of Victorian Literature* (Chichester, West Sussex: Wiley-Blackwell, 2009), 84.

72. Anon., "Modern Novels," *Christian Remembrancer* 4 (Dec. 1842): 581–611, 592.

73. Edgar Allan Poe, *The Literati* (New York: J. S. Redfield, 1850), 586.

74. T. S. Arthur, "Little Nell," in *The Brilliant: A Gift Book for 1850*, ed. T. S. Arthur (New York: Baker and Scribner, 1850), 74; David W. Bartlett, *What I Saw in London; Or, Men and Things in the Great Metropolis* (New York: C. M. Saxton, Barker, 1861), 74.

75. "H," review of *Dombey and Son*, *Westminster Review* 47 (April 1847): 5–11; repr. in *Dickens: The Critical Heritage*, ed. Philip Collins (London: Routledge and Kegan Paul, 1971), 225–26, 226.

76. John Forster to Charles Dickens, Jan. 16, 1841, *Letters of Charles Dickens*, ed. Madeline House, Graham Storey, and Kathleen Tillotson, 12 vols. (Oxford: Clarendon, 1965–2002), 2:187n.

## Chapter 7: On Influence

1. See Harold Bloom, *The Anxiety of Influence: A Theory of Poetry* (New York: Oxford University Press, 1973).

2. On the conjectural origins of influence see Leslie Brisman, *Romantic Origins* (Ithaca, NY: Cornell University Press, 1978), 11–20.

3. John Livingston Lowes, *The Road to Xanadu: A Study in the Ways of the Imagination* (1927; New York: Vintage, 1957), 391.

4. See Charles R. Fletcher and Susan T. Chrysler, "Surface Forms, Textbases, and Situation Models: Recognition Memory for Three Types of Textual Information," *Discourse Processes* 13, no. 2 (1990): 175–90.

5. Although the capacity limitations of working memory are widely attested in multiple domains, for a foundational article about working memory and reading see Meredyth Daneman and Patricia A. Carpenter, "Individual Differences in Working Memory and Reading," *Journal of Verbal Learning and Verbal Behavior* 19, no. 4 (1980): 450–66.

6. See Walter Kintsch, *Comprehension: A Paradigm for Cognition* (Cambridge: Cambridge University Press, 1998), 49–86.

7. David A. Balota and Robert F. Lorch Jr., "Depth of Automatic Spreading Activation: Mediated Priming Effects in Pronunciation but Not in Lexical Decision," in *Cognitive Psychology: Key Readings*, ed. David A. Balota and Elizabeth J. Marsh (New York: Psychology Press, 2004), 403–17.

8. See, e.g., Richard L. Marsh, Joshua D. Landau, and Jason L. Hicks, "Contributions of Inadequate Source Monitoring to Unconscious Plagiarism During Idea Generation," *Journal of Experimental Psychology: Learning, Memory, and Cognition* 23, no. 4 (1997): 886–97.

9. Oscar Wilde, *The Picture of Dorian Gray*, ed. Andrew Elfenbein (New York: Longman, 2007), 52. Subsequent citations of this source are referenced parenthetically in the text.

10. Rosina Bulwer-Lytton, quoted in an anonymous review of *Anti-Coningsby; or, The New Generation Grown Old*, *Fraser's* 31 (Feb. 1845): 218; Bayard Taylor, *Travels in Greece and Russia, with an Excursion to Crete* (New York: Putnam, 1859), 323; John Berwick Harwood, *Lord Ulswater*, 3 vols. (London: Bentley, 1867), 1:15; James Picciotto, review of *Daniel Deronda*, quoted in *George Eliot: The Critical Heritage*, ed. David Carroll (London: Routledge, 1995), 406.

11. See Jeroen G. W. Raaijmakers and Richard M. Shiffrin, "Search of Associative Memory," *Psychological Review* 88, no. 2 (1981): 93–134, esp. 129–30.

12. *John Keats: A Longman Critical Edition*, ed. Susan J. Wolfson (New York: Pearson/Longman, 2007), 371.

13. See James Najarian, *Victorian Keats: Manliness, Sexuality, and Desire* (Houndmills: Palgrave Macmillan, 2002), 11–52.

14. See *Tennyson's Poetry*, ed. Robert W. Hill Jr. (New York: Norton, 1971), 15.

15. See Jennifer Gribble, *The Lady of Shalott in the Victorian Novel* (London: Macmillan, 1983).

16. "A poetic 'text' . . . is not a gathering of signs on a page, but is a psychic battlefield upon which authentic forces struggle for the only victory worth winning, the divinating triumph over oblivion" (Harold Bloom, *Poetry and Repression: Revisionism from Blake to Stevens* [New Haven, CT: Yale University Press, 1976], 2).

17. Ronald T. Kellogg, *The Psychology of Writing* (New York: Oxford University Press, 1994), 26–28.

18. James Eli Adams, *A History of Victorian Literature* (Chichester, West Sussex: John Wiley and Sons, 2009), 368; for the best critical treatment of *Robert Elsmere* see Patricia Meyer Spacks, *Boredom: The Literary History of a State of Mind* (Chicago: University of Chicago Press, 1995), 151–63.

19. Oscar Wilde, "The Decay of Lying" (1889), in *The Soul of Man Under Socialism and Selected Critical Prose*, ed. Linda Dowling (Harmondsworth, Middlesex: Penguin, 2001), 170. "Green" refers to the Oxford philosopher Thomas Hill Green.

20. On the biographical background to the composition of *Dorian Gray* see Richard Ellman, *Oscar Wilde* (New York: Vintage, 1988), 313–14.

21. Mary Ward, *Robert Elsmere* (1888), ed. Clyde de L. Ryals (Lincoln: University of Nebraska Press, 1967), 353, 362. Subsequent citations of this source are referenced parenthetically in the text.

22. Wilde's manuscript is quoted in Horst Schroeder, "A Quotation in *The Picture of Dorian Gray*," *Notes and Queries* 38, no. 3 (1991): 327–28, 328. See Schroeder's article more generally on the Wilde-Ward relationship.

23. Pierre Bourdieu, *The Field of Cultural Production: Essays on Art and Literature*, ed. Randal Johnson (New York: Columbia University Press, 1993), 181.

24. Kerry Powell, "Tom, Dick, and Dorian Gray: Magic Picture Mania in Late-Victorian Fiction," *Philological Quarterly* 62, no. 2 (1983): 147–70.

25. Robert B. Cialdini, *Influence: Science and Practice*, 4th ed. (Boston: Allyn and Bacon, 2001), 209.

26. Sharon S. Brehm and Jack W. Brehm, *Psychological Reactance: A Theory of Freedom and Control* (New York: Academic, 1981), 5–6. The Brehms' book is the classic in the field; for more recent work on reactance see "New Directions in Reactance Research," ed. Sandra Sittenthaler, Eva Jonas, Eva Traut-Mattausch, and Jeff Greenberg, special issue, *Zeitschrift für Psychologie* 223, no. 4 (2015). Generally, recent work on reactance leaves the Brehms' definition intact, while expanding the areas in which reactance operates and the circumstances in which it can be overcome.

27. See David M. Erceg-Hurn and Lyndall G. Steed, "Does Exposure to Cigarette Health Warnings Elicit Psychological Reactance in Smokers?" *Journal of Applied Social Psychology* 41, no. 1 (2011): 219–37.

28. See Richard A. Chechile and Sal A. Soraci, "Evidence for a Multiple-Process Account of the Generation Effect," *Memory* 7, no. 4 (1999): 483–508.

29. Walter Pater, *The Renaissance: Studies in Art and Poetry,* ed. Adam Phillips (1873; Oxford: Oxford University Press, 1986), 80.

## Conclusion: On Methodology

1. Roman Jakobson, "Linguistics and Poetics" (1960), in *Language in Literature,* ed. Krystyna Pomorska and Stephen Rudy (Cambridge, MA: Harvard University Press, 1987), 62–94, 66.

2. For an especially useful treatment see also Nancy Armstrong and Leonard Tennenhouse, "The Mind of Milton," chap. 1 of *The Imaginary Puritan: Literature, Intellectual Labor, and the Origins of Personal Life* (Berkeley: University of California Press, 1992), 27–46.

3. Mary Poovey, "Mediums, Media, Mediation: A Response," *Victorian Studies* 48, no. 2 (2006): 249–55, 249; see also Rita Felski, "'Context Stinks!'" *New Literary History* 42, no. 4 (2011): 573–91.

4. See Morton A. Gernsbacher, Kathleen R. Varner, and Mark E. Faust, "Investigating Differences in General Comprehension Skill," *Journal of Experimental Psychology: Learning, Memory, and Cognition* 16, no. 3 (1990): 430–45.

5. John Guillory, "Monuments and Documents: Panofsky on the Object of Study in the Humanities," *History of Humanities* 1, no. 1 (2016): 9–30, 10n2.

# INDEX

processes; Relatedness; Religion; Transportation; Writing

Reading, sociology of, 40, 112; historical scholarship on, 40; and identification, 40–41

Real readers, 53–59, 89–110, 141–64; eighteenth-century readers, 142–45; nineteenth-century readers, 149–64, 175–83

Realism in fiction, 32–33

Relatedness, 171, 174, 178–79, 185

Religion, 18. *See also* Bible guides; Protestantism

Rhyme, 35

Richards, I. A., 98–99

Richardson, Samuel, 143–45

Roediger, Henry, 164

Ruskin, John: "Of Kings' Treasuries," 122–27, 131, 136

Ryan, Richard, 168–69, 171

Saler, Michael, 108–9

Sanford, Anthony, 22

Savile, Gertrude, 142–43

Schmitt, Cannon, 232n58

Schoch, Richard, 244n19

Scholastic Aptitude Test, 132–33

Scott, Walter, 102, 145–46, 155, 156–7, 159, 184, 186

Sedgwick, Eve and Adam Frank, 7–8

Self-enhancement, 174

Self-improvement, 174

Self-relevance, 174, 184, 187–89

Seward, Anna, 145

Sharpe, Rev. Lancelot, 145

Sherlock Holmes, 108–109

Singer, Murray, 41

Situation model, 103, 107, 115, 117, 151, 208

Smollett, Tobias, 143, 145

Southey, Robert, 175

St. Clair, William, 142

Standards of coherence, 89–90, 111–113

Stanovich, Keith, 2, 219n2

Steen, Francis F., 167, 169, 171

Steinbeck, John, 132

Sterne, Laurence, 144–45

Stevenson, Robert Louis, 158, 203

Stirling, Edward, 186

Stoddart, J. M., 201–2

Stow, David, 119–21

Strauss, Gustave: *The Old Ledger*, 176–79

Surface code, 103, 151, 208

Swift, Jonathan, 144

Swinburne, Algernon Charles, 106–108

Swinney, David, 24–25

Tennyson, Alfred, 197–99

Textbase, 103, 115, 151

Thackeray, William Makepeace, 160

Think-aloud protocols, 53–7, 75–83

Thirlwall, Connop, 157–58

Todd, Emily B., 152

Top-down processing, 14, 19, 23–24, 39–59, 226n11

Trabasso, Tom, 41

Transportation: and Dickens, 146–49, 187; eighteenth-century description, 141–42; and novels, 157–159, 175, 178, 184, 230n33; and poetry, 91–95, 97; and Scott, 146;

Trollope, Anthony, 156, 169

Van den Broek, Paul, 84–87, 111

Van Dijk, Teun, 103, 120

Vermeule, Blakey, 171

Vorderer, Peter, 167, 169, 171

Vulgarity, 172–73, 181–82

Walpole, Horace, 143

Warburton, William, Bishop of Gloucester, 144–45

Ward, Mary: *Robert Elsmere*, 200–11

Warner, William, 166

Wauchope, George Armstrong, 130

Wilde, Oscar: *The Picture of Dorian Gray*, 195–211; *The Decay of Lying*, 201, 203–4